THE COSTUME OF SCOTLAND

THE COSTUME
OF
SCOTLAND

John Telfer Dunbar

c. 1

B. T. BATSFORD LTD. LONDON

BY THE SAME AUTHOR:
The Lost Land, 1958
Highland Costume, 1977
History of Highland Dress, 1979
Herself
As Co-Author:
Old Highland Dress & Tartans, 1949
Old Irish & Highland Dress, 1950
The Official Tartan Map, 1976

Frontispiece *Sir John Sinclair, Champion of the Trews, c. 1794*

© John Telfer Dunbar 1981
First published 1981

ISBN 0 7134 2534 2

Typeset in Monophoto Baskerville by Willmer Brothers Limited,
Birkenhead, Merseyside
and printed in Great Britain by
Robert Maclehose Ltd
Glasgow, Scotland
for the publishers B. T. Batsford Ltd.
4 Fitzhardinge Street, London W1H 0AH

CONTENTS

LIST OF

ILLUSTRATIONS

Acknowledgments

The author and the publishers would like to thank the following for their permission to reproduce the illustrations used in this book: Bodleian Library, Oxford (11); Col. the Hon. T. Morgan-Grenville (14); the Duke of Atholl (28); the Duke of Roxburghe (23); the Rt. Hon. the Earl of Seafield (15, 16, 17, 56); the Earl of Wemyss (colour plate 2); Inverness City Council (18); Lord Macdonald (27); Anthony G. Murray (57); National Library of Scotland (35); the National Museum of Antiquities of Scotland (5, 7, 90); National Museum of Ireland (76); the Royal Company of Archers (colour plate 4); *The Scotsman* (88); the Scottish National Portrait Gallery (colour plate 1; 13, 20, 58, 59); The Scottish Tartan Society (45); Scottish United Services Museum, Edinburgh Castle (77, 80, 81). No. 30 is reproduced by courtesy of the Trustees of the British Museum. Colour plate 3 and No. 22 are reproduced by gracious permission of Her Majesty The Queen. Nos. 1–4, 6, 8–10, 12, 19, 21, 24, 25, 26, 29, 30–34, 36–44, 46–55, 60–75, 78, 79, 82–87 and 89 are from the author's collection.

To my wife Elizabeth
whose help has been invaluable

Introduction

THE HISTORY of the national dress of Scotland has been turbulent and emotive to an extent far beyond that of the folk costume or national dress of any other European country. This is because a number of Scottish writers have attempted to place the origins of the Highland kilt and the clan tartans in the 'mists of antiquity'.

Up to the 1800s early writers merely recorded what they saw, and it is to a great extent the objective nature of these accounts which has resulted in their being interpreted in different ways. It was only when the kilt and tartans became national symbols that attempts were made to give them an extensive ancestry. This was really unnecessary as during the nineteenth century the Highland costume, particularly in its military form, had acquired genuine historical merit far beyond the shores of Scotland. Attempts to prove that the dress in its modern form was the 'Garb of Old Gaul' were often motivated by the wish to make it 'Romantic'. The truth is that the elaborate costume of the 1820s bore little resemblance to the clothing worn in the Highlands a century before.

1 *Drawing of a group of Edinburgh citizens from life, c. 1830, by Walter Geikie*

The figures in the print carry the following captions:

Les Montagnards d'Ecosse en
leur habits accûtumés avec
un manteau pendant.

Berg-Schotten in gewöhnlichen
Aufzug mit herab hangen:
der Decke.

Un Montagnard d'Ecosse, qui prend son
manteau sur les epaules, quãd il va pleuvoir.
Ein seine Decke gegē dē Regē, gleich
einē Mantel über die Schul:
ter n schlagender Berg-
Schott.

2 *A well-drawn mid-eighteenth century foreign print showing how the belted plaid could be worn*

The kilt, as opposed to the tartan kilt of Scotland, was worn by the ancient Egyptians over 5,000 years ago, and thigh-length versions identical in shape to the modern Scottish kilt were worn by the warriors of Cyprus in the Archaic period of 600 BC. But perhaps Scotland has the last word, because on a tombstone in the kirkyard of Birnam, Perthshire, are carved the figures of Adam and Eve wearing kilts made of leaves.

In a letter dated 1825, Sir Walter Scott wrote to his friend Mrs Hughes, in reply to a query about clan tartans: 'I do not believe a word of the nonsense about every clan or name having a regular pattern which was undeviatingly adhered to . . .'. I agree entirely with him, but that does not mean that I disapprove of the modern clan tartan system. The fact that clan tartans and the kilt are merely short links in the long chain of Scottish costume history should neither alarm nor dismay.

The Victorian and Edwardian champions of the 'Romantic' theory may have been small in number but they were in tune with the mood of the period. The new landowners of the sporting estates wanted to acquire a Highland identity, the visitors to the Highland 'resorts' wanted tartan souvenirs, there was a growing number of Scottish, Highland and Clan Societies at home and abroad, and there were enterprising Scottish tradesmen eager to meet the demand.

But this enthusiasm was by no means entirely commercial. At an early stage, the Lowland poets and artists began to show enthusiasm for the 'romance' of the Highlands. Indeed, Allan Ramsay, who died in Edinburgh in 1758, expressed his poetic conception of a god-like ancestry wearing Highland dress – although I doubt if he ever visited the Highlands.

3 *Prince Charles Edward Stuart. One of several contemporary 'portraits' known as 'Harlequin type'*

Oh first of garbs, garments of happy fate;
So long employed, of such antique date;
Look back some thousand years till records fail,
And loose themselves in some romantic tale;
We'll find our god-like fathers nobly scorned
To be by any other dress adorned.

It was not only the Lowlanders who romanticised about the Highlanders of the past. In his *Records of Argyll* Lord Archibald Campbell writes:

To seek the 'origin of Tartan' is to seek for the first rude idea of decoration or ornamentation of stuffs, and simply goes back into the ages when women and men could first dye cloth; to seek the day the first lassie culled the first blaeberry to dye the cloth of her lover; to seek the primeval man who first used bullock's blood to dye the splendid red used in some of the clan colours. . . . Let us look into the composition of clan colours, sir, to see that they are older than the history of any costume that was ever written.

Some writers of the 'antique' school made it quite clear that they had little regard for anyone who might challenge their views. J. G. Mackay, who entitled his book on Highland dress as 'Romantic', wrote:

On the tower of St Clement's Church, in Rodel, Island of Harris, there is a sculpture representing a figure in the Highland dress, and showing the different parts of the dress in detail, the kilt, jacket, bonnet, and hose, with the plaid as distinct from the kilt. The date of the building is sometime in the thirteenth century, and there the figure stands . . . giving silent but most conclusive evidence of the age and authenticity of the dress, while generations of scribblers have been writing columns and columns of nonsense about it.

No sculpture which could be said to resemble this description has ever been found on the island of Harris. A thirteenth-century figure wearing a jacket and kilt would be an impossibility, nevertheless Mackay believed that he saw such a figure and records it as 'conclusive evidence'.

The whole subject of Highland dress history was bedevilled with racial and nationalistic feeling at the end of the nineteenth century. Dr William F. Skene, who became Historiographer Royal for Scotland in 1881, wrote of 'that extraordinary prejudice against the Celtic race in general and against the Scottish and Irish branches of that race in particular, which certainly biased the better judgement of our best historians . . .'

There were, of course, only a very few people studying the history of Scottish costume at this time and possibly the atmosphere of acrimony was not encouraging. Some extraordinary statements in even learned publications seem to have gone unchallenged. For instance, in *Archaeologia*, Volume XXI, James A. Robertson described his 'discovery' from the Antonine Wall: 'From a part of its ruins there was dug up, some years ago, a piece of sculpture (and which is now preserved at Croy), that represents three figures exactly dressed in the national garb of the Highlanders.' The figures are not, as he suggests, Highlanders in their 'national garb' but, as one might expect, they are three Romans in their every-day dress.

Robertson was equally determined to discover evidence that Highland tartan was

4 *Watercolour drawing entitled 'Reeling' by Williams, inspired by the visit of King George IV to Edinburgh in 1822*

5 *Woollen suit excavated at Barrock, Wick. It probably belonged to a local peasant,* c. *1690. With it was found a plaid about 8 ft by 5 ft*

6 *Plate from the* Book of the Club of True Highlanders *by C. N. McIntyre North, 1881*

of great antiquity too. Eventually he found what he was convinced 'exactly' proved his theory in a translation of the writings of Diodorus Siculus which described the Gauls as wearing 'coats stained with various colours'. Robertson concluded that: 'Thus we see the Caledonian Gael, when they first arrived in Britain, wore clothing exactly answering to the Highland tartan of this day, but of course not of the modern distinctions as to clans'. There are other translations of the original but to Robertson 'various colours' meant Highland tartan.

Evidence to prove that the modern kilt was of great antiquity was eagerly sought wherever it might be found. According to James Logan 'Alexander I is represented on his seal . . . with the feile-beag and round targe'. It certainly requires a great deal of imagination to see a Scottish king, living in the 1120s, seated on a horse and wearing a kilt. In fact the seal is of the usual conventional form which survived for centuries. It shows the king in the normal dress of a mounted warrior of the day, his so-called kilt being a coat of mail, whilst his 'round targe' is the top of the long Norman shield which can be seen on many seals of the period.

Unfortunately many of these extraordinary statements have been accepted by subsequent writers who have not examined the source material. In the late 1930s and the early 1960s the Scottish press published a number of letters from anonymous correspondents supporting the belief that the kilt and clan tartans must be of great antiquity. But that argument has been going on for over a century. In the *Ulster Journal of Archaeology* for 1858, a correspondent enquired whether 'Scottish antiquaries have been able to discover a period when the kilt was not worn by Highlanders?'

There have been, however, a number of well-informed historians of Scottish national dress including those whose profession gave them access to authentic and original material. Allied to this opportunity they had, in some cases, a considerable knowledge of the ways of life in the Highlands and the culture of the Gael. This enabled them to study the subject with an awareness of the conditions under which clothing could be made in the glens, and the actual conditions under which it would be worn. These factors are essential to a full understanding of the subject.

No close student of the Highland heritage or folk-lore can ignore the monumental

7 *Brooches from the National Museum of Antiquities of Scotland*

work of Alexander Carmichael who died in 1912 (9, 10). His splendid set of volumes entitled *Carmina Gadelica* has never been surpassed in the field of Gaelic poetry and song. But he also made several archaeological discoveries in the Western Isles and I have always regarded him as the pioneer collector of the early pre-clan tartans. Several of these I now have in my collection and the beauty of their colours and design puts the present-day tartans to shame.

These rare and precious specimens came to me from the collection of William Skeoch Cumming, the Scottish artist who was a friend of Carmichael's. Born in 1864, Cumming at the age of 21 had completed over 80 portraits for his famous composite picture of the Royal Company of Archers leaving Holyrood during the visit of Queen Victoria. He then began painting portraits of members of the legal profession which appeared in his picture entitled 'Bench and Bar'. In the course of this work he visited most of the great Scottish houses, and everywhere he went he made notes and sketches of any items of early costume, arms and armour, and he also made small reproductions of any family portraits showing interesting dress or uniform.

To his vast collection of notes, drawings and pictures, he added a great treasure – the manuscript business correspondence and records of the firm of William Wilson and Sons, Bannockburn. From the 1780s until the early twentieth century they supplied the bulk of the civilian tartans made in Scotland and also most of the Highland dress worn by the Highland regiments from the 1790s until the time of the Boer War. This collection, contained in five tea chests, was gifted to me by his widow after his death.

Unfortunately Cumming never published the results of his important and original research. His notes and sketches are now dispersed amongst a number of collections, my own included.

The first publication which really discounted the follies of former theories on the reputed antiquity of clan tartans, was written by Colonel M. M. Haldane. It was published in the *Scots Magazine* in 1931, and its title *The Great Clan Tartan Myth* made its purpose abundantly clear. This informed and extensive article has been almost totally ignored by recent writers on tartans.

The undisputed expert on Highland military uniform up to the time of his death in 1947, was Major I. H. Mackay Scobie, founder Curator of the Scottish United Services Museum. With a staff of three wardens, no telephone and no typewriter he created between the years 1930 and 1947 a magnificent collection of international importance. As a member of a distinguished Highland military family, a good piper and Gaelic speaker, he was welcome in many Highland castles and cottages. Although he wrote a regimental history and a book on pipers and piping, he never published anything on the history of Highland dress apart from articles and letters in the periodical press. This is unfortunate because he had a considerable knowledge of the subject which has only survived in the form of notes. I will refer to his article on 'Tartan and Clan Tartans' in the appropriate chapter.

The statement by a Lord Lyon King of Arms in 1948 that the development of clan tartans for many names was 'Humbug', was followed by a stunned silence. Perhaps the

8 *A young Edwardian Highlander whose outfit is hardly designed for play*

reason why this opinion was never challenged was because Lord Lyon was a Gaelic scholar, a skilled man of law, and a magnificent figure in his Highland dress.

Finally, there was Dr A. E. Haswell Miller, Keeper of the Scottish National Portrait Gallery, a fine artist and meticulous student of costume. His notes, which have been preserved in the gallery, are of primary importance, and I recall with pleasure his expertise and wit as we visited public and private collections together.

To Belle Skeoch Cumming, Major Mackay Scobie, Dr Haswell Miller and Sir Francis Grant I owe a great debt. They all generated an infectious enthusiasm, and they all maintained a high standard of academic integrity. They played a considerable part in the disposing of a 'Romantic' myth, and replacing it with a truthful tradition in which we can have honest pride.

1

◆

Shirts, Mantles and Plaids

A DISTINCTIVE Scottish Highland dress emerged very slowly from its Gaelic Irish
entanglements. It is not easy therefore to select a starting point for its history
which must rely on slight and fugitive references spread over a period of several
centuries. This 'dawn' period might be said to begin in the eleventh century and
continue on to the sixteenth, during which time the accounts are of bare legs, shirts and
mantles. But although these particular aspects caught the eyes of the early writers, they
were not entirely exclusive to the Scottish Highlanders.

These prototype costumes are, however, relevant and the most significant
references belonging to this early period have been published and discussed by H. F.
McClintock, and most writers on the subject have used the collection of accounts
published in 1834 by the Iona Society under the title *Notices of the Highland Dress and
Armour, collected from various sources*, by Donald Gregory and William F. Skene.

One important source which has been neglected by writers on Highland dress, is
the list of over a thousand accounts of Scotland compiled by Sir Arthur Mitchell,
K.C.B. In April 1901, he read a paper to the Society of Antiquaries of Scotland entitled
'A List of Travels, Tours, Journeys, Cruises, Excursions, Wanderings, Rambles, Visits,
etc., relating to Scotland' which was subsequently published. I was fortunate enough to
acquire his own copy into which he had added further references during the remainder
of his life.

It may be that Sir Arthur Mitchell published his list after reading P. Hume Brown's
Early Travellers in Scotland, published in 1891, and containing only two dozen entries
despite his statement in the Preface that it was 'as complete as I have been able to make
it'.

The accepted starting point for these early references is the account known as
Magnus Berfaet's Saga of AD 1093, of which McClintock gives the following literal
translation:

It is said when King Magnus returned from this expedition to the West, that he adopted the
costume in use in the Western Lands, and likewise many of his followers; that they went about
barelegged having short tunics [*kyrtlu*] and also upper garments [*yfir hafnir*], and so many men
called him 'Barelegged' or Barefoot.

This account does not tell us a great deal but it is interesting because of its early date. According to the Icelandic dictionary *kyrtlu* can be defined as a tunic or gown but the closest we can get to *yfir hafnir* is an upper garment. From early Irish writings and other sources this costume is now known as *Brat* and *Léine* and is described in detail by McClintock. It was worn by men and women alike in Ireland and Scotland up to at least the middle of the sixteenth century.

The word *Brat* is a native Irish word which has survived until the present day. When used to describe an item of costume it meant a woollen mantle or cloak worn as an outer garment. The word *Léine* indicates an outer garment resembling a shirt, and it is also a native Irish word. Although the appearance of this latter garment is usually described as *gel* – the word for 'bright', many modern writers have defined it as a 'saffron shirt'. It is unlikely that the true saffron dye was available in large quantities as it is made from the stigmas of the autumn crocus.

One reference which I have never seen quoted in Scottish costume histories is an early mention of Highland dress in a pilgrim's guide to Compostella, written between 1139 and 1173. It is reproduced in Vol. XXVIII of the *Scottish Historical Review* and the translation from the Latin is given as follows:

The Navarrese wear dark clothes, short, to the knee only, in the manner of the Scots, and shoes which they call lavarcas, of leather untanned, with the hair on, which they attach by straps about the feet, covering only the soles, and leaving the upper part bare. They were woollen mantles of dark colour (Palliolis vero laneis scilicet atris), hanging to the elbows, fringed like a cape, which they call saias.

This very interesting account was followed in the next volume of the *Scottish Historical Review* by an extract from a history of the First Crusade written by Guibert of Nogent between 1104 and 1112:

You might see [the soldiers] of the Scots, fierce in their own country, unwarlike elsewhere, bare-legged, with their shaggy cloaks, a scrip hang *ex humeris*, coming from their marshy homeland, and presenting the help of their faith and devotions to us, to whom their numerous arms would be ridiculous.

Both these references draw attention to the shaggy mantles and bare feet but the reference to the 'scrip' is of special interest. The original word is *sytarchia*, a medieval word for the scrip or pouch carried by pilgrims. In another context, Guibert described a pack of devils and the original Latin has been translated as 'wearing their scrips in the manner of the Scots, hanging forward from their haunches. . .'. This could be claimed as the earliest reference to the sporran.

There is now a gap of four centuries before our next reference to Highland dress. It was written by a Scot, John Major, whose *History of Greater Britain* was published in 1521. He was born in the Lowlands, near North Berwick, in 1470, and his *History*, written in Latin, describes the 'Wild Scots'.

Just as some writers have quoted the word *kyrtlu* used in Magnus Berfaet's Saga as evidence of a sort of Highland plaid in the tenth century, so others have seen the term *pannus lineus* used by Major, as evidence of a kilt. It is unnecessary to consider either of these fancies, but I quote McClintock's translation and his interpretation as evidence of scholarly consideration by an eminent costume historian:

Translation:

From the middle of the thigh to the foot they have no covering for the leg, clothing themselves with a mantle instead of an upper garment and a shirt dyed with saffron. . . . In time of war they cover their whole body with a shirt of mail of iron rings, and fight in that. The common people of the Highland Scots rush into battle having their body clothed with a linen garment manifoldly sewed and painted or daubed with pitch, with a covering of deerskin.

Interpretation:

The only uncertain point here is what exactly the 'pannus lineus' was. It was obviously different from the 'camisia' or 'shirt', and its interpretation must depend largely on what is assumed that Major meant by 'intersutum'. This particular compound of the verb 'suere', 'to sew', does not seem to occur in classical Latin though 'insuere' and 'consuere' are known. It might here mean either 'patched', 'pleated', or 'quilted', and each of these interpretations has been adopted by one or other of Major's translators.

'Pleated' would be a reasonable enough explanation if it applied to the shirts, seeing that we know that they often were pleated; but it does not apply to them. As the 'pannus lineus' was worn in battle and is mentioned in connection with arms and armour and not everyday dress, it is more natural to suppose that it meant quilted, or – to explain the phrase 'multipliciter intersutum' at length – 'made of two pieces of linen with a padding of hair or cotton between sewn together with many seams'. If so, it would be similar to the padded acton or *cotún* (to use the Irish word), worn as armour both in Ireland and in the Highlands – examples of which are to be seen on many tombs in Iona and the western Highlands. On the other hand 'pannus' is often used in the sense of a rag, so Major may, after all, only mean 'a tattered garment with many patches'. It is most likely, however, that the acton is intended.

I have quoted the above at length because it is the only reference which we have so far covering a period of many centuries, and also because it is a perfect example of the care which should be taken in translation. I would agree with McClintock that it is most likely the acton which Major describes.

A century and a half later, William Cleland wrote a satirical poem describing the manner in which the Highland Host waterproofed themselves by daubing on tar;

> *Its marvelous how in such weather,*
> *Ov'r hill and hop they came together;*
> *How in such stormes they came so farr;*
> *The reason is they'r smear'd with tar*
> *Which doth defend them heel and neck*
> *Just as it doth their sheep protect,*
> *But least ye doubt that this is true,*
> *They're just the colour of tar'd wool.*

When the Lordship of the Isles was forfeited in 1493 the kings of Scotland began to pay personal visits to the Highlands which for the first time encouraged them to wear some form of Highland dress. The Lord High Treasurer's Account dated 1538 records the details for a costume made for King James V as follows:

$2\frac{1}{4}$ ells of 'variant cullorit velvit' to be 'ane schort Heland Coit' at £6 the ell.
$3\frac{1}{4}$ ells of 'green taffatys to line the said coit with' at 10/- the ell.
3 ells of 'Heland tertane to be hoiss' at 4/4d the ell.
15 ells of 'Holland claith to be syde Heland Sarkis'

9 *Alexander Carmichael. Reproduced as frontispiece of* Carmina Gadelica *(Edinburgh 1900)*
10 *Alexander Carmichael, author of* Carmina Gadelica, *d. 1912*

This suit therefore consisted of a short jacket of vari-coloured velvet lined with green taffeta, but what was it that distinguished it as 'Highland'? Was it because the material was tartan or was it because of its short style? Then there is the question of the King's leg-covering. By 'hoiss' we can presume that these were what we would call 'trews' today, but does 'tertane' mean 'tartan' or does it mean the type of material known by that name and imported from France? Several latter-day writers have misquoted the original and given it as 'tartan' thereby providing a piece of 'evidence'.

One other item in the 1538 Inventory is '15 ells of "Holland claith to be syde Heland Sarkis"'. Some writers have translated 'syde' as 'three' but this is incorrect as the word means 'long' or 'hanging low'. Silk is also mentioned for sewing up the 'sarkis', and also ribbons for ornamenting the wrists. In 1578, Bishop Lesley described the use of silk thread in the stitching up of these large Highland shirts.

In the 'Inventair of the Jowellis Plenissings Artaillierie and Munitioun being within the Castell of Edinburgh pertaining to our Soverane Lord and his Hienes Derrest Moder MDLXXVIII' I came upon the following entries:

Ane hieland mantill of black freis pasmentit with gold and lynit with blak taffetie.
Ane blew hieland mantill.
Ane quhiet hieland mantill.

This entry throws a little more light on the previous one, written 40 years earlier, remembering that as both are inventories, the descriptions used would presumably be accurate. It describes three mantles, the first made of a rough black thick cloth braided with gold, the second and third being of blue and white respectively. These three mantles I assume to be the shaggy warm mantles of the type exported by the Irish in Tudor times and mentioned by Bishop Lesley in 1578 as 'villosas stragulas'. In view of this I presume that the words 'Heland' or 'hieland' used in the inventories, were descriptive of the style of the garments and not of the colour or pattern of the material.

Nicholaye d'Arfeville, a French cosmographer, who accompanied James V as a member of his naval expedition to the Western Isles, says of the natives: 'Ils portent, comme les Irlandois, une grande et ample chemise, safranée, et par desus un habit long jusque à genoux de grosse lain, à mode d'une soutane'.

About 1542 a Highland priest called John Elder wrote to Henry VIII proposing a Union between Scotland and England, the original letter now being in the British Museum. Once again there is emphasis on the bare legs of the Highlander and it is interesting to read the extent of Elder's explanation of the term 'Reddshanke'. However, it is from choice rather than poverty that the Highland shanks are bare. Despite the scorn of their more delicate fellow-countrymen, when the Reddshankes come to court they can hold their own in the world of fashion:

Moreover, wherfor they call us in Scotland Reddshanckes, and in your Graces dominion of England roghefootide Scottis, pleas it your Majestie to understande, that we of all people can tolleratt, suffir, and always best with colde, for boithe somer and wyntir, (excepte whene the froest is mooste vehement,) goynge alwaies bair leggide and bair footide . . . therfor, in so moche as we use and delite so to go alwaies, the tendir delicatt gentillmen of Scotland call us Reddshanckes. And agayne in wyntir, when the froest is mooste vehement (as I have saide) which we can not suffir bair footide, so weill as snow, whiche can never hurt us whene it cummes to our girdills, we go a huntynge, and after that we have slayne redd deir, we flaye of the skyne, bey and bey, and settinge of our bair foote on the insyde thereof . . . mesuringe so moche therof, as shall retche up to our ancklers, pryckynge the upper part therof also with holis, that the water may repas wher it entris, and stretchide up with a gtronge thwange of the same, meitand above our saide ancklers, so, and pleas your noble Grace, we make our schoois. . . . And althoughe a greate sorte of us Reddshanckes go after this manner in our countrethe, yeit never the les, and pleas your Grace, whene we come to the courte (the Kinges grace our great master beinge alyve) waitinge on our Lordes and maisters, who also, for velvettis and silkis be right well araide, we have as good garmentis as some of our fellowis whiche gyve attandaunce in the court every daye.

This delightful account obviously was meant to come as something of a revelation to the King, who Elder presumed had never even heard of Highland shoes. When 'Jo. Ben' visited Orkney in 1529 the only thing which he considered worth recording about the local costume was the fact that 'laymen heir have hair shoes made out of seal skins drawn together with a latchet – called in the vernacular rifflings.'

By now, the second half of the sixteenth century, there are many accounts containing references to Highland costume, but, on the other hand, there are also many which do not. Although the appearance of some Scots was undoubtedly distinctive, we cannot tell to what extent this was so. These accounts were written by a variety of native Scots and visitors with a variety of interests.

There is one account belonging to this period which illustrates the fact that even the Bishop of Ross found the dress of the Highlanders in his diocese worth recording. In 1578 his *De origine, moribus et rebus gestis Scotorum* was published in Rome, and the original Latin text is given by McClintock (1950). The following is a modern translation:

Their clothing was made for use (being chiefly suited for war) and not for ornament. All, both nobles and common people, wore mantles of one sort (except that the nobles preferred those of several colours). These were long and flowing, but capable of being neatly gathered up at pleasure into folds. I am inclined to believe that they were the same as those to which the ancients gave the name of Brachae. Wrapped up in these for their only covering, they would sleep comfortably. They had also shaggy rugs, such as the Irish use at the present day, some fitted for a journey, others to be placed on a bed. The rest of their garments consisted of a short woollen jacket, with the sleeve open below for the convenience of throwing their darts, and a covering for the thighs of the simplest kind, more for decency than for show or defence against cold. They made also linen very large shirts, with numerous folds and wide sleeves, which flowed abroad loosely to their knees. These, the rich coloured with saffron and others smeared with some grease to preserve them longer clean among the toils and exercises of the camp, which they held it of the highest consequence to practise continually. In the manufacture of these, ornament and a certain attention to taste were not altogether neglected, and they joined the different parts of their shirts very neatly with silk thread, chiefly of a red or green colour.

Having reached the period of the mid-sixteenth century we can seek pictorial evidence to add to the written accounts. However, again because of the Irish entanglements, we have no clear starting point. The great German artist, Albrecht Dürer, made a drawing in 1521 said to be of Irish soldiers and poor people. But Dürer never visited the British Isles so he must have met them on the Continent. The two soldiers, who are beautifully drawn, might well have been mercenaries and therefore possibly galloglasses – Hebridean professional soldiers found in nearly all Irish war-parties at this time. The 'poor people' all wear long tunics or shirts reaching to their shins, and mantles or jackets. Two are bare-footed whilst one wears brogues.

James Laudy, an eminent Belgian artist and costume historian, drew my attention to a picture in the Royal Museum of Fine Arts in Brussels, painted by Aertsen, a Dutch artist, about 1560. It depicts Jesus at the home of Martha and Mary but the costume is contemporary to the artist's time. One of the figures in the background shows a man wearing a heavy brown fringed mantle over a short-sleeved blue jacket with white or pale-coloured lines. From under these short sleeves protrudes a wrist-length sleeve of pale brown. The man is bare-legged. Laudy considers that this figure might represent one of the many Scots to be found wandering on the Continent at this time.

Whereas there may be some doubt about the nationality of these figures, there is none when we come to consider our next illustrations (*11*). They appear in the *Receuil de la diversité des Habits* published in Paris in 1562, and are entitled as 'Scottish', although clearly showing the similarity to Irish dress at this period. The man's cloak is possibly 'shaggy' and certainly fringed. He seems to have a bow and arrows, possibly a dagger, and a sword the scabbard of which has Irish characteristics. His helmet and his boots are unusual although McClintock suggests that they might be *cuarans*. I agree with him that the *Receuil* drawings might well be fanciful and made from descriptions rather than from life. The savage Scottish lady is wearing a voluminous sheepskin cloak.

It is interesting that even this, one of the earliest illustrations entitled as 'Scottish' has been quoted as 'evidence' of Highland dress. John Sobieski Stuart describes the male figure as being 'clothed in doublet, plaid and truis'!

The practice of costume artists using earlier illustrations as a basis of their own work is no new device. Half a century after the *Receuil*, a map of Ireland by Speed was published and six figures said to represent Irish men and women were used to decorate the margin. Two of them, entitled '*The Wilde Irish Man*' and '*The Wilde Irish Woman*' were clearly from the *Receuil* figures described above. Two Highland figures on Speed's map of Scotland appear to be wearing plaids.

11 *Scottish Highlanders portrayed by a French artist in the mid-sixteenth century. From the* Receuil de la diversité des habits, *published in Paris in 1562*

Unfortunately that great costume artist and engraver, Wenceslas Hollar, who worked in England from 1637 until 1687, never, as far as I know, drew a Scottish figure. Nevertheless, his 'Irish' woman in her long mantle with its shaggy collar, must surely depict a costume commonly seen in Scotland also. The linen kerchief which she wears wrapped around her head is typically Scottish.

Lucas de Heere, a native of the Low Countries, lived in England from 1567 to 1577. He had quite a sense of humour and regarded English fashion as lacking in imagination. He therefore drew an Englishman without any clothes but bearing over his arm a length of cloth and holding in his hand an outsize pair of scissors.

McClintock (1950) published a colour reproduction of one of de Heere's watercolour paintings of Irish people from the manuscript book in the Library of Ghent University, Belgium. The water-colour drawing of a 'Schotsche Hooglander' (*12*) is from the same source. Over his shoulders he wears the shaggy mantle hitched up to reveal a long-sleeved tunic with a short pleated skirt. This is a common European

12 *Line drawing after a watercolour drawing by Lucas de Heere, c. 1577, in the library of Ghent University*

garment of the period, but the cross-hatched lines might well indicate that the original had a tartan-like appearance. On his feet he wears flat shoes or brogues, and he carries a large sword of the Highland claymore type and a long dagger fastened to his belt.

This illustration has the appearance of a drawing done from life and not from hearsay. But what is really important is the fact that the drawings are coloured. When my *History of Highland Dress* was first published (1962), I only had a black and white reproduction of this drawing to examine. This was in a very rare limited edition of the de Heere manuscripts published in 1937, in Antwerp, under the title *Beschrijving der Britische Eilanden*. However, on the evidence of the lines half-way above the knees, I felt sure that our Highlander was wearing 'shorts', a garment which historians of Scottish costume have overlooked. Then, in 1964, James Laudy visited Brussels Museum and made an exact water-colour copy of the Highlander and sent it to me. It confirmed his opinion that the garment appeared to be 'very short trews, much like modern football shorts.' The colour drawing shows a distinct difference between the flesh-coloured legs and the pale blue-grey shorts.

McClintock drew attention to the evidence of Irish shorts which had been carved as early as the tenth century on a stone cross at Monasterboice in Co. Louth. Again, in the eighth-century *Book of Kells* we find a man carrying a spear and buckler and wearing what could be shorts.

If we examine some of the early references to trews we will find that they could refer to long or short leg coverings. Even Bishop Lesley's reference to 'foemoralia simplicissima', (1578) seems to translate as a simple covering for the *thighs*. When he goes on to say that they were worn more for decency than show or defence against the cold, the inference that they were shorts is stronger than ever.

There is an interesting engraving of the battle at Gembloux in 1578 showing Scottish troops described as 'Scoti nudi pugnantes'. They are in fact naked except for fairly heavy loin-cloths, some of which might be described as shorts. The habit of girding up loose garments between the legs when in action was practised by the ancient Romans and the eighteenth-century Highlanders.

By now there are many references to the style of sixteenth-century Scottish Highland costume, but it is not until 1581 that we have significant details about their colours. There is, of course, no mention of any form of 'clan tartan', the emphasis is, as one might expect, on camouflage. In that year George Buchanan published his *Rerum Scoticarum Historia*, and a translation (1827) has been made as follows:

They delight in variegated garments, especially stripes, and their favourite colours are purple and blue. Their ancestors wore plaids of many colours, and numbers still retain this custom, but the majority now in their dress prefer a dark brown, imitating nearly the leaves of the heather, that when lying upon the heath in the day, they may not be discovered by the appearance of their clothes; in these wrapped rather than covered, they brave the severest storms in the open air, and sometimes lay themselves down to sleep even in the midst of snow.

It is now, at the end of the sixteenth century, that we come to one of the great landmarks in the history of Highland dress – the clear identification of that very individualistic garment the belted plaid, direct ancestor of the kilt. When a party of Highland mercenaries arrived in Ireland in 1594 to assist Red Hugh O'Donnel against the English, their clothing could no longer be mistaken for Irish. Lughaidh O'Clery's description in Irish Gaelic has been translated as follows:

> They were recognised among the Irish Soldiers by the distinction of their arms and clothing, their habits and language, for their exterior dress was mottled cloaks of many colours with a fringe to their shins and calves, their belts were over their loins outside their cloaks.

Notice that these cloaks were fringed and no doubt had been worn over linen shirts in the Scottish Highlands and Islands for some time. There is no question of them being of a uniform pattern or colour, merely of many colours – *breacbhrait ioldathacha*.

Before describing the belted plaid in detail let us turn to a splendid description of the Highlander's costume of the early seventeenth century. John Taylor, who described himself as the 'Water Poet' and who walked from London to Edinburgh 'not carrying any Money to or fro, neither Begging, Borrowing, or asking Meate, Drinke, or Lodging'. This rollicking, good-humoured traveller met with prodigious hospitality including, in 1618, an invitation to attend a great Hunt on the Braes of Mar attended by most of the nobility and gentry of the district:

> . . . where they doe conforme themselves to the habite of the High-land-men. . . . Their habite is shooes with but one sole apiece; stockings, (which they call short hose) made of a warm stuffe of divers colours, which they call Tartane; as for breeches, many of them, nor their forefathers, never wore any, but a jerkin of the same stuffe that their hose is of, their garters being bands or wreathes of hay or straw, with a plead about their shoulders, which is a mantle of divers colours, much finer and lighter stuffe than their hose, with blue flat caps on their heads, a handkerchiefe knit with two knots about their necke; and thus they are attyred. . . . As for their attire, any man of what degree soever that comes amongst them, must not disdaine to weare it; for if he doe, then they will disdaine to hunt, or willingly to bring in their dogges; but if men be kind unto them, and be in their habit; then are they conquered with kindnesse. . . .

This is perhaps the most important description of the period because it is not only very detailed but also it emphasises the fact that on this great social occasion no-one must disdain to wear the 'right' attire. Attempts have been made to interpret the word 'jerkin' as meaning 'kilt' but I cannot accept this, and as Taylor was a very competent observer I think that he meant exactly what he said.

The 'plead' which he describes as being worn by the Highlanders was what is now referred to as the Belted Plaid, the simplest of garments which, nevertheless, has suffered from faulty description and mis-translation since the time of its origination. In fact, it was merely a large rectangular piece of material about five feet wide and roughly 14 to 16 feet long. Because of the difficulty of weaving a wide web on the old hand loom, it was made up two lengths of material about 30 inches wide sewn together.

The Gaelic word for a blanket is *plaide* and this is exactly what it was. At night, the owner merely had to roll up in it to have a fine warm bed – indoors or outdoors. In the morning, a little rearrangement converted it into a comfortable costume which could be adjusted to meet the wearer's needs in peace or war (2).

When it became a garment it acquired another Gaelic name, *Feileadh Mor*, meaning the big wrap or covering.

The conversion from bedding to clothing was achieved in rather an interesting manner. First of all the Highlander placed a belt on the ground and laid the plaid down lengthwise on top of it. This was next folded up in pleats over the belt and at right angles to it. He then lay down on top of the plaid with his back parallel to the pleats and the bottom edge behind his knees. Extending his arms to either side, he took hold of the edges of the material and folded them over his waist. Having fastened the belt he stood up, now wearing a rough replica of the modern kilt below the belt and a large amount of loose material hanging over it.

The many ways in which the top half of the belted plaid could be worn are illustrated in a number of eighteenth-century engravings, particularly the Van der Gucht drawings of the 1740s. In addition to military styles they illustrate 'The Highlanders in their accostumes clothes, and downwards hanging cloke' and 'A Highlander who put on his cloke about his schoulders when weather is sed to rain'. Whilst fighting, the belted plaid could be arranged in a number of ways to give easy access to the weapons and to leave the wearer's arms free to wield them (78).

There was also another manner of arranging the plaid which was noted by Skeoch Cumming but which, as far as I know, has never been published. It was used particularly in Inverness-shire by men and women alike. The plaid, in this case only about eight feet long, was held hanging behind the back with the arms widely extended outwards holding the top corners in each hand with the top centre drawn over the head like a hood. The hands were then brought together in front and the top corners knotted together. The arms were raised, lifting the knot over the head and placing it behind the neck. The hood could then be left in place or lowered and the mantle fastened over the breast with a pin or brooch. A belt could be worn around the waist but in this form the plaid was an outer garment.

John Taylor's admiration for the plaid was not shared throughout Scotland. In 1624 the Church Synod of Moray reported that 'ye brethern haunts to ye Presbitarie with uncomly habits, such as bonats and plaids, whairfor the assemblie ordains them not to haunt ye Presbitarie any mair with uncomly habbitts'.

There is evidence too that at least one Highland gentleman strongly disapproved of the native costume. About 1620, Sir Robert Gordon wrote to his nephew, the Earl of Sutherland, thus:

Use your diligence to take away the reliques of the Irishe barbaritie which as yet remains in your contrey, to wit, the Irishe langage, and the habit. Purge your countrey peice and peice from that unciwill kynd of cloithes, such as plaids, mantles, truses and blew bonnets. Mak sewere acts against those that shall weare them. Cause the inhabitants of the countrey to cloith them selves as the most ciwill prowinces of the Kingdome do, with doublet, hoise, cloiks and hats, which they may do with less chargs then the other. It is no excuse which some wold pretend alledgeing that unciwill habit to be the lightest among the montanes. They may cloith them selves (if they list) with coats and breiches of one colour, as light and handsome as plaid and trews.

It can be seen from this letter that attempts had previously been made to get the Highlanders to dispose of their plaids and trews, and that these had been met with counter-arguments by them in favour of the suitability of their native clothes to life in the mountains. Sir Robert was a bit of a kill-joy and insisted that the folk of Sutherland must 'eshew the footeball as a dangerous and unprofitable exercise'. Shooting and 'gofing', on the other hand, he described as 'honest exercise'.

By the mid-seventeenth century there are many references to Highland dress in travellers' accounts, estate and household records, Kirk Session Records, Burgh Court Books and other sources. Figures on maps and heraldic achievements are quoted as wearing plaids, trews and kilts and I have discussed the most important of these in my *History of Highland Dress*. I have described our next item of pictorial evidence also, but in view of the fact that it is unique and can be readily examined in the National Portrait Gallery of Scotland, it must be included here (*colour plate 1*).

The artist Michael Wright was an antiquary with an obvious interest in costume, and although he has been regarded as a Scot, I believe he was born a Londoner, and that he only made a relatively brief visit of four or five years to Scotland. Although Evelyn recorded in his Diary for 3 October 1662 that he had visited 'Mr Wright, a Scotsman, who had lived long at Rome', on the other hand we know that Wright was apprenticed to George Jameson in Edinburgh on 6 April 1636, as a 'citizen of London'. It would appear that he painted the Highlander about 1660, but who is this man attired in such splendour? Lord Archibald Campbell used this picture as a frontispiece and entitled it 'James, second Earl of Moray'. It has also been said to represent 'Sir Iain Campbell of Glenorchy, 1st Earl of Breadalbane'. The Scottish National Portrait Gallery catalogues it as a 'Highland Chieftain'. I believe that it is a portrait of an actor called Lacy 'an excellent low comedian and so pleasing to King Charles'.

I have discussed this picture fully in my *History* and here we will examine it purely as an excellent life-size illustration of mid-seventeenth century Highland dress. It shows that despite its simple form the belted plaid could be worn with dash and swagger. It is painted in several shades of brown and buff with crimson and black lines. The pattern of this plaid is highly complex, and despite very close examination, neither the late Dr Haswell Miller nor myself were able to work out any repeat. Unlike modern clan tartans, however, some of the early tartans did not have a repeat in the sett and I have specimens in my own collection showing this. The doublet, worn over a full and frilled shirt, is probably made of silk extensively embroidered in gold, and of the style which could have been seen at court at this period. The wide bonnet is probably made of velvet and it is decorated with an ostrich plume. The black and red hose are interesting as they have a horizontal join above the calf and a 'cock's comb' down the vertical back seam. No examples of this type of hose have survived as far as I know, but one would expect them to be worn out and discarded. However the same zig-zag is shown on the back seam of the hose worn by Alastair Grant the Champion, painted in 1714. Wright's Highlander wears long wide garters of gold ribbon with silver thread. His flat brogues have many holes punched in them, ankle straps and large tongues.

It is interesting to recall the importance which John Elder put on Highland shoes in the mid-sixteenth century. Likewise the attention of John Taylor was drawn to them in 1618, when he remarked on the thin single sole. This thin sole, which we see in the Wright portrait, is still being referred to 150 years later when the 'Generality now wear shooes having one thin Sole only.' It was about this time that shoes shaped to each individual foot *brogan cama*, were coming into use. The old *brogan direach* were straight shoes which chould be worn on either foot and were usually worn on alternate feet on alternate days. The Gaelic word *brog* has a number of meanings apart from 'shoe'. It can mean 'sock, socket, busk, busket, buskin', etc. Another word which usually meant old or shapeless shoes, was *bachaill, brachaill* or *sprachaill*, according to locality.

Alexander Carmichael recorded amongst his notes the words of a song entitled 'The Gaelic Shoe' which was sung or intoned during the stitching up of a brogue. The first verse takes the form of a tongue-twister, and the poem concludes:

> *Awl, last, tallow, waxen thong,*
> *Thrust through heel hen-feather-prong,*
> *Stitches eighteen up from toe,*
> *Down to heel right round a row,*
> *In the Gaelic shoe they go.*

Among the Statutes to be revived in the Burgh of Elgin in Moray, 1715, is the following entry regarding shoes; 'The best pair of men's shoes with leather heels, being double soled, of eleven inches or above, to be sold at thirty-six shillings Scots . . . the best pair of women's shoes, double-soled, timber on leather healed, at twenty shillings Scots.' Cheaper single-soled shoes were still being sold and bairn's shoes were six shillings.

With the dawn of the eighteenth century pictorial evidence of Highland dress becomes much more plentiful. A life-size portrait painted by Richard Waitt, and also now in the Scottish National Portrait Gallery, provides an interesting comparison to the 'Highland Chieftain'. Despite the equally splendid costume it is obviously not a 'theatrical' work, but a factual portrait. It shows Kenneth, 3rd Lord Duffus, a gallant Jacobite who took part in the Rising of 1715, and who died in 1734 (*13*).

He wears a handsome crimson doublet which was possibly made of velvet, and is lined with green material. It is slashed and pierced with small holes to form symmetrical patterns. The edges of the material are scalloped. His belted plaid has been allowed to fall over his belt in front and one corner is fastened to his left shoulder. His tartan hose are fastened with garters similar to those of the 'Highland Chieftain'.

Once again, despite careful examination of the original painting, it is impossible to find a satisfactory repeat in the sett of the tartan which consists of black, red, yellow and white stripes arranged in the typical complicated pattern to be found in the early specimens of the pre-clan tartan era.

The portrait of John Campbell, son of Lord Glenorchy, was probably painted by Charles Jervis in 1708 (*14*). The arrangement of the belted plaid is very clearly shown, bunched on the right hip and fastened to the left shoulder. As in the case of Lord Duffus his doublet is slashed and the skirts are also cut out in order to allow for the bunching of the belted plaid.

I have recorded six versions of this picture which is described by John Sobieski Stuart, and it has been suggested that it might have been painted by Kneller.

The colours used on both the Duffus and Campbell plaids are very similar, but the arrangement and the proportions differ. The shades of colour differ between one version of the picture and another. In fact one cannot be too dogmatic about the precise colours shown on an old painting which may have faded or even 'bled' together.

13 *Kenneth, Lord Duffus, painted by Richard Waitt, c. 1700. The upper part of the belted plaid hangs over the lower kilted part*

14 *John Campbell, son of Lord Glenorchy, probably painted in 1708 by C. Jervis. There are at least six versions of this portrait*

John Campbell's stocking-tops are interesting. They consist of a light blue or green zig-zag edged with brown, on a yellow background. Both the top and the bottom edges are scalloped. The hose themselves are of a red, green and black dicing.

The sporran is of leather and has the same long leather thongs as that of Lord Duffus. Very similar cords can be seen today fastened to game bags, particularly those used on the Continent. They are very practical for carrying game, the loop of the cord or thong being slipped over the head of the bird.

Another point of interest to be seen on John Campbell's portrait is the blue binding on the edge of his plaid. We find this on many portraits of the early and middle eighteenth century. The colour of the binding varies but the majority are of yellow.

Richard Waitt, who painted Lord Duffus, received patronage from the Grant families, the result of which is a fine series of pictures of Highland dress belonging to the first quarter of the eighteenth century. The most outstanding of these is a pair of full-length portraits of Alastair Grant the Champion (*15*), and William Grant the Piper (*16*). Both pictures are signed and dated 1714.

15 *Alastair Grant the Champion, painted by Richard Waitt, 1714*
16 *The Grant Piper, painted by Richard Waitt in 1714. The tartan, which is painted with great care, is unlike any Grant clan tartan worn today*

The Champion, Alastair Grant, was a man 'remarkable for strength, daring and courage'. He wears a brownish round bonnet bound in red with a red cockade, a blue jacket, a belted plaid and tartan stockings. His sporran is of leather with long cords terminating with tassels.

The Piper presents a more striking figure. He wears a scarlet jacket laced with silver and ornamented at the seams and edges with small rosettes, the sleeves being slashed and having wide cuffs.

The tartans worn by the two figures are very similar although the patterns of the hose differ. The edge of the Champion's plaid is bound in yellow whilst that of the Piper is bound in red.

The tartans of both plaids are bluey-grey, red, yellow and white with fine black lines and they only differ very slightly. John Sobieski Stuart described the tartan as 'Owr Spey', which he said was the description given by the people of Moray to 'gaudy sets of various colours on a white field, in the style of the mantles much worn on the South side of the Spey about a hundred years ago.'

Apart from the two large Grant portraits mentioned above, there is a fine series of half-length pictures of members of the family, all by Richard Waitt, signed and dated. Typical of these is the portrait of John Grant of Burnside (*17*). The tartans all differ from each other and none of them are of the sett worn today as a 'Clan Grant' tartan.

Plaids were not necessarily always made of tartan. On 11 January 1622, the Baron Court of Breadalbane fixed certain maximum charges for the weaving of cloth. For the weaving of a grey plaid of half hues the charges were fixed at two pecks of meal and two shillings silver. For a plaid that had only one sprang or stripe of hues the charges were one peck two lippies meal, and two shillings silver. For grey cloth, two pence and one peck meal the ell. And for tartan the charge was fourpence the ell and one peck two lippies meal. It was further ordained that every webster who should contravene these statutes would be compelled to pay ten pounds for each offence.

The value of clothing in the Highlands was high. In the *Scottish Historical Review* for January 1913, there is an account of a raid by 'loose and broken men' in 1698, on a farm near Aberfoyle. Isabell M'Clucky, the owner of the live-stock and goods which were plundered, made out a detailed inventory of them and it includes the following items of clothing:

of Cloath and wolen yaird estat to	£35
Eight plyds viz four qrof double and four single estat to	£48
ane pair of wollen Clats estat to	£1 –16/-
of mead neu harn in shirts 30 elns estat to	£12
of neu Linning in Shirts 24 elns estat to	£12
ten petticoats estat to	£30
four westcoats for women estat to	£4 – 6/-
thre gouns for women estat to	£12
2 pairs shoes & 2 pair stockings estat to	£5 – 8/-
two green aprons estat to	£3
ane buff belt	£1 – 4/-
two plyds estat to	£16

Some idea of the value of these items can be got by the fact that 'great southland Sheep' were estimated at 'thre pound Scots pice'. So thorough was Isabell M'Clucky in her claim that it includes 'a hundred cups of sheep muck' and 'Sixtie cups of cows muck'.

Fifty years earlier, Thomas M'Kenzie of Pluscardin put in a claim for clothing stolen by a gang of Highlanders which included 'ane whyt plaid worth eight punds With coat and trews and shoes worth four pund Scots with four pair of lining sheits worth four pund the pair, and pair of bed plaids worth twenty four punds tuo coverings worth four punds the peice Ten elne of new lining worth twentie shiling the elne Item ten elnes of tartan at threttie shilling the elne.'

And yet Captain Burt, who visited the Highlands in the 1730s, wrote of the Highland dress which 'distinguishes the native as a body of people distinct and separate', having the advantage of cheapness – 'A few shillings will buy this dress for an ordinary Highlander, who, very probably, might hardly be in condition to purchase a Lowland suit. . . .'

17 *Portrait of John Grant of Burnside by Richard Waitt, signed and dated 1725. The pattern of tartan is quite different in each of this series of accurate portraits*

18 *Major James Fraser of Castle Leather (1670–1750). The sporran is unusual but perhaps not out of keeping with its wearer*

By the time of the early eighteenth century the number of references to Highland dress throws some light on the extent to which it was worn. Highlanders in their plaids had been seen in the Lowlands for a century at least. When Sir William Brereton, a Cheshire gentleman, visited Leith about 1635, he was not very impressed by the appearance or habits of the local people, however:

Many Highlanders we observed in this town in their plaids, many without doublets, and those who have doublets have a kind of loose flap garment hanging loose about their breech, their knees bare; they inure themselves to cold, hardship, and will not diswont themselves; proper, personable, well-complectioned men, and able men; the very gentlemen in their blue caps and plaids.

The belted plaid was truly a unique garment. The Rev. Thomas Morer wrote in 1689 that the Lowlanders saw in the voluminous nature of that costume an additional advantage because, the Highlanders 'being too often men of prey, by this means they cover their booty the better, and carry it off without the owner's knowledge.' It must also surely be one of the only items of costume known to man having the advantage of being of great value when it was discarded. One tug at the belt and the Highlander was undressed for the fray. As the poet put it:

> *The Highlanders are pretty men*
> *For target and claymore;*
> *But yet they are but naked men*
> *To face the cannon's roar.*

Following in sequence the appearance of the 'Highland Chieftain', Lord Duffus, Lord Glenorchy, and the Grant Piper and Champion in their full-length portraits wearing the belted plaid, comes the portrait of Major James Fraser of Castle Leather (*18*). Painted about 1723, shortly after those mentioned above, it is the earliest known authentic portrait in oils showing the tartan trews. There are, of course, several line drawings of figures wearing this type of costume at an earlier date, and this might be an appropriate point at which to examine the history of the trews in greater detail.

2

The Trews

A GARMENT covering the body from the waist downwards to the ankles, and encasing the legs separately, has been in use in Europe since prehistoric times. Its origins were certainly not Scottish. W. F. Skene wrote, 'The third variety in the form of the dress worn by the Highlanders was that of the Truis, but this dress can be traced no further back than the year 1538'. By this he means that the first documentary account he has found refers to 'Heland tertane to be hoiss' and is dated 1538. It is only if we qualify the definition 'trews' with the word 'tartan' that we cannot date them to a much earlier period.

The trouserless Greeks and Romans were fascinated by the Celtic trews. The 70,000 Celtic warriors who marched towards Rome in 225 BC wore brightly coloured cloaks, shirts and trews. These early drawers are said to have been adopted by the British Celts after their first contacts with the Gauls of France. When the Romans conquered Gaul they called the new province *Gallia Braccata* (the land of the behosed Gauls). Although the Scottish Highland nobility and aristocracy of the eighteenth century were portrayed in trews, the Romans regarded with contempt the *bracae* as the dress of barbarians.

Coming nearer home, our modern word 'trews' is derived from the Irish *triubhas* or *truis*, a garment which we can see depicted in the eighth-century *Book of Kells*. They are shown in the two styles, one being ankle-length and the other taking the form of tight breeches.

In the 'Heimskringla' Icelandic Saga by Snorre Sturlason, there is a description of an Irishman who appeared in Norway about 1127 wearing 'trousers bound with ribands under his foot-soles'. In this and many other instances it is important to remember the close entanglement between Scottish and Irish culture and costume.

McClintock states that prior to the year 1200 trews were called '*bróc*', or some compound of that word. He also points out that both forms of costume, the *brat-and-léine* and the *jacket-and-trews* continued in use, in more or less altered forms, until the sixteenth century. Of the latter dress he writes:

> The *jacket-and-trews* dress on the other hand, close fitting covering the whole body and designed for warmth, is thoroughly Northern in type. Trousers or trews were worn by nearly all the 'Barbarian' peoples of Northern Europe with whom the Romans came in contact, such as the Gauls and Germans, so much that they were known among the Romans by the name adopted from the Gauls of *bracae* or *braccae*. Many representations of Gaulish *bracae* can be seen in Roman carvings or statuettes. They were sometimes tight, but more often loose and open at the ankles like modern trousers.

I have already referred to the drawing of a Highlander in short trews by Lucas de Heere, done about 1577. In 1581 John Derricke published his *Image of Ireland*, of which only one complete copy seems to have survived. One of the twelve woodcut engravings shows a chief and his officers at dinner in camp. There is no doubt about the trews worn by two of his followers as they are being lowered for obvious reasons. At this time there were many Scottish mercenaries fighting in Ireland – the so-called galloglasses.

The trews which had been worn in Ireland since pre-Christian times, must also have been widely known in the Scottish Highlands and Islands. However, John Derricke points out that their 'protractours' or foreign artists who tried to draw them, were often 'put out' by the form of the 'Irish trouzes'. In his own words – 'Irish trouzes more to put their strange protractours out'.

In the *Costume of the Clans*, John Sobieski Stuart refers to the *Image of Ireland* (1581) pointing out that in 'these impertinent lines are very accurately described the universal habits of the Hibernian and Scottish clans during the fifteenth and sixteenth centuries'.

Several travellers who visited Scotland during the late sixteenth and early seventeenth centuries have left us references to the trews. One says they were worn by gentlemen whilst another says the Highlanders wore them in 'the sharp winter weather'. As time passed the number of references to 'truces', 'truses', 'trowsis', and in the mid-seventeenth century our modern spelling 'trews' increases in use.

The seventeenth-century references end with the account by Martin Martin, a native of Skye who published his *Description* in 1703:

Many of the People wear *Trowis*, some of them very fine woven, like stockings of those made of Cloath; some are coloured and others striped; the latter are as well shap'd as the former, lying close to the Body from the middle downwards, and tied round with a Belt above the Haunches. There is a square piece of Cloth which hangs down before. The measure for shaping the *Trowis* is a Stick of Wood, whose length is a cubit, and that divided into the length of a finger, and half a finger, so that it requires more skill to make it, than the ordinary Habit . . . .'

There is a strange Gaelic rhyme describing the making of trews by rule of thumb entitled *Cumadh an Triubhais*. It includes the word 'nail' which was used as a measure of length for cloth in the fifteenth century. It represented the sixteenth part of a yard, or two-and-a-quarter inches. The poem could be translated as follows:

> *A full finger-length to the small,*
> *Eleven nails to the leg,*
> *Seven nails to the band;*
> *There are few whom that won't suffice,*
> *Let it be shaped straight,*
> *And three nails to the fork.*

The portrait of Major James Fraser to which I have already referred, (*18*) is the fore-runner to a series of great oil-paintings of Highland gentlemen painted during the first half of the eighteenth century. There are several versions of Fraser's portrait. He was a close friend of Lord Lovat who called him 'Major Bracks', and his pride in the Highland trews is well depicted in his portrait. The name of the artist is unknown and John Sobieski Stuart remarks rather unkindly that 'his portrait has been painted by a very bitter enemy to posthumous admiration.'

He wears a black cockade in his round bonnet, thereby showing his loyalty to the House of Hanover. The tartan of his jacket and trews is not very convincing, creating the effect of squares in two shades of green and red, all contained in black lines. The tartan of his small plaid consists of large squares of light red, smaller squares of light green, and white lines. Perhaps the most unusual feature is his well-filled oblong sporran with a small red 'tourie' at each bottom corner and two long thongs with gilt tassels – functional but hardly flattering.

This picture was probably painted in the early 1720s when Major Fraser was in his fifties. It has been suggested that the version in Inverness Town Hall was painted in 1715, whilst another copy of the picture was dated as '1723' by John Sobieski Stuart. For some reason the latter heartily disliked this picture. He described the coat as resembling 'the long and hideous stable waistcoat of a modern groom', the gartering of the trews as 'an inelegant fashion adopted at this period to prevent the tension of the cloth upon the knee', and the sporran as 'unsightly'. Because of its size, he considered that Fraser's plaid 'might have been his lady's shawl, had shawls been known to the Highlanders in 1723, . . . disposed with such base affectation of negligence that it must be supposed the lay study of a miserable artist rather than the natural usage of a Highland gentleman'. Even Fraser's shoes are described as 'square-toed clumsy clogs, which afford little association of feet which are said to have danced the "Gillie-Callum" before Caroline of Brandenburg.'

I would certainly not produce as contemporary evidence of the trews, Stuart's illustration in *Costume of the Clans* entitled 'Conflict; Katheran; trib; vocat; Clan Kaye et Clan Quhattan' and ascribed to 'Temp. Charles I.' This shows a highly ornate gentleman wearing skin-tight trews and a heavily fringed plaid flying high in the air behind him. He is poised on the top of a cliff and appears to be directing a battle taking place far below him. This extraordinary drawing is said to be 'From the original Drawing in a splendid MS copy of Boethius' Hist., in possession of Mr Hawkesly, Wardour Street, London.' The originals from which this and other illustrations in *Costume of the Clans* are said to have been taken would appear to have been seen by the Sobieski Stuart brothers only.

The next painting of this period showing the tartan jacket, trews and plaid has been the subject of debate (*19*). It was painted by Hans Hysing in 1726 and shows the 4th Duke of Leeds. In 1830, a copy of the picture was engraved by E. Scriven and published by C. Tilt as a portrait of the 'Young Pretender'. Then in 1908, the British Museum *Catalogue of Engraved British Portraits* produced a photograph of the picture with the title 'Prince Charles Edward Louis Philip Casimir, the Young Pretender when a Boy; W. L. standing in landscape, in a tartan dress. From picture in possession of Lord Rosebery.' Even Andrew Lang reproduced the picture in *Prince Charles Edward*, published in 1900. But in 1911 the truth was out. The catalogue of the Scottish Exhibition held in Glasgow that year described an engraving of Hans Hysing's portrait as 'said to be Prince Charles Edward but really a son of the Duke of Leeds.'

Now the interesting thing is that all during the time that Lord Rosebery's picture was entitled 'Prince Charles Edward Stuart' the life-size original painting signed and dated 'H. Hysing pinx. 1726' was hanging in Hornby Castle, the seat of the Duke of Leeds. It is, in fact, a portrait of his ancestor Thomas, fourth Duke of Leeds, when Earl of Danby.

As the Prince was born in 1720, he would have been only five or six years of age at the time the picture was painted, whereas the Duke of Leeds was 13 years of age. Furthermore, Hans Hysing was born in Stockholm in 1678 and came to London in 1700, where he stayed for the rest of his life painting many famous people including members of the Royal family. He could not have met the Prince.

Despite all these facts the picture continues to be wrongly entitled and appeared as a portrait of the Prince in a recent history of him.

Another fine illustration of the trews has also been the subject of faulty dating (20). The error was probably originally due to John Sobieski Stuart writing in the *Costume of the Clans* that this picture 'like many others in the Highland costume, has been supposed to be a portrait of the Prince Charles Edward.' whereas he believed the costume to belong to 'a period nearly half a century anterior'. I agree that it is not a portrait of the Prince and have never been able to trace any written claim to that effect. However I query Stuart's conclusion as to the name of the splendid Highlander in the portrait:

19 *The Duke of Leeds by Hans Hysing, 1726*

20 *Portrait by an unknown artist, probably depicting Andrew Macpherson of Cluny. The tartans of jacket, plaid and trews are of three different patterns*

From the traditionary recollections of the oldest member of the Cluny family, a lady ninety-two years of age, there is, however, no doubt that the original of the picture was the brave and 'beautiful' Andrew of Cluny, nineteenth chief of the clan Chattan, who died some time before the year 1701, with the costume of which period that of the picture perfectly corresponds.

This picture, when reproduced, is often dated 'circa 1660' and there are several versions of it with slight variations. In 1911 it was described in the Glasgow exhibition catalogue as 'Cluny Macpherson, 1649' and also 'Cluny Macpherson of the '45'.

I would be inclined to date it about the 1720s or 1730s. Painted by an unknown artist, it is almost certainly a portrait from life. The trews are of a green and brownish tartan with blue stripes whilst the plaid is of lighter tones of green with pinkish lines.

In an article entitled 'The Celtic Trews' by David MacRitchie, published in the *Scottish Historical Review*, 1904, the picture is reproduced with the title 'Andrew

Macpherson of Cluny, Painted in 1661'. How he identifies the picture and dates it with such certainty the author does not disclose.

Of the trews themselves he writes; 'This article requires to be emphasized, owing to popular misconceptions, not only among illiterate Cockneys, but also among many educated people in England, Scotland, and elsewhere'. As his 'earliest representation of a trews-wearing Highlander' he quotes a German playing-card 'printed in 1767', but the 'representation' evidently 'seems to date from the sixteenth or possibly the seventeenth century'.

21 *Jacket, trews and plaid worn by an English Jacobite during a visit to Scotland, 1744*

22 *An incident in the Battle of Culloden, painted by David Morier, an artist renowned for his accuracy, who is believed to have used Highland prisoners from the battle as models for this picture*

23 *A life-size portrait by F. de Troy of James, Duke of Perth, who died in 1746, as a young man in his thirties*

The wearing of the trews at the battle of Culloden is clearly depicted in David Morier's picture (*22*). They are worn with a tartan jacket by a charging clansman who carries a great bill-hook as he shouts defiance at the enemy. In contrast to this in the style is the very fine life-size portrait of James, Duke of Perth, who commanded the left wing at the battle and who died a young man in 1746 (*23*). There are at least three versions of this portrait with minor variations between them, and the artist was almost certainly F. de Troy. The colours of the coat, plaid and trews are the same narrow black stripes on a scarlet ground, but the sett varies. The coat is embellished with gold lace, as is his shoulder sword-belt which is rose-coloured and edged with blue.

The Duke's portrait shows the elegant effect which could be achieved by the tartan trews when worn by a man of good proportions. Indeed this fact had been remarked upon by Edward Burt of the Forfeited Estates Commission in his *Letters*, published in 1754 but written in the 1730s;

Few beside gentlemen wear the Trowze, that is, the Breeches and Stocking all of one piece, and drawn on together; over this Habit they wear a Plaid, which is usually three Yards long and two Breadths wide, and the whole Garb is made of chequered Tartan, or Plaiding; this, with the Sword and Pistol is called a *full dress*, and a well-proportioned Man, with any tolerable Air, it makes an agreeable Figure; but this you have seen in London, and it is chiefly their Mode of dressing when they are in the Lowlands, or when they make a neighbouring Visit, or go anywhere on Horseback; but those among them who travel on Foot, and have not attendants to carry them over the Waters, vary it into the *Quelt*, which is a Manner I am about to describe.

This is an interesting and important account written by an intelligent observer who spent several years in Scotland under the orders of General Wade. It tells us by whom and when the trews were worn and it also gives the dimensions of the little plaid or shoulder plaid. His *Letters* were written to a friend whom Burt presumed was familiar with the dress, having seen it in London, and this is the only reference of a documentary nature which tells us of the appearance of the Highland dress there before 1740.

In his book, Burt reproduces a drawing of Highlanders wearing their dress in a number of ways. These include the trews being worn with the belted plaid and also with the shoulder plaid (*21*).

The use and illustration of trews being worn during the Proscription period has been described elsewhere. But a portrait painted after the Repeal depicts the man who might be described as the Champion of the Trews (*24*) He is Sir John Sinclair of Ulbster, in his uniform as Colonel of the Rothesay and Caithness Fencibles which he raised in 1794, painted by Sir Henry Raeburn.

At that time Sir John was 40 years of age and already the first volumes of his monumental *Statistical Account of Scotland* had been published. This great work has provided material for students in every branch of Scottish history and all the profits from it were assigned by him to the Society for the Sons of the Clergy. He devoted his life to working for the benefit of his country.

Sir John Sinclair was an enthusiastic student of the history of Highland dress, and we will examine elsewhere his involvement in the early controversies regarding the antiquity of the kilt. However, his research convinced him of the necessity to preserve the use of the trews in view of their superior antiquity. Because of this, when he raised

his regiment, consisting of 600 men of Caithness, he dressed them in tartan pantaloons, small white sporrans and feathered bonnets. On the march they sang a regimental song which he had composed, one of the verses being:

> *Let others boast of philibeg,*
> *Of kilt and belted plaid,*
> *Whilst we the ancient trews will wear,*
> *In which our fathers bled.*

Sir John's great life-size portrait became widely popular and its mezzotint reproduction in colour by H. Macbeth-Raeburn was eagerly sought after. In 1800, the editor of the *British Military Journal* published a print based on the Raeburn portrait and dedicated to the Colonel and his officers in a 'correct representation of their uniform'.

This attempted revival of the wearing of trews, however, came at a time when there were other stronger influences at work which were to play a major part in the history of Highland dress. At the end of the eighteenth century and the beginning of the nineteenth, large numbers of men were being dressed in the kilt as the Highland regiments were being raised to meet the threat of Napoleon's great army.

It was also a time of change in the general fashion of men's wear throughout Britain. Breeches gradually went out of fashion and trousers began to replace them early in the nineteenth century and by the 1820s were in fairly general use. These early trousers were cut very tight – almost like pantaloons, or footless trews.

One cannot of course overlook the enormous effect which the Proscription Act of 1746 had upon the clothing of the Scottish Highlander. Revolution had interrupted the gentle pace of evolution and the day of mass-produced clothes was at hand. No other country has had a legal prohibition put on its costume so late in its history and the effect of the 'Diskilting Act' was so great that we must examine its origins in some detail.

24 *Sir John Sinclair, Champion of the Trews,* c. *1794*

3

♦

The Proscription and the Repeal

SUMPTUARY LAWS which attempted to curb extravangances in dress have been passed by many European countries for centuries. In the thirteenth century Venetian magistrates were appointed whose sole job was to enforce such regulations, and during the reign of Edward III English offenders were dealt with by Act of Parliament. These were economic measures, but the legal control of costume was also introduced for other reasons, one of these being the attempted suppression of political or racial symbolism.

During the reign of Henry VIII, an Act was introduced (1539) in Ireland, forbidding the people to dress their hair or wear any mantles, coats or hoods 'after the Irish fashion'. No man, nor man child, was to wear mantles in the street 'but cloakes or gowns . . . doublets and hose, shaped after the English fashion.'

But political symbolism continued in Ireland and in Scotland not only in dress but also in costume accessories. In the Victoria and Albert Museum, there is an ivory and paper fan painted with a scene of Queen Anne ascending to heaven, and a large white Stuart rose with two buds. This was obviously a drawing-room symbol of Jacobite sorrow on the death of the Queen in 1714.

During the early eighteenth century in Scotland, Acts were passed which attempted to disarm the Highlanders, but they were not successful. When General George Wade, Commander of the Forces in North Britain, arrived in Inverness in 1725, he attempted to enforce the 'Act for more effectual disarming the Highlands'. But only 20 years later the Hanoverian troops were met with a formidable display of steel.

After Culloden, in 1746, another Act for Disarming the Highlanders became law. One clause might be read as a compliment to the manner in which the Highland ladies denied any suggestion of weakness; 'If the person convicted shall be a woman, she shall, over and above the foresaid fine and imprisonment till payment, suffer imprisonment for the space of six calendar months, within the Tolbooth of the head burgh of the Shire or Stewartry within which she is convicted.'

But now the Highlanders had to part with more than their beloved arms. The Act of 1746 (19 Geo.II, c. 39) read:

And be it further enacted by the Authority aforesaid, That from and after the First Day of

August, One thousand seven hundred and forty seven, no Man or Boy, within that part of Great Britain called Scotland, other than such as shall be employed as Officers and Soldiers in His Majesty's Forces, shall, on any Pretence whatsoever, wear or put on the Clothes commonly called Highland Clothes (that is to say) the Plaid, Philebeg, or little Kilt, Trowse, Shoulder Belts, or any Part whatsoever of what peculiarly belongs to the Highland Garb; and that no Tartan, or party-coloured Plaid or Stuff shall be used for Great Coats, or for Upper Coats; and if any such Person shall presume after the said First Day of August, to wear or put on the aforesaid Garments, or any part of them, every such Person so offending, being convicted thereof by the Oath of One or more credible Witness or Witnesses, before any Court of Justiciary, or any One or more Justices of the Peace for the Shire or Stewartry, or Judge Ordinary of the Place where such Offence shall be committed, shall suffer Imprisonment, without Bail, during the Space of Six Months, and no longer; and being convicted for a second Offence before a Court of Justiciary, or at the Circuits, shall be liable to be transported to any of His Majesty's Plantations beyond the Seas, there to remain for the Space of Seven Years.

To be disarmed was something which the Highlanders could easily understand even if they did not completely obey. But commanding them to give up a costume in which they had considerable pride was another matter. This was an imposition of personal shame and they reacted with indignation – particularly the clans which had been loyal to the Government. The Gaelic bard, Alexander MacDonald, expressed his sentiments which were translated thus;

> *A coward was he not a king who did it,*
> *Banning with statutes the garb of the brave;*
> *But the breast that wears the plaidie,*
> *Ne'er was a home to the heart of a slave.*
>
> *Let them tear our bleeding bosoms,*
> *Let them drain our latest veins,*
> *In our hearts is Charlie, Charlie!*
> *While a spark of life remains.*

It is difficult to assess the exact extent to which the Diskilting Act was enforced. It was not put into immediate force and I have been unable to trace any prosecutions before 1748. Appeals to the Government to reconsider the Act came from several quarters including one from Lord President Forbes to the Lord Lyon, dated 8 July 1747. Forbes had been instrumental in maintaining a certain degree of reason amongst the Highland clans in previous years, and his plea to the Government was honest and reasonable. He saw the wisdom in the Disarming Act and the folly in the Diskilting Act. The following is an extract of that part of his letter which deals with the dress of the Highlander

The garb is certainly very loose, and fits men inured to it, to go through great fatigues, to make very quick Marches, to bear out against the Inclemency of the Weather, to wade through Rivers, and shelter in Huts, Woods and Rocks upon Occasion; which men dress'd in the Low Country Garb could not possibly endure. But then it is to be considered, that as the Highlands are circumstanced at present it is, at least it seems to me to be, an utter Impossiblity, without the advantage of this Dress, for the Inhabitants to tend their Cattle, and to go through the other parts of their Business, without which they could not subsist; not to speak of paying Rents to their Landlords. Now, because too many of the Highlanders have offended, to punish all the rest who have not, and who I will venture to say are the greatest Number, in so severe a manner seems to me unreasonable. . . .

Unfortunately the Lord President's advice was ignored, he was snubbed by the King and many of the funds which the Government owed him were never paid. In fact the Acts were now further enforced on those Highlanders who were under the slightest suspicion. They were made to take the following oath:

I, . . . do swear, and as I shall have to answer to God at the Great day of Judgement, I have not nor shall have in my possession, any gun, sword, pistol, or arm whatsoever; and never use any tartan, plaid, or any part of the Highland garb; and if I do so, may I be cursed in my undertakings, family, and property – may I never see my wife and children, father, mother and relations – may I be killed in battle as a coward, and lie without Christian burial, in a strange land, far from the graves of my forefathers and kindred; – may all this come across me if I break my oath.

This barbarous oath was totally in keeping with the savage reaction of the Duke of Cumberland to the Jacobite Rising. In December 1748 however, a *General Order to the Army in Scotland* decreed that those who offended against the Diskilting Act were to be taken before a magistrate in the prohibited clothing but that 'no insult or abuse be offered to the person or persons of those who shall be taken up and carried before the civil power . . .'

Strangely enough, one of the earliest offences which was reported in the Press, took place not in the Highlands but in the heart of Edinburgh. The *Scots Magazine* of 1749 reported that 'A Highlander was taken up on the street of Edinburgh, August 12, and carried prisoner to the castle, for wearing a philabeg. One Stewart, another Highlander, was taken into custody at Edinburgh, for the same crime, on September 18.'

About this time, according to a local tradition, the village football team at Petty in Invernesshire appeared for the annual match on Christmas Day clad in wide baggy trousers made of homespun by the Petty tailor. The crowd, accustomed to seeing the players in Highland dress, broke into roars of laughter, at which the team ran off home. When the result of the great match was received by the Laird of Cawdor, at that time resident in London, he was greatly upset at the plight of his tenants and wrote to his factor:

I had thought that the poor Highlanders who were depressed by wearing breeches might have been very agreeably accommodated by wearing wide trousers like seamen made of canvas. Nankeen might do for the more genteel, but I would have them short, as short as a philabeg and then they would be almost as good and yet lawful'

Drummond-Norie quotes a report from a Captain John Beckwith on duty at Strontian in Ardnamurchan, dated 26 May 1752. On that day the corporal in command of one of his patrols had taken up a man by the name of Cameron, servant to a Mrs Jane Cameron, who had a piece of tartan wrapped round him like a philabeg. The prisoner was sent to the Sheriff Substitute at Fort William who confined him.

Another report from a Captain Trapaud dated 25 June 1752, records the taking up of a certain William Cameron by 'the Glenmorriston party' for wearing the Highland dress. He was sentenced by the Sheriff of Invernesshire to six months imprisonment.

A third report for the same year from an officer in Lord George Beauclerck's Regiment referring to the people in North and South Morar states that:

> . . . the inhabitants of those countries begin to wear instead of breaches, stuff trousers much after the form of those the seamen use, but no longer than the kilt or philabeg. I am at a loss whether to look upon that as part of the highland dress, and take notice of such people as offenders against the law.

It is interesting that the same idea of a substitute for the philabeg seems to have occurred in Invernessshire and Argyllshire, within two or three years of each other, but there are other cases of stitching up the philabeg and transforming it 'into a pair of trousers like a Dutchman's'.

I cannot trace any cases of the Diskilting Act being enforced after 1760, and Drummond-Norie has this to say about the change in mood of the government:

> The accession of the third George to the throne that his great grandsire had wrested from the Stuarts, marked the commencement of a new and more enlightened policy on the part of the English Government towards the Highlanders, and Lochaber, in common with the other proscribed districts, benefited by the change. By the year 1760 militant Jacobitism was to all intents and purposes dead, and even the most fiery spirits among the adherents of the exiled Stuarts saw that it was useless to attempt to resuscitate it.'

Whilst the Diskilting Act was being enforced in some regions, it was being ignored in others. Ignorance of the Act was pleaded in some cases by those living in remote glens or on the Islands. Considering the state of communications at that time it is quite likely that many folk had never heard of the Act.

Before the Act was repealed in 1782, tartan was being made and sold in the shops of Edinburgh and Inverness, and in many of the smaller Scottish towns.

Stuart Maxwell, describing the references to the Highland dress in the Ross of Pitcalnie Papers, quotes evidence of the wearing of tartan costume during the Proscription period, and the common use of the words 'philibeg' and 'little kilt' at that time. In May 1757, a 'little kilt' was bought for three-year old Munro Ross, and another 'little kilt' for 'Sutherland' – possibly a servant. In 1761, a short coat, two vests, and a 'little kilt' were made for Munro, and in the same year his Grammar school master wrote to his mother to say that her son was well and wearing his 'short coat and Philabeg'.

Ladies too were defying the Act, and in 1755 Alexander Ross of Pitcalnie wrote to his wife to say that he had 'bespoke one of the finest and Pretiest Sets of Tartan I ever saw from Thomas Gardinar for your Ryding Cloathes.' In Edinburgh it became fashionable for a while to support the Jacobite cause and several society ladies wore tartan emblems. It would seem that the authorities were sensible enough not to arrest them.

There were, of course, many people in Scotland who were in favour of the legal banning of Highland dress. Sir Robert Gordon for instance described it as a relic of 'the Irish barbarity', an opinion which was shared by many Lowlanders. It has been said that the word 'Irish' was indeed often used by Lowlanders and Englishmen of the eighteenth century as an emotive word suggesting that the Highlanders were an alien people. Gaelic, although an older language than English, was frequently referred to as the 'Irish tongue'.

On the other hand several members of the Scottish nobility and aristocracy had large portraits painted of themselves and their families wearing tartans and Highland dress during the period of the proscription. In fact these include some of the finest paintings of the costume which have survived, and will be described in due course.

It is a fact that not a single man of political or social importance was arrested for wearing the tartan.

As an example of how the Diskilting Act was put into force, Charles Fraser-Mackintosh relates the story of a Sutherland man named Mackay who was seized in Inverness and charged with wearing the Highland dress. He pleaded ignorance and the fact that he had no other clothing. However he was sentenced to six months' imprisonment – barely two hours elapsing between his arrest and the sentence.

This unfortunate man was almost certainly John Mackay of Strathnaver the original judgement of whom is in the City Museum in Inverness and is reproduced in my *History of Highland Dress*. He had a 'short tartan coat upon him and a highland plaid party colouried wrapt lously about him'.

Fraser-Mackintosh expresses an interesting opinion that in one sense the diskilting statute did good 'because it gave rise to and originated the formation of societies and clubs exclusively connected with the Highlands, the people, and their language, which has tended so much to foster the ancient spirit'.

He then reproduces a letter, dated June 1748, from William Fraser, a member of a respectable Ross-shire family, to Bailie John Mackintosh of Inverness. Fraser's reaction to the Act is philosophical:

I'll be fond to have from you the Disarming Act for the Highland dress with amendments lately made by Parliament, how soon it comes to hand. Please give the bearer three yards and a half of good blew cloth for a great coat, with furniture. Do not forget to send good buttons, and as much coarse cloth as will make another to cover me when I attend the fishing . . . As we cannot appear in our country habit any more, may send me somè swatches of your cloths and fresees, and acquaint the prices . . .

How interesting it would be to know the story behind the arrest of 'Oronoce' a black servant of the Laird of Appin, Dugald Stewart. Probably legally a slave, he was arrested on 25 July 1750, and apprehended by the Commanding Officer of the Forces stationed in the Rannoch District 'for wearing the Highland garb, or being dressed in Tartan livery and was forthwith committed to prison.' The laird was too young at the time of the Forty-Five to be 'out' so he was not one of those attainted. But why did he dress his black servant in tartan livery? It may have been to draw attention to the absurdity of the Act.

In 1760, the *Edinburgh Evening Courant* advertised 'There is to be sold by roup in the shop of William Watson . . . of Edinburgh . . . the whole goods which belonged to the said William Watson consisting of Tartans of all kinds . . .' This was almost certainly a trading failure and nothing to do with the Act.

A little-known but very interesting account of Highland dress written during the Proscription period deserves more attention. Published in 1753 and written by one John Campbell, it is a now very rare pamphlet entitled *A Full and Particular Description of the Highlands of Scotland*. Apart from descriptions it contains a scheme whereby those who are disaffected might be persuaded to become 'zealously affected to his reigning Majesty'.

John Campbell held the Highlanders in high regard and declared that 'they are all gentlemen'. His description of their dress runs as follows:

. . . they make a most splendid and glorious Appearance, it being esteemed by all Judges to be the most heroic and majestic Habit ever wore by any Nation, but at present they are prohibited the Use of their ancient Cloathing, which may in Time prove hurtful to the Interest of *Great Britain*, seeing this Habit kept up the martial Spirit in them, they always delighting in Feats of War; next it is an active dress, seeing they have nothing to do when entering upon Action, but to throw off their Plaids, and draw their Swords and Pistols, and as they wear no Breeches, and tie their Garters below their knees, they are much more alert than those who are bound up like so many Dolls . . . Now by this Prohibition, they will quite forget their manly Exercises, their heroic Souls will melt away, or dwindle into Effeminacy, their Aversion to the Government will increase . . .'

There was much wisdom in John Campbell's opinion of the adverse effect which the Diskilting Act would have upon the martial spirit of the Highlanders. Had it been prolonged and enforced the outcome of the Napoleonic campaigns might have been quite different.

Meantime however, the Government wanted to know how effective the Acts had been, particularly in the districts where Jacobite sympathies had been shown. Blank forms entitled *Reports on the Annexed Estates 1755–1769*, were drawn up and sent out to various Factors. Amongst the many questions to be answered was 'Whether the laws prohibiting the Highland dress have taken full effect in that Estate'.

Of the Perthshire Baronies of Lix, Balquhidder and Callander, the answer is that 'they have taken full effect'. But regarding the Barony of Strathgartney, which lies in the parish of Callander, we read that although the laws have been observed, many of the people have substituted for the Highland dress

. . . short blue cloath coats or other short coats of one colour in place of tartan and trousers of one colour resembling the little kilts, with this difference, that they are sewed up in the middle and do not fall within the description of the Act of Parliament. This dress makes the people of that country easily distinguishable, but such of the tenants upon the estate of Perth as wore it have promised faithfully to conform themselves to the spirit and intention of the Act of Parliament and never more to be seen in that kind of dress.

This is further evidence of how comfortable and practical the Highlander found the kilt, and how widespread the practice was of substituting for it almost skirt-like short baggy trousers.

The Factors reported that the law had taken effect in the parishes of Comrie and Strowan, Muthil, the Barony of Kinbuck, Auchterarder, Stobhall and the estate of Arnprior. The Factor of the estate of Strowan was however a little more guarded in his reply. He pointed out that in the neighbourhood where troops were stationed the Acts were 'completely put in execution', but he could not say as much for other places where they were not stationed. However he would 'lay himself out to have these laws take effect in all that Districk of the Highlands where he has a concern or has occasion to travel.'

The Factor on the annexed estates of Lovat and Cromarty reported that the laws had taken full effect.

By now it was obvious that the Jacobite threat had subsided, and that the wearing of Highland dress did not signify any rebellion or defiance to the Government. In fact this might well be defined as the 'Doldrum' period in the history of Highland dress. Tartan had no clan or family significance, the Jacobite Risings were over and the glorious exploits of the Highland regiments had not yet begun. Enforcement of the Diskilting and Disarming Acts were no longer necessary.

Certainly by 1769 Highland dress was in evidence in Inverness. Thomas Pennant describes his visit to a fair which was held there in that year and being a man of science and a keen observer his account is of particular interest:

> The fair was a very agreeable circumstance and afforded a most singular groupe of Highlanders in all their motly dresses. Their *brechan*, or plaid, consists of twelve or thirteen yards of a narrow stuff, wrapt round the middle, and reaches to the knees; is often fastened round the middle with a belt, and is then called *brechan-feal*, but in cold weather, is large enough to wrap round the whole body from head to feet, and this often is their only cover, not only within doors, but on the open hills during the whole night. It is frequently fastened on the shoulders with a pin often of silver, and before with a brotche (like the *fibula* of the *Romans*), which is sometimes of silver and both large and expensive; the old ones have very frequently mottos.
>
> The stockings are short, and are tied below the knee. The *cuoranen* is a sort of laced shoe made of a skin with the hairy side out, but now seldom worn. The *truish* were worn by the gentry and were breeches and stockings made of one piece.
>
> The *fillebeg*, i.e. little plaid, also called *kelt*, is a sort of short petticoat reaching only to the knees, and is a modern substitute for the lower part of the plaid, being found to be less cumbersome, especially in time of action, when the Highlanders used to tuck their *brechan* into their girdle. Almost all have a large pouch of badger and other skins, with tassels dangling before. In this they keep their tobacco and money.

Here we have an excellent description of Highlanders in their native dress only 23 years after the Act of Proscription and whilst it was still in force. The reference to the kilt as a 'modern substitute for the lower part of the plaid' is important, as presumably Pennant got his information from the Highlanders themselves. His account of their arms and the dress of the women is described elsewhere.

As an appendix to his *Tour*, Thomas Pennant gives a long list of questions under the title 'Queries, addressed to the Gentlemen and Clergy of *North-Britain*, respecting the Antiquities and Natural History of their respective Parishes, with a View of exciting them to favour the World with a fuller and more satisfactory Account of their Country, than it is in the power of a Stranger and transient Visitant to give.'

Although he does not include any queries about costume, it would be interesting to know what response his appeal received. It is highly likely that Sir John Sinclair of Ulbster read Pennant's *Tour* and I wonder if it inspired his *Statistical Account?*

Whereas Pennant saw Highlanders sporting their 'motly dresses' in Inverness in

1769, Dr Samuel Johnson, during his very extensive tour of Scotland and the Western Islands in 1773, only saw one man wearing the 'ancient Habit' although the little kilt was 'very common' – at a time when the Diskilting Act was still in force. he wrote:

> In the islands the plaid is rarely worn. The law by which the Highlanders have been obliged to change the form of their dress, has, in all the places that we have visited, been universally obeyed. I have seen only one gentleman completely clothed in the ancient habit, and by him it was worn only occasionally and wantonly. The common people do not think themselves under any legal necessity of having coats; for they say that the law against plaids was made by Lord Hardwicke, and was in force only for his life; but the same poverty that made it then difficult for them to change their clothing, hinders them now from changing it again.
>
> The fillibeg, or lower garment, is still very common, and the bonnet almost universal; but their attire is such as produces, in a sufficient degree, the effect intended by the law of abolishing the dissimilitude of appearance between the Highlanders and the other inhabitants of Britain; and, if dress be supposed to have much influence, facilitates their coalition with their fellow-subjects.
>
> What we have long used we naturally like, and therefore the Highlanders were unwilling to lay aside their plaid, which yet to an unprejudiced spectator must appear an incommodious and cumbersome dress; for hanging loose about the body, it must flutter in a quick motion, or require one of the hands to keep it close. The Romans always laid aside the gown when they had any thing to do. It was a dress so unsuitable to war, that the same word which signified a gown signified peace. The chief use of a plaid seems to be this, that they could commodiously wrap themselves in it, when they were obliged to sleep without a better cover.

Doctor Johnson was, of course, accompanied by James Boswell, a Scot educated in Edinburgh, who published his own account of the tour in 1785, and a third edition with some amendments in 1786. In it he states that the Doctor showed the spirit of a Highlander throughout the tour. 'One night, in Col, he strutted about the room with a broad-sword and target, and made a formidable appearance; and another night, I took the liberty to put a large blue bonnet on his head. His age, his size, and his bushy grey wig, with this covering on it, presented the image of a venerable *Senachi* . . .'

Boswell describes two gentlemen wearing the Highland dress. The first is 'Mr Malcolm Macleod, one of the Rasay family, celebrated in the year 1745–6.' He was a 62-year old man, bearded, hale and well proportioned:

> He wore a pair of brogues – Tartan hose which came up only near to his knees and left them bare, – a purple camblet kilt, – a black waistcoat, – a short green cloth coat bound with gold cord, – a yellowish bushy wig, – a large blue bonnet with a gold thread button. I never saw a figure that gave a more perfect representation of a Highland gentleman.

Although Doctor Johnson gives a full description of the island of Raasay and even mentions Malcolm Macleod, he makes no reference to him wearing Highland dress.

Boswell's second description is of the laird of Kingsburgh on the island of Skye:

> Kingsburgh was completely the figure of a gallant highlander, – exhibiting 'the grace mien and manly looks' which our popular Scotch song has justly attributed to that character. He had his Tartan plaid thrown about him, a large blue bonnet with a knot of black ribband like a cockade, a brown short coat of a kind of duffil, a Tartan waistcoat with gold buttons and gold button-holes, a bluish philibeg, and Tartan hose.

This description of an imposing costume contrasts vividly with that of the youths of Dunvegan, who followed the distinguished visitors along the road. 'The usual figure of a Sky-boy, is a *lown* with bare legs and feet, a dirty *kilt*, ragged coat and waistcoat, a bare head, and a stick in his hand, which, I suppose, is partly to help the lazy rogue to walk, partly to serve as a kind of defensive weapon.'

Just how imposing Highland dress could be can be seen from an examination of the portraits which were painted at this period. Despite the Proscription these large canvases were exhibited quite openly and their existence must have been widely known.

In 1745 the young Francis Charteris, Earl of Wemyss, married the daughter of the Duke of Gordon, and two or three years later they had a beautiful picture of themselves painted by Allan Ramsay (*colour plate 2*). Allan Ramsay was born in Edinburgh in 1713, and he was the son of the poet of the same name who was the author of *The Gentle Shepherd*. The vivacity and charm of Ramsay's portraits appealed to several members of the great Scottish families and his Edinburgh studio was crowded. Like many of his contemporaries he used a 'drapery painter', but obviously under close supervision as the detail of the costume shows.

When Ramsay painted the Weymss portraits he was producing some of his finest work. George Vertue praised 'his silks and satins, etc., shineing beautiful and clean'. The Earl wears a simple coat and a pair of gartered trews. The tartan of both is

25 *Broad bonnet and shoulder plaid worn with breeches. From* The Gentle Shepherd *painted by David Allan in 1786*

26 *Lowland country lasses. From* The Gentle Shepherd, *David Allan, 1786*

27 *The Macdonald Boys. Artist unknown. Sir Alexander and Sir James painted during the period when the Highland dress was proscribed.*

identical and gives the impression of a black and red check. The tartan of his shoulder plaid is of similar proportion but the colours are blue and red. In his left hand he carries a blue bonnet and he is armed with a basket-hilted broadsword and a dirk having a small knife and fork side by side in the scabbard.

Also belonging to the Proscription period is Allan Ramsay's portrait of Norman, the 22nd Chief of MacLeod. The similarity of his costume to that of the Earl of Wemyss is striking and conducive to a number of theories. It consists of coat, gartered trews, buckled shoes, basked-hilted broadsword and dirk almost identical to the Earl's. Only the tartan of the shoulder plaid differs. The sett is of black and red, but defies attempts to record. It has even been suggested that two seperate setts can be distinguished which infer two separate pieces of material, and that produces a real problem.

The picture of 'The Macdonald Boys' painted by an unknown artist, but probably Jeremiah Davison, about 1749 or 1750, is well-known to costume and golf historians (27). Sir Alexander was born in 1744 and stands with his golf club on the left of the picture, whilst Sir James, born in 1740, stands on the right, holding his flint-lock gun. Sir Alexander wears gartered trews, and the short hose of the kilted Sir James seems to be made of the same large red and white checked material. The four garments consisting of two jackets, a long waist-coat and a kilt are of four different red, black and green tartans.

28 *John, 4th Duke of Atholl, with his wife and family. A delightful conversation piece painted c. 1780 by David Allan*

David Allan, who has been described as 'The Scottish Hogarth', was born in 1744, and his charming and skilful drawings and paintings are of great assistance to the student of Scottish costume, Highland and Lowland. He came up to Edinburgh from London about 1780 towards the end of the Proscription period, and in that year he painted his delightful conversation piece of John, the 4th Duke of Atholl with his wife and family, his personal servant and his dogs. The Duke wears a pork-pie blue bonnet with red and white dicing and a large black feather. He has a brown jacket, a cream-coloured waist-coat, a kilt, badger-head sporran and red and white diced hose. His servant is also wearing a kilt.

In contrast to these grand portraits there is the rather pathetic Highlander seated on the ground in the corner of William Hogarth's picture entitled 'The Gate of Calais'. Painted in 1749, it provides good evidence of the costume worn at Culloden. The forelorn Jacobite exile clasps his hands and looks with dismay at his toes sticking through his thin shoes. He wears a round blue bonnet to which is still attached his white cockade – the only means of identifying on which side he had fought at the battle. The tartan of his trews and coat is well enough painted to give the impression that this is a portrait from life. His sporran is a simple pouch fastened to his waistbelt and in it is stuck his clay pipe.

One important piece of evidence depicting the wearing of Highland dress in

Edinburgh in 1751 has, as far as I know, never been published. In one of the note-books which belonged to Skeoch Cumming, and which is now in my collection, there is a note headed 'Visit to British Museum Print Room'. Then follow a number of references and sketches including figures from a sketch by Paul Sandby inscribed 'Drawn in the High Street at Edinburgh 1751' (*30*). I subsequently examined the album of Sandby drawings in the British Museum which shows the figures exactly as copied by Skeoch Cumming and inscribed with the place and date in Sandby's handwriting. Such is the detail in Sandby's sketch that a sign above an entrance bears the words 'Good Eating down this Close, 1751'. The Highlander wears a grey belted plaid with thin red stripes, diced hose, a round blue bonnet, a small sporran attached to his waist-belt and a sword suspended from a shoulder belt. Thus he defies both the Diskilting Act and the Disarming Act.

Now Paul Sandby was no ordinary artist. In 1741 he held an appointment in the military drawing department of the Tower of London. In 1746 he served with Colonel David Watson and assisted him on the military survey of the Highlands up to 1751. He was a member of the Royal Academy and exhibited over a period of 30 years, and he introduced the aquatint process of engraving into England.

His drawings are undoubtedly done from life and must be regarded as important items of costume evidence. Apart from the 1751 sketch there is a self portrait which

29 *An unfinished drawing of a Highland dance by Paul Sandby*

indicates his close interest in costumes. It consists of the artist seated on the ground, and drawing 'from the antique'. Below, on an ornamental cartouche is inscribed *A Book of Figures with the Prospect of Edinburgh Castle by Paul Sandby 1746–7*. Below that are the lines:

> *Tis not a trifling Beauty to Express,*
> *The various Shapes and Folding of the Dress.*

In the same British Museum collection there are other Indian ink, wash and pen drawings including one of 'Jacobite Prisoners' showing two handcuffed Highlanders wearing round blue bonnets, short coats, kilts, shoulder plaids and diced hose. Another is entitled *Street Scene in Edinburgh* and is dated 1750. It shows ten principal figures but no Highland dress, the men being in breeches and two of them wearing broad bonnets. A black and red chalk drawing is inscribed '*A Scotch Washerwoman*' and shows a girl trampling clothes in a tub with her clothes girded up around her waist. Another Indian ink, wash and pen drawing is inscribed *A Highland Laird's Will found among some papers taken from the Rebels in the year 1745*. It shows a man wearing breeches and seated on the floor of a cottage reading a paper. Above him stands a woman wringing her hands whilst two dogs and a goat look on with interest.

But undoubtedly the most interesting Sandby drawing in this collection is an unfinished sketch or working draft in pencil and wash inscribed 'Sketch for a picture'. It shows a Highland laird, his wife and family, watching figures dancing before them.

30 *Copy by Skeoch Cumming of a Paul Sandby drawing, Edinburgh 1751*

The laird wears tartan trews, a diced bonnet, a long-tailed coat and he holds a curved horn snuff-box. Two of the dancing figures wear plain material kilts and diced hose with garters, whilst two pipers standing behind the laird are wearing kilts (29).

I have already mentioned the portrait of the Duke of Atholl and his family which David Allan painted in 1780, but in the same year he also made a painting which is entitled 'Highland Dance' (31). This picture has strong similarities with Sandby's study of the laird watching the dancers as described above.

Robert Burns wrote of David Allan as 'the only artist who has hit genuine pastoral costume', and certainly the figures in the 'Highland Dance' have the air of authenticity. They include Neil Gow, the famous Scottish fiddler and composer, wearing the tartan breeches and hose in which Sir Henry Raeburn painted him some years later.

There are two versions of Allan's picture one of which shows the principal dancer wearing trews whilst the other shows him in the kilt. The latter picture is not so well known and it is possible that Sandby saw the 'trews' version, or the engraving of it, and based his pencil and wash sketch on that.

The greatest demand for the restoration of the traditions and culture of the Scottish Highlanders after the need for the Proscription Acts had gone did not come from Scotland. It came from a group of patriotic Scottish gentlemen in London. They wished to put on the 'Garb of Old Gaul' once again, to sing and recite in the old Gaelic tongue, and to listen to the music of their ancestors. But they also wanted to stimulate interest in the old Highland traditions and preserve them from extinction. And so, in 1778, the Highland Society of London was founded with Lieutenant-General Simon Frazer of Lovat as President, or more correctly 'Chieftain'. Immediately the Society was organised they set to work promoting Highland language, literature and piping competitions for which they provided the prizes.

Four years after their foundation, the Society appointed a committee whose job it was to have the Diskilting Act repealed. They chose as their spokesman James Graham, the talented 27-year-old Marquess of Graham, a Member of Parliament who later became the third Duke of Montrose.

With commendable speed the Bill of Repeal was agreed, passed by the House of Commons, approved by the House of Lords and given the Royal assent. Within weeks a caricature was going the round of the London clubs. It was entitled *The Scotch made happy by a late Act of Parliament*, and it showed 16 men taking off their breeches and putting on kilts, whilst three young women are peeping at them from behind a screen. It was obviously intended to portray the 16 representative peers of Scotland.

One Englishman was not at all happy at the thought of the Highlanders appearing in England in their native dress. Sir Philip Jennings Clerke told Parliament that he remembered that there were six Highlanders once quartered in a house in Hampshire, who were really as well-behaved soldiers as he had seen, but still the singularity of their dress had put the man of the house to very great inconvenience; for finding that his wife and daughter could not keep their eyes off the Highlanders, he was obliged to find a lodging for them both.

OVERLEAF **31** *Highland dance, by David Allan. Niel Gow wears tartan breeches*

Immediately a satirical print appeared entitled 'Sir P. J. C . . . . e's 'Hampshire Story'. It shows two Highlanders seated at a table in the kitchen of an inn. The landady is so enamoured with them that she pours the wine over the table instead of into a glass, while the daughter gazes at them with rapture, spilling the contents of the frying-pan onto the floor and over the unfortunate cat.

In Scotland reaction to the Repeal took several forms. The Rev Joseph Robertson Macgregor, the eccentric minister of the Gaelic chapel in Edinburgh, immediately attired himself in a complete suit of Macgregor tartan and paraded conspicuously throughout the city. The ladies of the capital broke out into a tartan rash.

In certain areas of the Highlands it appears that the the event was ignored whilst in others the following notice proclaimed in Gaelic:

Listen Men

This is bringing before all the sons of the Gael that the King and Parliament of Britain have for ever abolished the Act against the Highland dress that came down to the clans from the beginning of the world to the year 1746. This must bring great joy to every Highland heart. You are no longer bound down to the unmanly dress of the lowlander. This is declaring to every man, young and old, simple and gentle, that they may after this put on and wear the trews, the little kilt, the doublet and hose, along with the belted plaid, without fear of the law of the land or the spite of enemies.

It is easy to imagine when one reads these rapturous comments that the Highlander would leap with joy and, casting off his breeches, don the costume which his ancestors had worn 'from the beginning of the world.' The truth is that it was the fashion-conscious city folk who rushed off to their drapers and demanded tartan, whilst the fact which governed the reaction of the people in the mountains and glens was finance not fashion.

But we must be grateful that the eyes of the poets were not blinded by the mundane facts of economics. When Duncan ban Macintyre wrote his stirring Gaelic poem *Oran do'n éideadh Ghàidhealach* he did not express a hope but stated what he thought must surely be a fact. The breeks were already cast into the dust and the great belted plaid of the pleats was being worn in all its glory. His poems has been translated thus:

News have I got which is fresh,
And fulfills the desire of my heart
We shall get us the national dress,
Which we use at our era's first start.
Since we're furnished with glass that o'erflows,
Talking all in a hum of delight,
Then here's to the health of Montrose
Who for us has asserted this right.

I saw, met in Dunedin today,
The social kind association,
And the letter of luck which did say
That began our great jubilation,
The pipes played in tune charmingly

On the smooth clear expanse of the knoll;
We have brought our own garb publicly –
Us rebels who'll venture to call?

For thirty years, aye, more than that,
On our backs was a cloth cassock vile,
A cloak we received and a hat,
And that did not suit us, that style;
And buckles to fasten our shoes,
The thong we prettier deemed;
Our base garb did us so abuse
That dottards our handsome youth seemed.

We have got at this present fair play
Which to every land's love will appeal,
The power to put on our array
Never asking the wily brood's seal;
We now are arrayed as is just,
And pleasing the style to our eye;
We have put down the breeks in the dust –
They'll ne'er come from the nook where they lie.

Upon us we have put the dress
That is gay, and to us suited both,
The great-belted plaid of the pleats,
And a waistcoat made of fresh cloth;
Coat of cloth of the tartan with checks
In which the red thickly will be,
Hose which never trammel our pace,
Within a span reach to the knee.

This poem illustrates extremely well a major change in the development of what the poet himself calls the 'national' dress. It was no longer a style of costume which could identify the people living in the wild glens of the Highlands. It was now a costume which was 'pleasing' and 'gay'. One wonders what might have been the thoughts of the real Highlanders living in poverty and hunger had they read this poem written by one of themselves?

Macintyre, 'a maker of songs to sing', was born in 1724, and served in the Argyll Regiment of Militia fighting on the Government side, although in his poetry he shows strong sympathy for Prince Charles Edward Stuart and the Jacobite cause. After his military service he was employed as a forester and subsequently came to Edinburgh in 1767, where he enrolled in the City Guard – 'the black banditti'. He won several Highland Society of London poetry prizes and the first edition of his poems was published in 1768. He died in 1812.

In addition to his *Song to the Highland Garb* already quoted, he wrote another spirited ditty, possibly just after the Diskilting Act was published. It was called *Oran do'n bhriogais*, or *The Song of the Breeches*, and after expressing his sentiment that 'the Young

Prince' should be on the throne, he gives his opinion of King George:

> *What disgust he caused us*
> *What annoyance and contention,*
> *Forcibly to disclothe us*
> *By subjecting us to tyranny.*

As the poem goes on, Macintyre points out that apart from the physical discomfort of the breeches there is another objection. Surely, he says, it is unfair that the clans which were loyal to the Government should be punished:

> *Since we adopted breeches,*
> *That garb is not approved by us;*
> *As round the houghs we tighten them,*
> *It irks us to be clad in them.*
> *Erstwhile we were mettlesome,*
> *Wearing tartan underneath the belts,*
> *Though nowadays in general,*
> *We put on the saddle cloths.*
> *Methinks it is an ill reward*
> *For the men who went campaigning*
> *To deprive them of their raiment,*
> *Though by their help Duke William won.*

Macintyre lived long enough to see the Highland raiment worn once again and, just as many of the men from the Highlands had helped the Government to victory during the Jacobite Risings, so they were now to come forward in their thousands to fight in the ranks of the British Army.

This period between the Proscription in the middle of the eighteenth century and the raising of the Highland regiments at the end of it, was the great milestone in the history of Highland dress. Up to the time of the Jacobite Risings the dress of the Highlander had been, for centuries, his clothing purely and simply. A multipurpose covering ideally suited to his way of life and completely devoid of the influence of fashion, it had served him well. And then, within a very short time, it had become a symbol of rebellion and because of this it was banned.

It is at this point that the evolution of Highland dress became unique in terms of history of costume. Banned because of its implications of nationalism, it was to be revived as a national dress. Formerly the natural clothing of the people living in a remote region of Scotland, it now became worn with pride by Scots at home and abroad as a symbol of the entire Scottish nation.

At the end of the eighteenth century the Highland dress as worn by the civilian was to be entirely swamped by the Highland dress worn by the soldier. For a number of reasons, not least the effects of the industrial revolution and the changes taking place in the Scottish economy, there was little tartan to be seen. And then with the last few declining years of the century the ascendancy of the kilt began.

4

◆

The Kilt

'IT IS TRUE that the history of the Highland dress from the national point of view is at any time debatable and hotly-disputed ground upon which a prudent man would no more think of lightly entering than he would of committing himself on a moot point in theology.' So wrote Lord Archibald Campbell almost a century ago and the statement still applies today.

As far as the kilt is concerned, the trouble began in March 1785, when part of a letter was published in the *Edinburgh Magazine*. It was entitled 'The FELIE-BEG, no part of the Ancient Highland Dress. Part of a letter from Ivan Baillie of Aberiachan, Esq.'

According to J. G. Mackay, 'Ivan Baillie of Aberiachan was son of Alexander Baillie of Dochfur and brother of William Baillie of Rosehall, County Sutherland, who gave much useful information during 1745–6, and uncle of Major Hugh Robert Duff, whose wife was the only daughter of Arthur Forbes of Culloden.' Baillie was in fact a reliable witness being a Highlander of good position giving first-hand evidence. In view of the importance of this letter therefore I will quote it in full:

In answer to your enquiry, I do report, according to the best of my knowledge, and the intelligence of persons of credit, and very advanced ages, that the piece of Highland dress, termed in the Gaelic *felie-beg*, and in our Scots *little kilt*, is rather of late than ancient usage.

The upper garment of the Highlanders was the tartan or party-coloured plaid, termed in the Gaelic 'breccan', when buckled round by a belt and the lower part plaited and the upper loose from the shoulders. The dress was termed in the Gaelic *felie*, and in the Scots *kilt*. It was a cumbersome unwieldy habit to men at work or travelling in a hurry, and *the lower class could not afford the expense of the belted trousers or breeches*. They wore short coats, waistcoats, and shirts of as great length as they could afford; and such parts as were not covered by these remained naked to the tying of garters on their hose.

About 50 years ago, one Thomas Rawlinson, an Englishman, conducted an iron work carried on in the countries of Glengarie and Lochaber; he had a throng of Highlanders employed in the service, and became very fond of the Highland dress, and wore it in the neatest form; which I can aver, as I became personally acquainted with him above 40 years ago. He was a man of genius and quick parts, and thought it no great stretch of invention to abridge the dress, and make it handy and convenient for his workmen: and accordingly directed the using of the lower part plaited of what is called the *felie* or *kilt* as above, and the upper part was set aside; and this piece of dress, so modelled as a diminutive of the former, was in the gaelic termed *felie-beg* (*beg* in that tongue signifies *little*) and in our Scots termed *little kilt*; and it was found so handy and convenient that, in the shortest space, the use of it became frequent in all the Highland Countries, and in many of our northern Low Countries also. This is all I can say about the date and form of the *felie-beg*, and what was formerly used in place of it. And I certify from my own knowledge, that till I returned from Edinburgh to reside in this Country in the year 1725, after serving seven or eight years with writers to the signet, I never saw the *felie-beg* used, nor heard any mention of such a piece of dress, not (even) from my father, who was very intelligent and well-known to Highlanders, and lived to the age of 83 years, and died in the year 1738, born in May, 1655.

The *felie-beg* is in its form and make somewhat similar to a woman's petticoat, termed in the Gaelic *boilicoat*; but differs in this, that the former is not so long nor sewed in the forepart, but made to overlap a little. The great *felie* or *kilt* was formed of the plaid double or twofold; the *felie-beg* of it single.

I used *f* and not *ph* in spelling *felie-beg*, as, in my esteem, more adapted to the Gaelic. 22 March 1768.

To the great majority of people it would be of little interest to know who had unpicked the seam down the middle of the belted plaid and then sewn up a little kilt. To most of us it would not appear to be a matter of great importance, but to a small group of people the suggestion that the credit of the invention of the kilt should be given to an Englishman was unthinkable. What was more, the idea that the kilt dated from the first quarter of the eighteenth century and not from the 'mists of antiquity' was unbearable. By these few the whole thing was seen as an attack on Highland traditions and they christened it the 'Rawlinson Myth'.

In fact the assertion that the little kilt was of recent origin was widely accepted during the late eighteenth century. Richard Gough published an edition of Camden's *Britannia* in 1789, in which he writes about the Highlanders in Breadalbane:

The dress of the men is the 'brechan' or plaid, 12 or 13 yards of narrow stuff wrapped round the middle and reaching to the knees, often put round the waist, and in cold weather covering the whole body, even on the open hills, at night, and fastened on the shoulders with a broche; short stockings tied below the knee; 'truish' a genteeler kind of breeches and stockings of one piece; 'cuoranen' a laced shoe of skin with the hairy side out, rather disused; 'kelt' or 'fillibeg' q.d. little plaid or short petticoat reaching to the knees, substituted of late to the longer end of the plaid; and lastly the pouch of badger or other skins with tassels hanging before them.

Neither at the time of the publication of Ivan Baillie's letter nor of Richard Gough's *Britannia* can I trace a single word of protest. Now the number of people in Scotland at this time who took a scholarly interest in Highland dress was very few indeed. Perhaps the greatest of these was Sir John Sinclair, compiler of the *First Statistical Account of Scotland*, who, apart from his own knowledge of the history of his fellow Highlanders, had collected a vast amount of information on the dress and habits of the people of all Scotland.

On 15 May 1796 he wrote a letter to John Pinkerton the Antiquary which was subsequently published in the latter's *Literary Correspondence* (1830). In it Sir John writes that:

. . . it is well known that the phillibeg was invented by an Englishman in Lochaber about sixty years ago, who naturally thought his workmen could be more active in that light petticoat than in the belted plaid, and that it was more decent to wear it than to have no clothing at all which was the case with some of those employed by him in cutting down the woods in Lochaber.

The dispute on the origin of the kilt started about the turn of the century, and an indication of this was given by Sir John Sinclair in the year 1804. He then published a paper addressed to the Highland Societies of London and Scotland entitled 'Observations on the propriety of preserving the Dress, Language, etc of the ancient inhabitants of Scotland', in which he says:

Whether the *philibeg*, or short petticoat, is an old part of the dress, or a modern alteration, is disputed. Many contend that it was first substituted, on account of its lightness, for the belted plaid, by Highland woodcutters employed by English companies in Argleshire and Lochaber, about the year 1730.

One of the earliest adverse reactions to this statement was made by General David Stewart of Garth, author of *Sketches of the Character of the Highlanders of Scotland*, published in 1822, in which he says:

The fealdag was the same as the philibeg only not plaited. The mode of sewing the Kilt into plaits or folds, in the same manner as the plaid, is said to have been introduced by an Englishman of the name of Parkinson, early in the last century, which has given rise to an opinion entertained by many that the kilt is modern and was never known till that period. This opinion is founded on a memorandum left by a gentleman whose name is not mentioned, and published in the Edinburgh Magazine ... I am the less willing to coincide in the modern opinion founded on such a slight unauthenticated notice, than in the universal belief of the people, that the philibeg had been part of their garb, as far back as tradition reaches.

This observation is mildly expressed in comparison with some of those who shared his opinion. Nevertheless the General's statement contains some errors and confusion. He refers to 'Parkinson' where the correct name is 'Rawlinson' but he may have become confused over the name of Parkinson who, according to John Sobieski Stuart, was Rawlinson's tailor. The 'memorandum left by a gentleman whose name is not mentioned, and published in the Edinburgh Magazine' must surely refer to that clearly stated therein as 'Part of a letter from Ivan Baillie of Aberiachan'

One might also query General Stewart's claim to know 'the universal belief of the people'. Major McClintock (1949), who made a close study of this controversy, evaluates the opinions of General Stewart and Sir John Sinclair in detail, pointing out that when the General published his *Sketches* in 1822, 'Except for his boyhood, therefore, and for any intervals of leave that he may have had, all but six years of his life had been spent out of Scotland or, if at times with his regiment in Scotland, had been spent in the performance of military duties.' Sir John Sinclair was born 18 years earlier, inherited large estates, became President of the Highland Society of London, raised a regiment of Highland Fencibles, played a major part in the development of Scottish agriculture, and championed the wearing of Highland dress in which he was portrayed by Raeburn. I agree with Major McClintock that 'with such a life and experience behind him he was in 1798 much better qualified to weigh and give an opinion as to the truth or otherwise of the story under discussion than was general Stewart 24 years later.'

It must be assumed that by 'philibeg' General Stewart means the tartan kilt of the Scottish Highlander, but that being so, could anyone seriously claim that it 'had been part of their garb, as far back as tradition reaches'?

One cannot help wondering if any of this argument would have arisen if it had been claimed that the kilt was invented in the early eighteenth century by a Highlander. It cannot be doubted that both the General and Sir John were very patriotic Highlanders with a genuine love for the traditions of their native land. The difference of their opinions was based on strongly held and very sincere beliefs. It was only when the argument was interpreted as an attack on Highland tradition that it became regrettable, and when it declined into a personal level it became deplorable.

Certainly the argument will continue but one hopes that it will not be in the style of the irascible Pinkerton, who was not above inventing a few bogus ballads, and wrote of the 'tasteless regularity and vulgar glare of the tartan'. Is it because of the fraudulent *Vestiarium Scoticum* that writers on the subject generally ignore the opinion of John Sobieski Stuart? His *Costume of the Clans* contains a great deal of valuable information and his theory of the origin of the kilt deserves careful assessment. One cannot dismiss the possibility that Glengarry deserves the title of 'Father of the Kilt'

Perhaps too much emphasis has been placed on the supposition that one particular individual might have invented the kilt. After all, the ancient Egyptians wore kilts as did men throughout the world from the earliest times. It is all a matter of definition. There is a certain amount of evidence that the little kilt appeared in a number of widespread places throughout the Highlands at about the same time. My own opinion, based on the evidence which we have to date, is that the little tartan kilt similar to the one which we wear today, made its general appearance in the Highlands during the first quarter of the eighteenth century.

It would be wrong to imagine that at one point in time the Highlander discarded his great belted plaid and put on a little kilt. After all by discarding the old garb he was discarding not only his clothing but also his extremely handy shelter on the hill in peacetime, and on the march in wartime. He certainly did not put on the kilt to show the world that he was a Scot – although less than a century was to pass before he did do so.

Our knowledge of the use of Highland dress up to the time of the eighteenth century is largely based on the written accounts of visitors. We have little information on the Highlanders' own opinions of their dress, because there was little or no reason why they should remark upon it. It is abundantly clear that they wore it because it was ideally suited to their way of life. It was a dress the style of which was based on function and not on fashion. If the function was to change so would the style of the dress. It is true that the belted plaid was an ideal garment if you had to sleep on the hill, but if that necessity ceased surely one of its chief virtues had gone, and its cumbersome nature had to be reconsidered. The variety of ways in which it could be worn by a fighting man to accommodate his weapons was of little value when the country had achieved a more peaceful state.

I doubt if the fact that you could sleep three to a bed would have a permanent appeal to the Highlandman. However, in John Dalrymple's account of the *Characteristic Traits of the Ancient Scots Highlanders* published in the *Scots Magazine* of July 1796, we read;

In rain, they formed the plaid into folds, and, laying it on the shoulders, were covered as with a roof. When they were obliged to lie abroad in the hills, in their hunting parties, or tending their cattle, or in war, the plaid served them both for bed and for covering; for, when three men slept together, they could spread three folds of cloth below and six above them.

The wearing of a number of distinct forms of costume within a fairly restricted area was not unusual in a highly populated district at this period of history. Fashion and a variety of occupation would be responsible for this. But when we seek comparison with other countries having a similar topography, land-use and population density, we find that the Scottish Highlands had a much higher than average variety in native dress. Not only that, but the survival in styles continued for a longer period.

At the end of the eighteenth century a number of people were wearing a transition garment bridging the change in style between the belted plaid unstitched in any way, and the tailored kilt. Although its existence has been ignored by most writers it could be regarded as a very close ancestor of the kilt.

It was described in 1796, when Charles Grant, Vicomte de Vaux, published his *Mémoires historiques, généalogiques, politiques, militaires, etc.* He set forth the complete equipment of a 'Seigneur des Montagnes d'Ecosse' as follows; 'A full trimmed bonnet. A tartan jacket, vest, kilt and cross-belt. A tartan belted plaid. A tartan pair of hose, made up [original]. A tartan pair of stockings ditto, with yellow garters. A pair of brogs. A silver-mounted purse and belt. A target with spear. A broad-sword. A pair of pistols and bullet mould. A dirk knife, fork and belt.'

Had previous writers been as meticulous as this in their descriptions, how much fuller our knowledge of the earlier forms of costume would be. Here we have the belted plaid, the trews and the kilt, all in the same wardrobe, and this inventory is followed by a description of the method of putting on the belted plaid:

Being sewed, and the broad belt within the keepers, the gentleman stands with nothing on but his shirt; when the servant gets the plaid and belt round, he must hold both ends of the belt, till the gentleman adjusts and puts across, in a proper manner the two folds or flaps before; that done, he tightens the belt to the degree wanted; then the purse and purse-belt is put on loosely; afterwards, the coat and waistcoat is put on, and the great low part hanging down behind, where a loop is fixed, is to be pinned up to the right shoulder, immediately under the shoulder-strap, to be pinned in such a manner that the corner or low-flyer behind, hangs as low as the kilt or hough, and no lower; that properly adjusted, the pointed corner or flap that hangs at the left thigh, to be taken through the purse-belt, and to hang, having a cast back very near as low as the belt, putting at the same time any awkward bulky part of the plaid on the left side back from the haunch, stuffed under the purse-belt. When the shoulder or sword-belt is put on, the flyer that hangs behind is to be taken through, and hang over the shoulder-belt. N.B. – No kilt ought ever to hang lower than the hough or knee – scarcely that far down.

This account contains many salient points. It shows, for instance, that the part of the belted plaid hanging below the belt was known as the 'kilt' before it was separated from the plaid. It also shows that this lower portion was sewn up in the manner of the modern kilt and that keepers, or loops, were also sewn on in order to keep the belt in place.

In a note published in the *Proceedings of the Society of Antiquaries of Scotland* Vol. 105, A. V. B. Norman draws attention to a letter written in 1769 from Sir Robert Murray

32 *Sir Robert Murray Keith in the uniform of the 87th Regiment of Highland Volunteers which he raised in 1759*

Keith in Dresden to his father in Scotland. The Elector having expressed a wish to see him in the uniform of the 87th Regiment of Highland Volunteers which he had raised ten years previously, Sir Robert requested amongst other items 'a handsome *bonnet*, a pair or two of the finest knit *hose*, and a plaid of *my colours*, sewed and *plaited* on a waist belt.' This plaid was obviously stitched up in the same manner as that described by Charles Grant, and the brevity of Sir Robert's request infers that this style of plaid was well enough known not to require a detailed description. It is also interesting to read his specification of the plaid being in 'my colours', no named tartan.

Sir Robert was painted by Anton Graff in Dresden the following year (1770), presumably wearing the plaid from Scotland. Nine years later this portrait was engraved in Vienna (*32*). Mr Norman traced the original painting to the British Royal Collection where he examined it and found the plaid to be of dark green and black tartan.

The following letter from a Scottish firm of clothiers is addressed to William Wilson and Son, who, at the time it was written had captured the market for civilian and military tartans in Scotland. Within two years, the output from their mills in Bannockburn was to increase tenfold:

Gentn. A young Gentn of our acquaintance in London want a Highland Kilt & Plaid in one pice as the Highland solders wear them, he wants a good dale of Blue in the patron 12 yards we believe will do, if you could favour us with the quantity of a good quality as soon as possible, it may be a mean to introduce more of your Manuftr there, and if you could get it made up in the trew Calladonian way so much the better, we are

> Gentn your very abd sirs
> *Ure & Dobbie*

Glasgow 25th Sept 1792.

This stitched-up belted plaid enjoyed a considerable revival when King George IV visited Edinburgh in 1822. Apart from dressing some of their followers in it, some of the Highland chiefs themselves put it on. For the man with the figure to carry it, the stitched-up belted plaid looked very well.

The Highland regiments were raised early enough for some of them to be dressed in the belted plaid, but the increasing use of the little kilt coincided with the widespread raising of the fighting men required to face the Napoleonic threat. It was therefore on this wave of regimental recruiting that the kilt was brought before the eyes of Europe and became a Scottish national symbol. Its origins continued to be argued, but no-one could deny that this was the first time that it became the national costume of the Scottish nation as a whole and not the regional dress of those who lived in the remote mountains and glens of the Highlands.

There is one account of Highland dress which has been widely ignored but which is of considerable importance. It was written by a trained observer at a time of particular significance – immediately after the Repeal of the Proscription Act. About 1784, Faujas Saint-Fond, a professor of geology in the Museum of Natural History in Paris, visited Scotland and his account of his travels was published in 1799. On arrival at Dalmally in Argyll he observed 15 Highlanders. 'All of them wore the same remarkable garb', which he went on to describe:

Their dress is very remarkable. It consists in a military jacket, with sleeves and facings of a woollen stuff, in which the colours cross each other, so as to form large squares of red, green, blue and white; in a mantle of the same stuff, tucked up and pinned on the left shoulder, called the plaid; and in a kind of petticoat, short and plaited like the lower part of the military dress of the Romans. This last serves them instead of breeches, but it does not descend much lower than the middle of the thigh. Their legs also are partly naked, being covered only with woollen half-stockings of vivid colours, so disposed in cross bars as to imitate very nearly the ancient buskin. Their head is covered with a blue bonnet surrounded with a narrow variegated border of red, blue, and green, and decorated with one long and waving plume . . . Their shoes, which, in general, each makes for himself, in a coarse but stout manner, are tied with strings of leather; this kind of shoes are known by the name of *brogues*. They keep their money in a waist-belt of otter skin, which serves at the same time as an ornament. It is so formed that the skin of the animal's head hangs down before. The eyes are edged round with red woollen tape, and the whole is furnished with a number of small tassels of different colours. This skin covers a pouch, which serves them by way of purse.

Such is the attire which the Scotch highlanders, as well as the inhabitants of the Hebrides, have worn from a very remote antiquity. Did they copy them from the Romans at the time when those lords of the world attempted in vain to conquer them; or have they received them by a more ancient derivation from their ancestors, the Celtic? This is a question of difficult solution.

It is however, well-known that the modern descendants of the ancient Caledonians are so attached to this form of vesture, which reminds them of their ancient valour and independence, that the English government found its repeated attempts to induce them to lay it aside, completely frustrated; though this dress is certainly the least adapted to a people who inhabit so cold and humid a climate.

This informative account shows that already the jacket was identified with the military style, and that the little kilt and shoulder plaid were being worn. The details of the bonnet and the sporran are most informative, as are his opinions of the antiquity of the dress and the attachment it has to the hearts of the people.

Saint-Fond's *Travels* contains a coloured plate designed by himself and entitled *Inside of the Cottage of MacNab a Blacksmith at Dalmally*. It shows the traveller receiving refreshment from a bare-footed woman wearing a striped jacket and a tartan skirt reaching down to her shins. Another woman, also wearing a long tartan skirt, is seated behind her. There are three men, all wearing diced bonnets, shoulder plaids, kilts, and diced or tartan hose. One of them wears a large elaborate sporran with at least eight tassels.

Costume has always been used in a symbolic manner by artists, and Saint-Fond's illustration must be viewed with that in mind. It is highly unlikely that inside Macnab's cottage we would have found four Highland persons dressed in such a uniform manner, but the kilt, and any other form of tartan clothing, was now a means of instant recognition of the Highlander. This in turn gave the faulty impression that everyone who lived in the Highlands wore the Highland dress.

Drummond-Norie considered that the Diskilting Act 'was probably an ingenious effort on the part of the Government to abolish that national distinction which the Highland dress largely assisted in maintaining, while at the same time it offered an gratuitous insult to a large number of their late enemies, and afforded an excuse for the infliction of still further punishment'. He saw it as a victory of might over right the result of which was that by the year 1760 'militant Jacobitism was to all intents and purposes dead.'

I would agree with his description of the Government's intention, but I think that depriving the Highlander of his natural every-day dress played only a very small part in the destruction of Jacobitism. But it certainly did not help to make the Highlander sympathetic to the new masters.

Within a lifetime, any suggestion that the kilt and the tartan signified that the wearer was a rebel seeking to overthrow the reigning house was out of the question. In fact the reverse was true. Within the space of one week in the year 1822, more tartan was seen in Edinburgh than had probably been seen in the whole of the Highlands during the previous century. And it was to be worn as a symbol of loyalty to the reigning Hanoverian monarch who himself was to wear what would be described as 'The Garb of Old Gaul'.

5

♦

George IV and Queen Victoria

URING the first 20 years of the nineteenth century, the kilt and the tartan were being widely associated with military uniforms at home and abroad, whilst as a form of civilian dress in Scotland they were going through what might be described as a 'pastoral' period.

When Professor Garnett visited Inverness in the late 1790s he used words such as 'picturesque' and 'graceful', which were soon to become common expressions when applied to the Highland dress:

> The highland dress is very common in this town and neighbourhood, and is undoubtedly much more picturesque and beautiful than the formal, tight, stiff habit of the English. . . . The highland bonnet is in particular very ornamental; so are the graceful folds of the plaid; the modern habit has however convenience to recommend it, and in a few years this ancient dress of the highlanders, which resembles very much that of the ancient Romans, will probably be scarcely seen.

When Garnett arrived at Kenmore in Perthshire, he found the Highland dress far more common than in any other district in Scotland. And once more his description is that of a picturesque folk costume becoming fasionable and incorporating modern styles:

> It consists of a short jacket of tartan, or woollen cloth, woven in squares of the most vivid colours, in which green and red are however predominant; the Philabeg, or kilt, which is a sort of short petticoat reaching to the middle of the thigh, of the same stuff; of hose, or half stockings, which do not reach the knee, knit or wove in diamonds of red and white. They have generally, when dressed, a pouch made of the skin of the badger or fox hanging before, in which they keep their tobacco and money. They wear a mantle, or plaid of tartan, which is folded in a graceful manner over the shoulder, but covers the whole body when it rains. Instead of a hat, they wear a blue bonnet, with a border of red and white. This dress which is much more picturesque than the modern, is fast wearing out in the Highlands; many dress in the English manner, and still more have a mixture of the Highland and English; for instance many have a hat and short coat, with kilt and hose; while others have no other part of this dress than the hose and bonnet.

Dorothy Wordsworth, who visited Scotland in 1803, has been described as one of the early tourists who came to the Highlands in search of the 'picturesque noble savages'. As she passed through the Lowlands her eye was caught by a shepherd sitting 'screened by his plaid', then by 'a women sitting right in the middle of a field, alone, wrapped up in a grey cloak or plaid', and then 'an old man, the first we had seen in a Highland bonnet.' The dresses of the Scottish lasses were 'so simple, so much alike, yet from their being folded garments, admitting of an endless variety, and falling often so gracefully.'

Near Luss, playing in the Highland dress and philabeg, were a group of school boys, and then, at Loch Katrine, a splendid Highlander, complete 'in dress, figure and face, and a very fine-looking man, hardy and vigorous, though past his prime.' This Highlander 'upon the naked heath' was one of the most memorable encounters during the tour. 'While he stood waiting for us in his bonnet and plaid, which never look more graceful than on horseback, I forgot our errand and only felt glad that we were in the Highlands.'

On another occasion she saw a party returning from church. Their appearance was far from dismal as the men were in tartan plaids and the women wore scarlet cloaks and carried green umbrellas. The latter fascinated her and later, near Tarbet, she noticed a hut:

A number of good clothes were hanging against the walls, and a green silk umbrella was set up in a corner. I should have been surprised to see an umbrella in such a place before we came into the Highlands; but umbrellas are not so common anywhere as there – a plain proof of the wetness of the climate; even five minutes after this a girl passed us without shoes and stockings, whose gown and petticoat were not worth half-a-crown, holding an umbrella above her head.

However the day of the 'Comic Highlander' was at hand. In 1821, *The Tour of Doctor Prosody in Search of the Antique and Picturesque* was published in London. The author, William Coombe, illustrated his satire with 'Twenty Elegant Embellishments'. These show the majority of Scots wearing round blue diced bonnets, short jackets and tartan trousers. The kilted figures display a large amount of bare leg above short diced hose. In the neighbourhood of Stirling the doctor is apprehended as a poacher, and his captor is illustrated as a tall Highlander in the unlikely costume of a kilt worn over a pair of blue breeches.

On reaching the island of Mull, Prosody dons the kilt himself and is portrayed flourishing a large feathered bonnet. A waggish native had assured him that his air and figure 'would the graceful dress of Scotia's mountaineer become.' He was then told that as a visitor to the island it was expected that he should pay the customary compliment by wearing the native costume immediately upon landing. The native assured him that there would be no difficulty in obtaining the necessary outfit:

> *I travel in the Glasgow trade,*
> *And therefore can get quickly made*
> *Among my customers a dress*
> *Of tartans, such as might well grace*
> *Some Island Chieftain's feudal pride.*

The doctor having accepted the offer:

> *The dress was soon prepar'd and made,*
> *Even to the bonnet for his head.*

And so, fully attired, the doctor was presented to Laird MacAlpine, who, upon finding out that Prosody was a doctor of divinity, made some pawky remarks about parsons going abroad without their breeks.

But it was the visit of a much more illustrious Englishman that was to illuminate with conscious and unconscious humour the next chapter in the history of Highland Dress. In 1822, King George IV was persuaded to visit Scotland, and, as at that time his popularity hung in the balance, the success or otherwise of the visit was of vital importance. However, under the skilful guidance of Sir Walter Scott and General Stewart of Garth all went well and the King won the hearts of the great majority of the Scottish people.

It was now accepted that the wearing of the kilt and tartan was an expression of patriotism and not of rebellion. Moreover the news leaked out that the King himself would appear in the 'Garb of Old Gaul'. The result was a tartan explosion giving birth to hundreds of 'clan tartans' being demanded by all ranks of society. It also gave birth to the fearsome tartan arguments which have bedevilled the subject ever since.

Even the Celtic Society, created only two years before, and of which General Steward was a co-founder, came under attack. One of its objects was 'to promote the general use of the ancient Highland dress in the Highlands of Scotland'. This aroused fierce jealousy amongst some of the Highland chiefs and others, including the great Alastair, Macdonell of Glengarry who wrote to the *Edinburgh Observer* that he could not pass over that 'non-descript convention of anything rather than highlanders, – the Celtic Society – an incongruous assembly of all ranks that have no one common band of union among them. They neither speak the language nor know how to put on correctly the garb of the Gael . . .'

Our evidence regarding the appearance of the King in Highland dress ranges from his tailor's account and his official portraits to the scurrilous prints of the period. He made his appearance in Royal Stewart tartan on 17 August at a levée held at Holyrood.

According to the accounts of George Hunter & Company who supplied his outfit, the most expensive item was 'a fine gold chased Head Ornament for Bonnet, consisting of Royal Scots Crown in miniature, set with Diamonds, Pearls, Rubies and emeralds, supported on a wreath of chased gold Thistles surrounding a sea-green emerald, large size.' His goatskin Highland Purse had a massive gold top and nine rich gold bullion tassels, whilst his powder horn was gold-mounted and attached to a massive gold chain. His dirk was inlaid with gold and encased in a crimson velvet scabbard richly ornamented with chased gold mountings with the Royal Arms of Saint Andrew, Thistle, etc. He had a fine basket-hilted sword and a pair of Highland pistols. His costume included 61 yards of 'Royal Sattin Plaid', 31 yards of 'Royal Plaid Velvet' and $17\frac{1}{2}$ yards of 'Royal Plaid Casemere'.

Mrs Harriet Scott wrote to her daughter, 'His Majesty wore tartan Highland dress, with buff-coloured trousers like flesh to imitate his royal knees, and little bits of tartan stockings like other Highlanders half up his legs, and he looked very well, only a little *huffle-buffle*.' Sir David Wilkie, who did a splendid portrait of the King in Highland dress, wrote: 'He looked exceedingly well in tartan; he had on the kilt and hose, with a kind of flesh-coloured pantaloons underneath.'

33 *Sir William Curtis, Lord Mayor of London, who accompanied King George IV to Scotland in 1822*

Unfortunately, however, the King's friend, Sir William Curtis, Lord Mayor of London and Member of Parliament, also decided to wear the kilt. His corpulent figure encased in tartan was a perfect subject for the English satirists who immediately produced a number of caricatures. One of the most famous of these was entitled 'Bonnie Willie' and was engraved by George Cruikshank (*33*).

The caricaturists were not of course interested in historical accuracy and one anonymous print entitled *A Thousand Warm Receptions in the North*, shows the King and

Sir William in short kilts at the Drawing Room held at Holyrood. In fact the King wore the uniform of a Field Marshal on this occasion.

The enthusiasm to make this a 'Highland' occasion was shared by the poets, one of whom wrote:

The whisky shall flow in a stream to his health,
We'll bumper it roun' till we fa';
Our bonnets, with shouts, we'll toss high in the air,
For our ain George that's comin', hurra, hurra!

We'll cock our blue bonnets, aha, aha,
Our Scottish blue bonnets, aha, aha;
We'll busk on our tartans – the gatherin' blaw –
King George the Fourth's comin', huzza, huzza!

Costume in the 1820s reflected the enthusiasm for romanticism. The classical styles of the years immediately following the French Revolution were relinquished, but the inspiration of Paris remained. Although the fashionable ladies of Edinburgh shared in the current modes and manners, many of them gave their dresses that little touch of tartan. But it was the men who applied Highland dress in such a manner as to reflect the spirit of the age. In the portraits by Sir Henry Raeburn we can see great Scottish gentleman perpetuated in the Byronic pose. George, 5th Duke of Gordon is portrayed in tartan kilt, jacket, waistcoat and plaid, whilst John, 2nd Marquess of Bute, wears the normal clothes of the Lowlander but around his shoulders is draped a splendid red and green tartan cloak with brilliant scarlet lapels.

This latter portrait was painted just before the visit of George IV whilst the Duke was painted just afterwards. The two portraits might be quoted as examples of the budding use of Highland dress as a Romantic expression before 1822, and the full flowering after the Royal visit. Too often it has been suggested that George IV and Queen Victoria created a wearing of the national costume which had been moribund before their arrival. A closer examination of the subject will show that this was not so. In both cases their visits coincided with a rising wave of tartan fashion which they took up and thereby greatly accelerated.

A number of costumes worn at the 1822 visit have survived, including examples from my own collection which can be seen in Edinburgh Canongate Tolbooth. Almost without exception they are based on the military style. There were, of course, many quasi-military Highland costumes worn by such bodies as the Royal Company of Archers, the Celtic Society and the 'tails' or followers of the clan chiefs. Indeed more than one chief spent almost the entire family fortune in one-upmanship.

Once the cheers had died and the King had sailed out of sight down the Firth of Forth, many of the Highland costumes were put away. Their use in the outdoor was almost entirely limited to special occasions although they remained *à la mode* in the ballroom (*4*).

The most conspicuous public display of tartan in the Scottish countryside at this time was at the Highland Games and Gatherings. It is said that the Scottish King, Malcolm Canmore, organised the first Games at Braemar in the eleventh century, but

34 '*The Macnab' by Sir Henry Raeburn, c. 1806. A civilian costume of a very military nature*

probably the earliest gathering on modern lines was held at St Fillans, Perthshire, in 1819. Here the Highland dress was in great evidence amongst spectators and athletes alike, and for the latter it soon became compulsory. About the year 1836, a weaver from the neighbouring town of Crieff, Willie Lury, won the long jump but was disqualified because he did not wear the kilt. However, the Statistical Account of 1845 for the parish of Comrie sadly records that 'the Highland dress is entirely disused.'

In the year 1830 an event took place which enlivened the history of Highland dress at this period. Charles X abdicated from the throne of France and sought refuge with his family in Scotland. His grandson, the Duke of Bordeaux, had been appointed King of France with the title Henry V, but he too was amongst the party of exiles. He was fascinated by the Scottish national costume and by right of his connection with the Royal House of Stewart he had assumed the right to wear the Stewart tartan. He had a number of Highland costumes made and these he wore whenever possible in the company of Edinburgh society.

In 1835 a book was published in Paris entitled *Souvenir des Highlands, voyage à la suite de Henri V en 1832*. It was written and illustrated by an artist named D'Hardiviller whose romantic style was highly successful. He described an occasion outside Dunkeld where Henri was greatly impressed by 'les fiers Highlanders revêtus de leur riche costume, le front couvert de la toque ornée de feuillage ou ombragée de plumes.' D'Hardiviller illustrated the occasion with an engraving showing a splendidly dressed Chief describing to Henri a march past of his retainers including four pipers and a standard bearer.

There are other illustrations of Highland dress including a portrait of 'le vénérable Mac-Grégor', a splendid old man wearing a tartan jacket and kilt, and signed 'Duncan MacGregor'.

The most striking illustration however is the frontispiece which shows Henri himself 'en costume de Highlander', wearing a large bonnet with two feathers, kilt and shoulder plaid, and short tartan hose (*35*).

This drawing was very popular and it was the source of many subsequent portraits and prints. Various embellishments were added in the form of a bow and arrows, a more elaborate bonnet and a larger sporran, often with a badger-head top. There is also a version showing trews being worn under the kilt.

One contemporary print of Henri is described as showing the most perfect form of the Highland dress which 'far excels every other style of dress described in history.' However the writer was much mistaken when he concluded that the costume of the Highlanders 'may pass away'.

One highly colourful event which played a part in the history of costume in Scotland was the Eglinton Tournament, organised at Eglinton Castle, Ayrshire in 1839. The rich young Earl of Eglinton, disgruntled by the lack of ceremony at Queen Victoria's Coronation, decided to re-create the splendour of a medieval tournay followed by a grand banquet and ball.

Despite the weather this splendid folly was greatly enjoyed by thousands of people. The host, as Lord of the tournament, wore a suit of full Gothic gilt armour, and 13 knights likewise fully equipped, took part in the contests. The Earl of Craven wore a suit of engraved Milanese armour inlaid with gold, and the Marquis of Waterford a suit of polished steel fluted German armour, whilst other knights were clad in black armour and polished steel plate. All were mounted on burdened chargers and accompanied by men-at-arms in demi-suits of armour. These were surrounded by esquires, pages and grooms. There were musicians wearing rich costumes of silk, mounted on horses trapped and caparisoned, trumpeters in full costume with emblazoned banners, heralds, poursuivants, and halberdiers.

The Queen of Beauty, the lovely Lady Seymour, wore a long violet velvet skirt covered with gold heraldic wings, an ermine and miniver jacket, and a superb crimson velvet mantle. Around her throat she wore a number of diamond chains, and on her head she carried a pearl-encrusted crown. Her maids-of-honour and her suite were also splendidly costumed, as were the hundreds of ladies who attended the tournament as spectators dressed in medieval styles.

The evening banquet, lit by thousands of candles and attended by 400 people, was a splendid affair. It was followed by a Ball at which 2,000 guests danced to the music of the band of the 2nd Dragoon Guards who were dressed like minstrels.

In his delightful account of the tournament, Ian Anstruther describes the ladies appearance as follows:

> Certainly many of the company's dresses were of hardly mortal description. Aunt Jane was in dahlia satin with an Indian veil embroidered with gold; Lady Montgomerie, in rich cerise, had a headdress 'tastely adorned with cameos'; Lady Graham, a popular beauty, her jewelled bosom swathed in green, had a string of pearls about her waist which might have been used for a skipping rope; a Mrs Campbell was 'trimmed with bullion'; Lady Charleville, a friend of the Lambs', was 'festooned with bouquets of precious stones'; many an aristocratic waist – like the Duchess of Montrose's, in ruby velvet, was hidden beneath a diamond stomacher, fastened with emeralds, amethysts and sapphires in place of hooks or buttons.
>
> Most of the men too were dressed magnificently. Lord Chelsea was suited in emerald velvet, Lord Maidstone mantled in golden lace, Lord Saltoun robed in crimson satin, Sir Charles Lamb in sky blue silk . . .

There are a number of pictures, prints and cartoons of the tournament, and at Blair Castle we can see the suit of armour worn by Lord Glenlyon, heir to the 5th Duke of Atholl. This suit is most interestingly documented as both the detailed estimate and the final account have survived. The printed estimate quotes a plain suit of knights *cap-à-pie* armour, lined with leather and with Tilting pieces complete, for 150 guineas, or for hire at 60 guineas. Lord Glenlyon bought his body armour, armour for his horse, and many extras including an emblazoned shield with armorial bearings, a silk banner, a chain mail hauberk shirt, a 'beautiful model of *cap-à-pie* suit of armour on jointed figure' and several other items totalling £346. Included was a 'rich evening costume out of tartan velvet supplied by Lord G. with cap and plume and a pair of superior scarlet silk hose pantaloons'.

His Lordship, who fought as Knight of the Gael, brought with him 73 Atholl Highlanders, including four officers and four pipers. They wore kilts and shoulder plaids of Atholl tartan, blue coatees, blue Glengarry caps and some carried

35 *Henry V of France, who visited Scotland in 1832. A print from Hardivilliers'* Souvenir des Highlands

broadswords and targes. He hired a large tent and two pavilions to form his own encampment, and the presence of his own private retinue cost him over £1,000.

The Eglinton tournament is a significant example of the 'Gothic Revival' of that period. The novels of Sir Walter Scott were greatly responsible for this Romantic Movement in Scotland and we can trace a strong affinity between the description of a tournament in *Ivanhoe* and the procedure at Eglinton Castle. One of the results of this romantic Gothic fever which struck some of the richer families, took the form of a desire to set up a private collection of antique arms and armour.

A year before the Eglinton tournament took place, a young dealer in such relics, Samuel Luke Pratt, opened up a gallery in Bond Street, London. On show was a fine collection of authentic items and many excellent reproductions some of which have puzzled collectors ever since.

It was from Samuel Pratt that Lord Eglinton sought advice on the arms and armour required for the tournament, and the original arrangements were all made in his gallery. Everyone spoke highly of Pratt's enthusiasm and expertise. In every possible case, the Eglinton costumes were based on authentic illustrations or specimens. Many of the arms and pieces of armour which were finally selected were original, and where copies were made, they were of a high standard. Unfortunately few of these items have survived.

There are however two interesting suits in the possession of John Balfour of Balbirnie worn by his ancestor of the same name who was Esquire to the Knight of the Gael. These were on show at the 'Clothes from Scottish Houses' Exhibition in Edinburgh, 1969.

The first costume consists of a silk tunic made from Murray of Athole tartan and lined with white silk. The bodice of the tunic is padded with cotton wool, indicating that a breastplate was to be worn over it. The tight undersleeves are of red tartan, whilst the elbow-length oversleeves are of the same Murray of Athole tartan as the tunic which has a full pleated skirt. The round hat is made of red silk tartan with a blue satin brim. It is interesting to note that some of the dye from the green tartan has run, which means that the suit was probably worn on the opening day when a deluge caused the jousting to be postponed.

The second suit was probably worn at the ball given in Eglinton Castle. It consists of a tunic of a dark bluish-green velvet with full sleeves to the elbow which are slashed with red silk. The sides of the skirt of the tunic are also slashed to reveal the long sleeved splendid undertunic of crimson damask woven with silver and gilt metal thread. The red velvet waistbelt is trimmed with gilt metal braid.

There was one man at the Eglinton tournament who was to play a most significant part in the subsequent popularity of the Highland dress. On this particular occasion he played the part of the Jester and Ian Anstruther describes him thus:

He was an actor called Robert M'Ian who had made a name for himself portraying Robin Oig M'Combich in *The Two Drovers* and other plays that were drawn from Sir Walter Scott. Riding a donkey, and dressed in cap and bells, he jogged about and made some feeble jokes. But, like many people of the same profession, without a script he was just a bore, and nobody thought him amusing. 'His repartees were like a series of slight electric shocks', wrote one of the journalists, trying hard to be nice about him. In the end he lost his temper and handed his wand to the Eglinton Herald . . .

But this short-tempered jester is probably better remembered today than anyone else who took part in the great tournament. His sentimental and theatrical paintings of so-called Scottish Highlanders are to be seen on the walls of hotels, public houses and restaurants throughout Scotland.

I have already mentioned the visit of King George IV to Scotland in 1822, and there is no doubt that he did much to make Highland costume 'fashionable', and to stimulate the invention of clan tartans. But many writers would have us believe that after that nothing much happened in the history of the national dress until the arrival of his niece, the young Queen Victoria, in 1842. She is then said to have invented 'Balmoralism' and started a tartan epidemic throughout Scotland. This is not so, and if we examine contemporary evidence we will see that the Romantic Revival in all aspects of Highland costumes was in full flood long before she came north. At Dunkeld she was surrounded by hundreds of Highlanders in their 'picturesque' garb, and then at

36 *Finlay the deerstalker photographed by D. O. Hill during his visit to Colonsay, 1830*

Taymouth there was Lord Breadalbane at the head of his men – all in Campbell tartan, Sir Neil Menzies and his men 'in the Menzies red and white tartan' and a kilted company of the 92nd Highlanders.

In order to discover the early sources of this Romantic revival we must retrace our steps to a decade before the Eglinton tournament! North Britain had become a land of romance epitomised by the tales of Sir Walter Scott, the verses of Ossian, and two talented 'Princes', the Sobieski Stuarts, whom we will discuss later.

The demand for tartan and kilts as symbols of a visionary Scotland was awakened, and the means of meeting it was to hand. The manufacture of tartan was no longer a cottage industry. The mills of William Wilson and Sons of Bannockburn turned out tartan by the mile. Only the stage managers were required – the 'experts' who would advise and direct the 'correct' patterns, and the 'correct' styles.

Two men were largely responsible for supplying the link between commerce and romance. One of these we have already met, the actor who turned artist, Robert Ronald McIan, the other was James Logan, law student and artist turned writer, born in Aberdeen, about 1794.

Logan as a young man studied to be a lawyer but when he was still at college he suffered an unfortunate accident which effected his whole life. Whilst attending as a spectator at a Highland games meeting he was struck on the head by a 17-pound hammer being used in one of the events. As a result of this he had to spend the rest of his life with a four-inch square metal plate attached to his forehead. In March 1840 he wrote a letter to the Highland Society of London apologising for the affliction of his mind caused by this wound. Later he was to write 'Give me my eyesight as it once was and take away this terrible pain in my temples, and I could still be very happy among my books, even here in London'.

Despite the pain and his meagre livelihood, he began a pedestrian tour of Scotland in the year 1826, his object being to collect material for a book about the manners and customs of the Scottish Highlanders. In 1828, having returned to London, he joined the 'Club of True Highlanders' where, according to their records, he helped to form 'a brilliant record of the ancient garb, manners and customs which it was the object of the club to perpetuate' (6).

According to McIntyre North, Logan whilst studying at the Royal Academy had found the atmosphere 'severe and repressing . . . and when it came to making copies of the nude, and we are afraid sometimes naughty, models of those days, he, who had seen the well-shaped foot of the "Highland Lassie", soon discovered that he had no vocation in that line . . ..'

Logan now set to work on his proposed book, at the same time writing essays and giving lectures on Scottish antiquarian subjects. At first he intended that it would appear in 12 parts and issued a Prospectus to that effect, endorsed 'No. 1 will appear on the first of Jan 1831'. However, when it did appear it was published in 1831 in two volumes entitled *The Scottish Gael; or Celtic Manners as preserved among the Highlanders*.

For some time Logan had been in touch with Wilsons of Bannockburn and in my *History* I have quoted the contents of some of their letters. The importance of the *Scottish Gael* is that it published the first list of clan tartans, but Wilsons pointed out that this list contained 'several Fictitious and Fancy patterns' and that there was 'a want of correctness in the Specimens . . .' This will be discussed in the chapter on tartans.

Logan's book was in great demand from the moment of its publication. What is not generally realised, however is that he himself designed new patterns, and not only for the home market. On 29 October 1835, Logan wrote a long letter from London to William Wilson and Sons:

Gentlemen,

At the time I received the patterns of Tartan, which you were so obliging as to send me, for my guidance in preparing my 'History of the Clans' I intended writing to you on the subject, in reply to your esteemed observations thereon . . .

I now trouble you on a little matter of business. My friend Roderick MacDonald, Esq., of Castle Tirim, Prince Edward Island, has lately arrived in London, and has informed me, that by his influence among his clansmen, and other Scotsmen, there established, a *Caledonian Society* has been formed the objects of which are to cherish early recollections and social intercourse, by wearing their national dress and practising their fondly remembered and benevolent customs, as well as to promote the cause of Education, in their distant land.

Logan then goes on to describe more about the Society and to state that Roderick MacDonald has been authorised to procure for the members 2,000 yards of tartan. He continues: 'He has applied to me on the subject, and I have designed a Tartan for the Society, to which no one can lay individual claim. The pattern is annexed, and I have to request the favour of your informing us, at your first convenience, what the above quantity of Stuff will cost?'

After explaining that Mr MacDonald does not expect to have any benefit from the transaction, Wilson says that it is expected that tartan will become the national dress of the Scots 'of whom there are no fewer than 25,000 on the Island . . . their countrymen being not more strongly attached to the Costume of their Fathers, than zealous of the honour of their mother country.'

After discussing delivery and payment, Logan refers to 40 yards of plaid which had been made by Wilsons 'a few years since, for my late Brother, Alexander' and which had cost 1/6d per yard. The letter then concludes with a request that Wilsons obtain the lowest price which they can for 250 plain and 250 chequered bonnets.

The *History of the Clans* to which Logan refers in the above letter, was not published until 1845, when it appeared under the title *The Clans of the Scottish Highlands*. I have a rare Prospectus advertising the publication of the two lavish volumes of *The Clans* by Ackerman and Co., of the Strand, London. The dedication is to 'Her Most excellent Majesty, The Queen, who has graciously deigned to visit the country of The Clans, and patronised their Manufactures & Costumes.' This is followed by an acknowledgement of the patronage of the book by the Highland Society of London.

The opening paragraph of the Introduction reads:

There is no more extraordinary spectacle in Europe than that of the Gael of Scotland, who retains a language the most ancient, and once the most widely diffused, and preserve the manners and customs which distinguished their ancestors in ages the most remote. Among all the habitudes which characterize this 'peculiar people', none is more remarkable than their fond adherence to a garb the most primitive.

The Scots on far-away Prince Edward Island, and James Logan living in London, shared that enthusiasm for their native country so often found amongst exiled Scots. And yet the history of our national costume is unique in one respect which is the very opposite to agreement. No other national costume in the world has been the subject of such bitter and discouraging argument. In the Introduction to *The Clans* Logan refers to 'the discomfiture of the prophets who pronounced "its tasteless regularity and vulgar glare" as sufficient to prevent for ever its adoption anywhere except in the Highlands'.

The prophet to whom Logan referred was John Pinkerton who, in 1783, published a collection of 'ancient' ballads but which he had to admit subsequently were mostly written by himself. In 1797 he published *Iconographia Scotica, or Portraits of Illustrious Persons of Scotland*, followed in 1799 by *The Scotish Gallery*.

Pinkerton was corresponding with Sir John Sinclair in 1796 about the *Iconographia*, but in the previous year they had been discussing Highland dress when Pinkerton wrote that he was highly pleased to read that Sir John had appeared at court wearing his tartan trousers as they were 'far more ancient than the philabeg'. On the publication of this statement by Pinkerton, plus his remark that 'Highland dress is, in fact, quite modern', he and Logan became life-long enemies.

Any denial that Highland dress was of great antiquity was regarded by James Logan as a display of anti-Celtic feeling; however he was confident that by his own theories 'the arguments of those who assert its recent adoption are overthrown.' His argument runs as follows:

While, however, some authors have written in ignorance, many have done so from a feeling of prejudice and silly jealousy of the Scottish mountaineers; but it will be proved that this primitive costume, so well suited to the warrior, so well adapted for the avocations of the hunter and shepherd, has not only been the invariable dress of the Highlanders from time immemorial, but is to be derived from the most remote antiquity; and that neither their clothing, arms, language, poetry, nor music has been adopted from any nation whatever, but received from the primaeval people whence they sprang. Their country and pursuits rendered the belted plaid and kilt the most convenient apparel, they were not likely to lay it aside for any other. It is still less probable, that had the Truis been worn before the adoption of the Feile-beag, the inhabitants of a cold climate would have denuded themselves of so essential a part of the dress of all other nations. Nor would a people so strongly attached to their primitive customs, and opposed to change, have become so partial to a dress introduced by strangers. All who ever settled in the Highlands, as far as we can ascertain, conformed to the manners of their adopted country.

Logan regarded Highland dress as 'a venerated badge of national distinction' with unbounded assets. It was 'a dress the most convenient and economical, and greatly conducive to the preservation of health; while the sociality of the meetings connected with the object, where all classes mix in cordial animation, has a most beneficial effect'. It might be true that the sociality of the kilt might be beneficial amongst the Highlanders living in London, but I doubt if this would apply to the poverty-stricken people living in the mountains and glens of the Scottish Highlands at that time.

James Logan was undoubtedly one of the men most responsible for the adoption of Highland dress by Victorian Highlanders, Lowlanders and indeed non-Scots also. Its style and fashions were by now far removed from the days of its use as genuine peasant clothing. I wonder what the reaction of the people living in the Highlands at that time would have been had they read his lines: 'In the various modes of its arrangement this is undeniably the most picturesque and original costume in Europe, partaking of the graceful flow of Oriental drapery, with more of the advantages of European attire, and while it can be worn in great plainness, it is susceptible of the highest enrichment.'

The romantic words of James Logan in *The Clans* were illustrated by Robert Ronald McIan, another exiled Scot with deep nationalistic feelings. Having played as an actor in the south-west of England he moved to London where he performed the parts of some of Sir Walter Scott's more dramatic characters. At the age of 36 he abandoned the stage and became an artist.

It may have been McIan's dramatic style that attracted Logan; certainly such pictures as his 'Highland Cearnach defending a Pass' would be likely to stir the heart of a Victorian Scot. Anyway when the two large quarto volumes of *The Clans* were published, McIan's highly theatrically posed illustrations of 'Highlanders' made an immediate appeal to London society. After all the author could claim with genuine pride that amongst the list of subscribers were the Queen, Prince Albert and several members of the Royal Family, the King of France, members of the nobility, Highland chiefs and Charles Dickens.

McIan devised a special formula for the illustrations of *The Clans* and his subsequent publications. As a starting point he copied a number of original portraits, altering the costume to suit his own ideas, and dramatising the pose. Then to widen their appeal he painted the tartans to conform with the 'clan' tartans of his day. In all he produced over a hundred studies of Highland dress and it is unlikely that their popularity will ever be eclipsed. However, as evidence of what the Highlanders looked like during the centuries he portrays, I would have certain reservations about them. (*37*)

37 *MacNeil, painted by R. R. McIan who applied modern tartans to imaginative drawings and conflicting costume periods*

In 1845 J. Menzies of Edinburgh, D. Bogue of London, M. Amoyat of Paris, L. Michelsen of Leipzig and G. H. Söhne of Prague published *The Costume of the Clans* by John Sobieski Stolberg Stuart and Charles Edward Stuart. This vast tome (my copy weighs 22 pounds) was the result of many years careful research in the British Museum, the National Library of Scotland and the Highlands of Scotland. It is unfortunate that, perhaps owing to the doubtful reputation of the authors, no costume historian has· published a critical edition of this work. It is now very rare, and although a considerable number of their original notes survive these are not easy to decypher.

I have discussed and described this book at some length in my *History*, and whereas some of the illustrations are unlikely, and some of the written evidence and opinions doubtful, there is a great deal of valuable and unique information in *The Costume of the Clans*. There is too a realisation by the authors of some truths about the true and false use of Highland dress which many other writers of their generation chose to ignore.

The so-called Stuart brothers were not afraid to express their opinions and personal attitudes, and when they published the following lines they met with severe criticism:

> Since the days of Johnson, the beau-ideal of the Scott novels, the glory of the Highland regiments, and the interest with which foreigners admired in the late Glengarry the last of the chiefs, have increased the popularity of the Highland garb as a fancy costume. It has pleased some of those dissatisfied with the funereal monotony of modern dress to adopt for balls and dinner parties a habit which allows with impunity the indulgence of colours and decorations inadmissible under the despotism of fashion. But this indulgence, like other licenses of luxury, has the same reference to national manners as the splendours of the stage or the pageants of a throne; and the Highlanders of Scotland shall no more return to the costume of their ancestors because it is paraded in a ballroom or worn at a feast, than the people of England will resume the cloak, the plume, and the trunk-hose of the cavalier because they strut in a melodrama or pomp at a coronation. Those who assume the tartans only at the tables of the Crown and Anchor, and in the Assembly Rooms of Edinburgh; or in the sunshine of a summer's day, flutter for a few hours in a fair, or disturb the apathy of a church – do not reflect that they are emulating the delusion of those classic enthusiasts who in 1792 exhibited in the streets of Paris the astonishing apparition of French democrats stalking with severe brows and naked heads, in the toga of Brutus and the tunic of Lycurgus. The people of France, however, still continue to cover their heads with hats and their legs with trousers.

The reference to stage and pageant costume is interesting because these were the pioneer days of historical accuracy on the stage, largely due to the efforts of J. R. Planché. However, Macready as 'Macbeth' still wore a 'fashionable flowered chintz dressing gown' in the murder night scene, whilst in the same role, Sir Herbert Tree would appear dressed as a Viking.

Macbeth continued to pose a problem to stage costumiers. In 1873 Doré sought to obtain information on authentic dress for his forthcoming illustrations of Shakespeare's plays. In reply, Robert Young, a historian living in Elgin, suggested 'a kind of armour' but advised that the best Edinburgh antiquaries be consulted. Then Professor Innes of Edinburgh wrote to E. Dunbar Dunbar that 'it might suit M. Doré to presume that Scotland and Scots of the upper class dressed after French fashions of their time.' He adds the rather obvious piece of information that 'One thing we are pretty sure of, that

Macbeth wore *some* dress.' Although the Professor of History gives a few hints on possible costume to Dunbar Dunbar, he finally suggests that the matter be 'left absolutely open for a man of M. Doré's sense and admirable taste, to dress Macbeth as he pleases.'

Finally, William F. Skene, the Historiographer Royal of Scotland, was appealed to regarding the costume of Macbeth. His advice was that *The Costume of the Clans* be consulted as 'the letterpress contains every notice that exists regarding the dress from the earliest period, and there are very accurate drawings of every representation of it either on monumental stones or in pictures.'

Before leaving this slight digression to the world of the stage I must refer to two delightful French interpretations of Highland costume to be worn in a dramatisation of Scott's *Lady of the Lake*. (*38, 39*). They were published in the five-volume '*Petite Galerie Dramatique ou Recueil des Differents Costumes et Auteurs*, as hand-coloured etchings.

38 and **39** *Pair of French theatrical prints of costume worn in* La Dame du Lac, *c. 1830s*

The contrast in life-style between the rich and the poor, the aristocracy and the peasantry, was greater in Victorian times than it has ever been before. Life in the Highlands for the common people was still largely a matter of the survival of the fittest. But for those using the mountains and moorland as a playground, there was a formalised 'correct' wear for the sporting gentleman. In many cases these sporting tenants and landlords were newcomers replacing the old lairds and chiefs who had left their native glens.

It is wrong to imagine that Queen Victoria 're-introduced' Highland dress and tartans to Scotland when she came to the Highlands in 1842. All she and Prince Albert did was to give it Royal approval. They both wore it with dignity and – in comparison with many of their contemporaries – with considerable restraint.

After all, other members of the Royal family had worn it before. In 1746, George III had been portrayed as a boy wearing tartan; and the Queen must have been familiar with Sir David Wilkie's picture of George IV in full Highland dress, and Sir William Beechey's life-size portrait of Augustus Frederick Duke of Sussex wearing the Highland costume with the insignia of the Garter.

Pictorial evidence of the Highland costumes worn by the Victorians is vast. It ranges from drawings and paintings in thousands, to the early photographs which tell us exactly what people looked like. Nor must we neglect the sketchbooks of the Queen herself. Victoria was a skilled artist in line and watercolour, and her albums in the Royal Collection which cover the period 1827 to 1890, contain hundreds of costume sketches.

During her stay at Balmoral the Queen spent much time sketching the tenants and their children. She also sketched Highlanders spearing salmon in the river Dee, ghillies out on the hills deer-stalking, and the kilted attendants at the innumerable picnics. Even the Prince of Wales and Prince Arthur had to pose on several occasions wearing their kilts and shoulder plaids, tartan hose, blue bonnets and long hairy sporrans.

The Queen delighted in the use of tartan, and the sincerity of her enthusiasm was completely genuine. She would have been horrified at the subsequent commercialism of tartan for which some writers have blamed her. When she wore it she did so with moderation, and when Prince Albert wore the kilt, he did so with dignity (40).

By Victorian times, Highland dress worn with a sense of dignity and pride was well established. As early as 1817, David Webster described it as a costume 'often worn by gentlemen on particular occasions'. When Henry V of France visited Scotland in 1832, he was greeted by chiefs in picturesque Highland dress accompanied by their clansmen in similar costume. He reciprocated their sentiments by donning it himself.

In September 1848, the Queen and Prince Albert visited Balmoral. Once again the appearance of her 'faithful Highlanders' fascinated her. Gamekeepers and ghillies were photographed, and kilted tenants were sketched. But already the fertile imaginations of the cartoonists were in full flight. A lithograph by 'H. H.' entitled 'A Scotch Polka on board the *Victoria and Albert*, on the way to Scotland, August 1847' shows the Queen in a tartan dress, and Albert wearing a tartan shoulder plaid and feathered Glengarry bonnet.

40 *HRH Prince Albert in 1858. An engraving after John Philip, RA*

At the opening of the Great Exhibition in 1851, the young Prince of Wales wore a kilt, velvet jacket, white collar and feathered cap. Both the Prince of Wales and Prince Albert had had their portraits painted by Winterhalter in 1849, and the subsequent lithograph by Leon Noel was extremely popular. From now on Highland dress became very fashionable for children's wear at formal society occasions in Britain, France and America. *The Englishwoman's Domestic Magazine* praised its advantages. 'As soon as little people leave off their suits they should be put into Highland costumes, which are not only the prettiest dresses for boys and girls, but also the most healthy.' (*8*).

In September 1852, the Queen described in her *Journal* an open-air torchlight ball at which, 'I wore a white bonnet, a grey watered silk and (according to Highland fashion) my plaid scarf over my shoulder, and Albert his Highland dress which he wears every evening'. In September 1859 they attended the Highland Games given for members of the British Association. 'Albert and the boys were in their kilts, and I and the girls in Royal Stuart skirts and shawls over black velvet bodies.'

The famous picture by William Powell Frith of the wedding of the Prince of Wales to Princess Alexandra in 1863, is almost dominated by the figures of two boys in Highland dress standing in the foreground. They are Prince Leopold aged ten, and Prince Arthur aged thirteen, and their costume shows very clearly the strong military style being applied to Highland dress at this period. Their doublets are of the pattern being worn by the men of the Highland regiments, having two flaps in front and two flaps behind, braided with three buttons and long button-loops on each flap. The gauntlet cuff is also of the military style. They wear kilts and shoulder-plaids of the Royal Stuart tartan, diced hose with red garters, and they carry Glengarry bonnets mounted with eagle feathers. Frith has given them a fine air of dignity and even the white 'Eton' collars seem in context.

In the Royal archives there is a photograph of Prince Leopold, afterwards Duke of Albany, and Prince Arthur, afterwards Duke of Connaught, taken by Mayall in March 1863. The costume appears to be that shown in Frith's picture but Prince Arthur is armed with a basket-hilted broadsword and a dirk. Whether he wore these arms at the Royal wedding is not clear from the picture, although he did carry them at the wedding of the Princess Royal in 1858.

In the background of the wedding picture is a small impish figure wearing a similar Highland costume. This is Prince William, the future Kaiser Wilhelm II, every inch a Teutonic Highlander, Whilst the Royal family waited for the arrival of the bride, Prince William managed to prise off the large Cairngorm stone from the dirk which his young uncle, Prince Leopold, had lent him. Having hurled this trophy across the floor, he proceeded to bite the bare knees of Prince Arthur and Prince Leopold.

Sir Edwin Landseer painted the activities of Queen Victoria and Prince Albert in Scotland on many occasions. To many people these scenes, in the form of engravings, were the only insight into the life of the Royal family in the Highlands. Because of this, the dignified manner in which he portrayed Highland costume had a considerable effect upon its acceptance and use. The detail of his draughtsmanship provides useful information to the costume historian.

There is a misconception that the Queen introduced Landseer to Scotland. In fact, it was when she first visited Ardverikie in 1847, that she first saw the 'beautiful drawings

1 *'Highland Chieftain'. A life-size painting by Michael Wright, c. 1660.*

ancii Charteris 5t Earl of Wemyss
Katharine his Wife Daughter of
Alexr 2d Duke of Gordon.

2 *The 5th Earl of Wemyss and his wife, by Allan Ramsay. The picture was painted shortly after their marriage in 1745, during the period when Highland dress was proscribed.*

3 *Detail from David Morier's painting of the Battle of Culloden showing the many patterns of tartan worn. None of these corresponds to modern 'clan' tartans.*

4 *Portrait by an unknown artist, c. 1715, showing the uniform of the Queen's Bodyguard for Scotland, The Royal Company of Archers. Probably of James, 5th Earl of Wemyss.*

of stags, by Landseer'. His paintings of country folk may have over-obvious sentiment but they demonstrate the symbolic use of costume. Two contemporary genre scenes in the Victoria and Albert Museum show this clearly. *The Stonebreaker and his Daughter* portrays an interesting romantic interpretation of working clothes. The man wears a blue bonnet, a greenish nondescript jacket and breeches, and a pale cream and brown checked plaid covering his head, shoulders and knees. His cream-coloured hose are secured with red and yellow garters. His daughter wears a small red tartan plaid around her shoulders. *The Drover's Departure* shows a grey checked shoulder-plaid being worn by a kilted Highlander, Both pictures are painted with great attention to detail. The tidiness and orderly arrangement of all the costumes is questionable, but one feels that the items of clothing are factual.

In addition to the many paintings of the Royal family in Scottish costume there is a vast collection of photographs both in the Royal albums and elsewhere. George Washington Wilson of Aberdeen took many excellent photographs at Balmoral and was appointed Photographer Royal for Scotland. The many lithographs which were taken from photographs are, because of their accuracy, of great value to the costume historian. For example, the photograph of the young Prince of Wales, later King Edward VII, taken by Lake Price, was produced by Richard James Lane, lithographer to the Queen. It shows the Prince wearing a kilt and shoulder plaid, the tartan of which is depicted in detail. The formality of his costume is interesting because it is what he actually wore whilst shooting out on the moors.

Specimens of the tartan costume and accessories which belonged to Queen Victoria and which are now outside the Royal collection are rare. I have, however, a few items which were presented to me by Sir Edward and Lady Reid of Ellon. Sir Edward's father, Doctor James Reid, was appointed resident physician at Balmoral in 1881. These relics include three silk tartan shoulder scarfs which the Queen wore at Balmoral. They measure nine feet in length, including their fringes, and they are 18 inches wide. The three seperate tartans are 'Royal', 'Dress' and 'Hunting' Stewart, the latter with a slight difference from the usual sett.

Queen Victoria altered the setts of the Stewart tartan to suit her personal preferences, although most of these alterations were slight. She was not, however, the first member of the Royal Family to take an interest in tartan. In 1812, her father, H.R.H. the Duke of Kent and Strathearn, being Colonel of the Royal Scots, made an effort to clothe the regiment in 'Strathearn' tartan. I have an interesting letter dated 22 September 1821, written by Gloag Cochran and Company to Wilsons of Bannockburn, the tartan manufacturers, asking 'whether or not there is a pattern of Tartan called the Strathearn . . . as it is for a member of the Royal Family.'

The artist who portrays the Victorian Highlanders with the greatest dignity is, in my opinion, Kenneth MacLeay RSA. His drawings were lithographed by Vincent Brooks and published in 1870, under the title *Portraits Illustrative of the Principal Clans and Followings, and the Retainers of the Royal Household at Balmoral, in the Reign of Her Majesty Queen Victoria* (41–44) MacLeay made hundreds of detailed drawings of jackets, waistcoats, kilts, sporrans, guns, pistols, swords and dirks including many family relics. He then made watercolour drawings of his subjects from life usually in pairs. When the finished portraits were finally exhibited at 'Mr Mitchell's Royal Library, Old Bond

41 *Lachlan McPherson, Standard bearer, and Ewan McPherson, sword bearer. By Kenneth MacLeay, 1869*

42 *John Grant with Lochaber Axe, and John Fraser, by Kenneth MacLeay, 1869*

43 *Four figures contrasting 'full' dress with 'day' dress. By Kenneth MacLeay, 1869*

44 *Three Sutherland Highlanders, the figure on the left in the uniform of a Volunteer. By Kenneth MacLeay, 1868*

Street, London' they caused a minor sensation. It was known that they had received the Queen's personal approval and when Mitchell published them, the edition was immediately bought up.

Every detail is carefully shown, from the clan badge on the bonnet down to the exact detail of the footwear. But it is the pose of the figures that is so natural and yet conveys the pride of these dignified men. Each one is named and he and his costume described. Some have biographical notes as for instance Farquar Macdonald who was born in 1831 on the Island of Scalpa (off Skye). He was a famous salmon fisher who 'could shoot a salmon in the act of leaping the falls, with a single bullet.'

There is a fine portrait of John Brown painted by Carl Sohn, Junior, at the Queen's command in 1883. She thought it 'wonderfully fine' and it certainly is very flattering (45). Brown was painted and photographed in a number of costumes, but his favourite everyday wear was a kilt of plain material with matching stockings and a dark jacket and waistcoat. He wears one of these outfits in his picture in the illustrated edition of the Queen's *Journal*. This was made from a photograph reproduced as a wood engraving, and there are a number of photographs of this non-tartan outfit in the Royal Collection. However, he was not always so conservative in his dress. I have a hand-coloured photograph entitled 'John Brown Esq. Her Majesty's Personal Attendant.' On his head he wears a large Glengarry with a large square black cockade on which is fastened a silver brooch carrying the Royal Arms. Behind the brooch is a small bunch of flowers indicating a clan plant but which cannot be identified with certainty. Over a white shirt with a small bow tie he wears a pale purple jacket with black silver-edged lapels and silver laced gauntlet cuffs. His bulky Royal Stuart kilt hangs to the centre of the knee, and his matching shoulder plaid is fastened with a large circular silver brooch with a cairngorm in the centre. His wide sword-belt has silver slides and buckle and the waist-belt has a rectangular silver buckle. He is armed with two matching silver pistols and a sword with a heavy silver basket hilt of an unusual pattern encased in a silver-mounted scabbard. He also has a hunting horn suspended from his shoulder by a silver chain. His white hair sporran has a large silver top and extends downwards to the top of his tartan hose. Lying on a rustic table, a stag's head gazes up at him with admiration.

Portraits of John Brown range from cartoons in *Punch* and the notorious one in *The Tomahawk* of 1866, at one end of the scale, to portraits by Landseer and sketches by the Queen herself at the other. He had a considerable wardrobe, and a number of genuine and not-so-genuine items from it have survived. He had strongly held views on the correct dress of the outdoor servants and pipers at Balmoral and no doubt the Queen closed her ears to many an argument.

It might be fitting to conclude these observations on the Victorian kilt-wearers with the words of that great enthusiast, McIntyre North, which he published in his now rare *Book of True Highlanders* in 1881. Having declared the usual Lowland dress of his day as standing 'pre-eminent as a model of ugliness', he then describes it:

On his body he has a flannel undershirt. Then, if he wears an open shirt front, a chest protector, or else some of the hundred and one fads advertised; over that he has a shirt proper; then a waistcoat, collar and necktie then a coat; and then to protect the coat, a greatcoat. He has a hat to put on his head, which neither covers it nor protects it from the weather; and to protect the greatcoat and the hat he has an umbrella, and when it is dry he has a cover to protect the

45 *John Brown, painted by Carl Sohn Jnr., 1883, by command of Queen Victoria, who described the picture as 'so like'*

umbrella. With regard to the bifurcation; he has stockings to cover him from the tips of his toes to his knees, and then a pair of drawers to cover him from his knees to his waist, and to protect these; he has a pair of tight-fitting leather boots to protect his feet (the smaller and the less like the human foot the better), and a pair of trousers to protect his stockings, drawers, etc . . .'

In contrast to this diabolical dress, North describes the 'immense superiority' that the Highland dress possesses;

The kilt, leaving the legs free, the wearer has the advantage of the *air bath*, which is so invigorating to the human frame, the friction of the lower part of the kilt maintains the warmth in the cold weather; and the upper part fitting closely round the waist, supports and protects the loins in a manner especially beneficial in warm climates; the want of which support in the Lowland dress frequently rendering the use of cholera belts, etc, necessary; in wet weather, the rain being immediately shaken off, the wretched and dangerous effects arising from standing or walking about in sodden bags (which chill the system and necessitate the use of stimulants) is entirely avoided . . . A celebrated physician, whose name we forget, was so impressed with the unwholesomeness of the modern dress that he used frequently in warm weather to take off his unmentionables, and sit writing for an hour or two without them, in order to have an *air bath*.

And so the Victorian 'Highland outfit' was now in full fashion. Here was a costume that, if one ignored the draught, would promote health. Not only that, despite the cartoons in *Punch*, it was highly respectable and worn frequently by many members of the Royal family. As a fashionable outfit it began to have 'correct' and 'incorrect' items of wear and styles for various occasions (*46, 47*).

46 *The kilt being worn in a natural manner in an appropriate environment. Photograph by W. Skeoch Cumming*

47 *A Skye Piper, c. 1908, wearing three different setts of tartan. This was his dress for weddings, funerals and formal occasions*

48 *Edwardian deer stalker. Gaiters were popular in all shooting costumes and were even worn with the kilt*

And then the big question arose, Who had the 'right' to wear it? It was unlikely that anyone would argue with the kilted Highlander who held the pony in the background at the shooting party. He had been clothed at the expense of the estate (*48*). Whenever he got home he could hang his kilt up in the cupboard and put on his comfortable old unmentionables. But what about the unfortunate new 'laird' whose name was not included in the lists which hung in the tailors' shops in Edinburgh? *'If your Name is here we have your Tartan'* they proclaimed. However there was no need for him to despair, the lists were highly elastic and would stretch with the passage of time. Even if he could not enter the ranks of the top league there were always the 'septs'.

No other piece of material with the exception of the club tie has ever achieved the distinctions of the tartan. Its status was widespread. The Empress herself proclaimed her ancestry by wearing the 'Royal Stewart' tartan; some of the finest regiments in the world were dressed in it, so why shouldn't the ordinary civilian adopt what one commentator called 'the poor man's heraldry'? Well the answer is that he did, and within a decade the tartan lists grew from under 50 to nearly 500.

6

The Tartan

BY SETTING UP the most primitive loom in the simplest manner anyone who can weave can produce a tartan. Dr A. E. Haswell Miller wrote in 1956: 'The type of pattern commonly known as "tartan", far from being peculiarly Scottish, is one of the simplest types of design to invent, and there are few quarters of the world where it is not to be found as a native production.'

The word itself originally meant a light woollen material of any colour and was derived from the French *tiretaine* and the Spanish *tiritana*. James Logan stated that the word 'tartan' was derived 'from the Gaelic tarsan, or tarsuin, across' and then went on to claim that the 'French tyretaine, a sort of woollen cloth, is certainly of Gallic origin.' In fact, the Scottish Highlander never used this word when he spoke Gaelic. He used the word *breacan* which simply means 'spotted like a trout, banded like a zebra, or striped cross-wise'. For those with an interest in origins, *cadadh* or tartan cloth, is defined in MacBain's *Etymological Dictionary of the Gaelic Language* (1911), as 'doubtless from the English *caddis*, worsted, crewel work.' But we also find the kilt hose or stockings described by the words *cados* and *cathdos*. Just to make it more difficult, *cadûd* in the early Irish writings can refer to wrapping, as of a blanket.

Writers of the past have declared some strange definitions of Scottish tartan. For instance, J. G. Mackay states that 'We have it on the authority of Blind Harry that the patriot Wallace wore tartan.' In an attempt to support this claim he quotes lines from Blind Harry's poem describing William Wallace as being dressed 'In till a gyde of gudly ganand greyne' and 'Ane Ersche mantill'. I find it difficult to accept these quotations as proof that Wallace wore tartan.

Several writers have been preoccupied with giving clan tartans – that is, tartans which are identified with a particular name – an antiquity which cannot however be substantiated. There is no present clear evidence that these clan, or named tartans existed before the middle of the eighteenth century.

The factual evidence which must be examined regarding tartan is found in authentic and contemporary written accounts by Scots or visitors to Scotland, pictorial evidence, genuine traditions and folk-lore and the actual specimens of the material which have survived. With this in view, let us consider the opinions of the specialists who have had the greatest opportunities and experience in their own particular fields of research.

Scotland owes a great debt to J. F. Campbell of Islay for preserving so much folk-lore which otherwise would have been lost. He was a profound and scholarly collector of Gaelic texts many of which were published in his *Popular Tales of the West Highlands*.

On 2 October 1882, he wrote as follows to Lord Archibald Campbell who in turn published the letter in *Records of Argyll*. I have never seen it quoted by historians of the tartan.

My Dear Lord Archy,

You are kindly welcome to come here and copy every document that I have which bears upon your subject.

1st. As collector of the popular tales of the West Highlands, I have twenty-two volumes in Gaelic. Dress is repeatedly and minutely described in one particular class of stories, and is incidentally mentioned in others. It is the dress of the Iona tombstones apparently. I have a very good memory for useless knowledge. I am nearly certain that there is no mention of any tartan at all in any story orally collected by me or for me.

Having examined Campbell's vast collection of original material, I can find no mention of clan tartans, and, if such a system existed, find it difficult to understand why none of the many poets and story-tellers describe it.

Dr Alexander Carmichael's well-known collection of five volumes of Gaelic poetry are not mentioned in the clan tartan argument. But I consider it significant that neither there, or in his unpublished collection is there any reference to such a system.

One must also wonder why the great poets of the Jacobite era such as Duncan Bàn McIntyre, John MacCodrum and Alexander Macdonald make no mention of the Highlanders being dressed in clan tartans.

Dr A. E. Haswell Miller, as Keeper of the Scottish National Portrait Gallery, had unique opportunities to study the pictorial evidence regarding Highland dress, a subject in which he was deeply interested. As an artist of considerable merit he made copious records of pictures in private and public collections, including the Royal Collection. In an authoritative publication by the Historical Association in 1956, entitled *Common Errors in Scottish History*, he wrote:

The bearers of certain Scottish names frequently claim – and would even reserve – the right to wear one of these patterns as a more or less heraldic badge. But the 'Scottish Clan Tartans' as we know them from numerous books, post-cards and other productions were never systematised before the appearance of such publications in the nineteenth century.

Authentic documentation of the tartan previous to the nineteenth century is limited to a comparitively small number of contemporary portraits, and is negative so far as it provides any suggestion of heraldic significance or 'clan badge' intention. . . .

Haswell Miller pointed out that common sense 'hesitates to accept the feasibility of an organised and agreed system of design for tartan throughout the Highlands of Scotland in the eighteenth or earlier centuries.' His conclusion was that the heraldic or 'family badge' significance of the tartan had no original documentary support, 'and the establishment of the myth can be accounted for by a happy coincidence of the desires of the potential customer, the manufacturer and the salesman.'

Major I. H. Mackay Scobie spent a lifetime collecting information on Highland dress in all its forms, military and civilian. Unfortunately, although he wrote many articles which were published in his regimental magazine *Caber Feidh*, and in other Scottish publications such as *The Celtic Monthly*, he never published a book on the subject of Highland dress. His *Old Highland Fencible Corps* (1915) and *Pipers and Pipe*

Music in a Highland Regiment (1924) contain much information on Highland uniforms. His family lived in the clan country for close on two centuries and he was a Gaelic scholar: his opinion therefore is authoritative. In *Chamber's Journal* June 1942, he made this opinion quite clear: 'The antiquity of Highland *Breacan* (tartan, of course, was not unknown in other countries) is beyond dispute. On the other hand, "clan" tartans – as defined and known at the present day – cannot be shown to have existed as such prior to the 1745 period, and, indeed, are even later.'

After collecting early specimens of tartan for almost 50 years I do not have a single example of a clan tartan dating before the very late eighteenth century. Of the specimens dating before that time, a great many show a difference between the pattern of warp and weft. Such an arrangement could not possibly produce the modern clan tartan the sett of which depends on the exact duplication of colour and pattern between warp and weft.

I have collected several hundred documentary references to Highland dress between 1600 and 1800 but they contain no mention of clan tartans before the late eighteenth century.

Before leaving the subject of early tartans which have survived, it might be appropriate to mention something about their classification and attribution. The number said to have been worn by 'Bonnie Prince Charlie' are legion, as are the number of those said to be from the battlefield of Culloden. But the question is whether it is possible to identify an old piece of tartan, and furthermore to date it with any degree of accuracy. As far as identifying the original owner is concerned this will depend on the age of the tartan; the more modern it is the more accurate is its pedigree *likely* to be. Where the original ownership is known with complete certainty this fact can undoubtedly add to the interest and value of the specimen. The silk tartan scarves which belonged to Queen Victoria are of great appeal to the student of tartans because of their superb manufacture. They are also of interest to the historian concerned with the life of the Queen Empress.

But what of the pieces of tartan claimed to be 'Jacobite'? I have managed to acquire some of these, but not one of them can be said with complete certainty to have been worn by a particular individual or on a particular occasion. And as far as I am concerned this makes very little difference to their value; they have their own intrinsic beauty and fascination. The fact that they were spun and woven over two centuries ago, the beauty of their colours and the excellence of their texture give pleasure enough.

The only collection of tartans which, over a period of a century, can be dated to a day, are those attached to the records of William Wilson and Sons of Bannockburn. There is a special fascination in reading a letter to the Quartermaster of a Highland regiment discussing their tartan, particularly when it has a sample attached to it with a little rusty pin. Even more fascinating is the fact that this is the tartan which the regiment is to wear on the field of Waterloo, or on the Heights of Balaclava.

Laboratory tests can provide worthwhile information when applied to the yarn of any textile, but personal knowledge brings greater understanding and pleasure to the student of tartans. By learning how to spin and weave, using the techniques of the eighteenth century in the Highlands, it is possible to add greatly to one's knowledge.

Having acquired these skills, however, the ability to give a close date to an early tartan will not be achieved, but the problems which faced our ancestors will be better appreciated.

The production of organic dyes presents a challenge. The collection of the ingredients is difficult enough, but the subsequent processes are sometimes highly odoriferous. Organic dyeing is an art to be practised in the open air.

Methods of documenting the pattern or sett of a tartan have varied in the past, but the simple thread count has been the most successful for ordinary purposes. I employed that method in the *Official Tartan Map*, and described its application. The recording of modern clan tartans is not difficult but the setts of the old pre-clan tartans are more demanding. Apart from the fact that the warp and the weft frequently differ, very often the sett does not repeat or pivot as it does in the modern clan tartan.

I use a photographic method to record the early tartans and by taking a colour-slide and projecting it at a fixed distance, I obtain an exact scale reproduction. Where a large sett is involved, as it often is, a mosaic or overlap series of several slides must be employed. With experience and experimentation good enough colour reproduction can be obtained, but if a greater degree of accuracy is required, then a set of commercial colour-matching sheets can be used.

The student will search in vain for published details of eighteenth-century tartans. This very important aspect of the history of Highland dress has been completely ignored. The number of specimens extant is not large and a publication giving their location and details of the setts would be most useful.

There is no doubt that the earliest lists of setts were published to meet the demand of Scots, and others, wishing to know what their 'correct' clan tartan was. The publication in 1831 by James Logan of the first list of the clan tartans in his *Scottish Gael* brought satisfaction to customer and tailor alike.

I have written at some length on the compilation of Logan's list and of the lists in pattern books which followed thereafter in my *History*. Unfortunately Logan gave no details regarding his source material and for a century after the publication of his book no one seems to have questioned this. It is a quite extraordinary fact that although by 1830 the firm of William Wilson and Sons, Bannockburn, has produced literally hundreds of miles of clan and military tartans, by the early twentieth century their records had vanished and their whereabouts remained unknown for a further half-century.

It has been stated that the Wilsons obtained details of tartan setts from Logan. In actual fact the correspondence of the firm shows that Logan hardly knew of them before the publication of his book. Indeed it now appears that they had more than a little to do with the design of some of the clan tartans which appeared in the *Scottish Gael*. The fact is that Wilsons were selling tartans long before Logan was born.

The authors of the many books listing and illustrating clan tartans have never described the part played by Wilsons of Bannockburn in Scotland's tartan trade. And yet for over a century they had a monopoly at home and abroad. In hundreds of the firm's letters dealing with the supply of military tartans for half a century from 1797, every Highland regiment in the British army is mentioned. A decade before the publication of the *Scottish Gael*, patterns of Wilson's clan tartans were available from clothiers' shops in most of the Scottish towns. Had the tea-chests containing the correspondence and records of this great family business been lost, we would be completely ignorant of perhaps the most important chapter in the history of tartan.

William Wilson was born in 1727, married Janet Paterson, and had two sons, John born in 1754 and Alexander born in 1771. William was entered with the Incorporation of Chapmen, Bannockburn by William Wingate, Lord Principal, having paid his dues as a weaver in September 1759. John, his son, was entered with the Chapmen exactly ten years later. He died in 1789 but one of his sons James, born in 1780, worked with his uncle Alexander. However this arrangement did not work out very well and when Alexander's two sons, William born in 1800, and John born in 1802, grew up and joined the firm, James left. He then joined his two brothers John and William in a firm entitled J. & W. Wilson which manufacturerd tartans and textiles for a time and then turned to the manufacture of carpets.

I have not yet completed the deciphering and cataloguing of this large collection, but so far the earliest document which I have discovered, and which is of considerable interest, is dated 1763. It is entitled *Extract Petition and Act of the Justices anent the Weaving of Plaids and Tartans in St Ninian's Parish*. It reads:

At Stirling the sixteenth day of Jany . . . in presence of the Justices of Peace Stirlingshire mett in theire adjourned Quarter Sessions, anent the Petitions of the Makers of Tartan or Plaid in Bannockburn St. Ninians Camsbarron and at Newhouse betwixt Stirling and St. Ninian's Shewing that the Tartan trade labours under great Discouragment at present as not being esteemed in the foreign Mircate occasioned by everyone being at liberty to weave them in what Breadths and Girths they think proper. Being under no legall restraint either as to Breadth Quality or Sufficiency, which induced but too many to Committ Gross frauds by not making the web from end to end of the same thickness Sett and Colour making the foreend of a much better consistency than the rest foolishly thinking that by that means if they once get off their work without Suspicion there can be no after Quarrell not considering that these frauds discredit that great Article of Business in Foreign and even in home markets. . . .

In order to prevent these shady practices the weavers put forward a scheme whereby their Corporation would appoint inspectors empowered by the Justices to inspect the tartans woven locally. The names of the inspectors would be given to the Justices, be appointed for a limited period, and replaced at regular intervals.

. . . if a web is found defective by the Inspector it shall be cut in lengths of ten or twelve yards and given back to the owners to be Sold in parcells to prevent fraud he paying a penalty proportioned to the Offence not exceeding half a crown for a web of fifty yards be at the disposal of the Inspectors . . . That the breadth of the Tartan at the reed be twenty inches and a half and equall in colour and quality from end to end. Lastly Inspectors transgressing shall be liable in Double the penalties of the other weavers as to all or any articles of their duty And shall be answerable before any one or more Justices of the Peace on Complaint. . . .'

This very interesting document, written during the time when the Highland dress was proscribed, is evidence of the concern and pride which the weavers took in their craft. But it also indicates that even at this early date they were looking to their export trade and were anxious not to be discredited in the foreign markets.

Following the Treaty of Union of 1707, the ports of Glasgow and Greenock found themselves ideally situated for trade with the North American colonies and the rich plantations of the West Indies. Clyde ship-building flourished and the importation of tobacco increased rapidly. By the time the Wilsons began business there were many Scottish businessmen and agents in Canada, North and South America, and the West Indies. Scottish settlement in America had reached a recognisable proportion by the early eighteenth century. In February 1736, Governor Oglethorpe of Georgia visited Darien, where he found a colony of Highlanders in their native dress and as a compliment to them, put it on himself. In 1746, John Mitchell of Fredericksburg advertised in the *Virginia Gazette* for a servant boy who had run away and whom he described as 'A Scots Highland Boy . . . speaks broken English and has his hair cut. He carried with him a Tartan Waistcoat.' In 1775, Donald McLeod petitioned the New York congress for permission to recruit a hundred Highland Immigrants 'in defence of our liberties . . . with the Proviso of having the liberty to wear their own Country Dress, Commonly called the Highland Habit.' The following year a gentleman in Philadelphia wrote to a friend in London that 'Messrs Sproat, Semple and Milligen, merchants in Front Street . . . have raised companies of their own countrymen of a hundred men each, who are equipped in the Scottish dress.'

By the year 1784, William Wilson and Son had established a good trade in tartans with merchants on the island of Grenada. A letter dated 8 August, from a merchant named Walter McAllan, encloses a draft for £175 with some 'Dollers to make up the amount' in payment of 'Tartan Cloaths.' A flourishing trade was also established with Jamaica through agents called John and James Christie. For the years 1784 and 1785 they sold over £700 worth of Wilson tartans.

In order to meet this demand the Wilsons were now employing as many weavers as they could find. A Petition of the Co-operative Tartan Weavers of Bannockburn which 'Humbly Sheweth that your Petitioners hopes that you will take it into Consideration to advance the prices, and likewise to be paid still by the Measured Yard' is signed by 80 men and women.

Trade with Kingston, Jamaica, was established at the turn of the century, and by 1818 tartans were being shipped out every month. The cost of carriage, dues, insurance, freight, postages and commission worked out at about £4 per bale.

But by far the greatest overseas trade was to Rio de Janeiro. This was handled by a Glasgow agent, John Jameson of Brunswick Street, to a firm of merchants in Rio called Messrs Ewing and Hodson. Apart from large quantities of tartan cloth, Wilsons supplied consignments of tartan cloaks at a hundred a time. These lots were made up one half of 'dark patterns' and one half of 'the lighter kind', and they were 'all lined with green baise or blue flannel as most convenient.' A special consignment ordered by Messrs Freese Blankenhagen & Company was for a hundred tartan cloaks 'some with velveteen and shag collars, and 25 of full breadths of Tartan for Stout People.'

Meanwhile in New York Wilson tartans had already become a rage by the 1820s. The McDuff pattern was particularly popular and Wilsons' list included over 40 clan setts in addition to the Wellington, Regent, Glencoe, Prince Royal, Glen Lyon and other 'fancy' tartans. In November 1823, David Hadded, their New York agent, wrote to William Wilson describing how well worsted tartans were selling. In the previous three months he had sold over a thousand dollars' worth amongst which the Glengarry and Clanranald patterns were the most popular. On 24 September 1823, Wilsons shipped out to William Hadden two bales of tartan on the Black Ball ship 'William Thompson'. On 15 November they were auctioned in New York for £1,019.

The little village, dating back to the middle ages, built on the banks of the Bannock Burn in Stirlingshire had, by the end of the eighteenth century become a small industrial town. Thanks to the initiative and exertions of the Wilson family a stout stone mill and dye sheds had been built in the 1770s and were being constantly expanded until two large mills named 'Skeoch' and 'Royal George' stood over three stories high.

It is unfortunate that James Logan, when he came to Scotland about 1826, did not visit the Wilsons at Bannockburn. When he did contact them in 1831 his book was already in course of publication and it was too late to avail himself of their information. It is also unfortunate that Logan does not give us particulars regarding his sources and authorities.

Although Logan's list is the first to be published in book form it is perhaps not the first to be printed. In 1831, the well-known firm of Romanes and Paterson, 'Scottish Tartan, Shawl & Silk Warehouse', had a printed list, a copy of which lies before me now. It is not identical with Logan's list either in content or definition, and it must be remembered that this Scottish firm had been producing clan tartans in large quantity and that these had been accepted as 'correct' for many years. They stocked the tartans in 'Worsted, Silk and Worsted, Sarsenet, Satin and Tweeled Silk', and some of the more popular tartans in 'Tabbinet, Spun Silk, Velvet, and Superfine Worsted'.

The next tartan pattern book was without doubt a forgery. Entitled *Vestiarum Scoticum* it was published in 1842, and I have described it, and its creators, in considerable detail in my *History*. John Sobieski Stolberg Stuart and his brother Charles Edward Stuart claimed that the 75 tartans which they depict were based on a 'small black-leather quarto of the sixteenth century'. They had a strong reason for publishing this forgery as it could help their claim to Royal descent. Many of the tartans which they illustrated were taken into use, and most of these are still worn today.

It is not possible to state how many tartans are in use today as they are being invented all the time. When the *Official Tartan Map* was published in 1976, the number of setts illustrated was 141, but there were at that time several hundred setts to choose from. Who had the right to wear them?:

With the exception of tartans blazoned with the appropriate chief's approval in the Public Register of All Arms and Bearings in Scotland, there is no legality for or against their use. The right to wear a tartan should be carefully considered, as a matter of individual conscience. Because clan tartans can be regarded with sincere and fully justified pride, their misuse can cause considerable offence. The ultimate authority for a clan tartan is the clan chief.

The early methods of manufacturing the materials from which the clothing of the Highlanders were made is an important aspect of the subject. The final appearance of any costume must depend on the raw materials and the means employed to make them. The wool, the dye pots, the water, the organic ingredients, the spinning and weaving equipment would all affect the colour and texture of the cloth. Nor can we ignore the variety of skill possessed by the people engaged in the many processes. There is also the fact that most of these people were fighting for existence in a poverty-stricken country. In many cases the quantity and quality of their home-dyed, home-spun, home-woven clothing would depend on the amount of time available for making it.

When we study the techniques and materials used in the making of textiles in the Highlands, it becomes clear that there must have been certain regional differences. But to suggest what these differences were is not easy. Within the Highlands and Islands there was a great variety of climate and geology, and therefore a great variety of plant ecology. There was also a variety in the quantity of sheep and the nature of their wool. Even the acidity of the water varies considerably.

Unprejudiced and factual accounts of the lives of the humble Highlanders are few. We really know little about their movements locally, nor do we know a great deal about their local trading methods. We can speculate, but nevertheless I believe that to the costume historian a study of the methods used by the Highlanders to produce their clothing is of importance and interest.

49 *Sheep shearing in western Argyll, c. 1920. Note the uniformity of dress worn generally by agricultural workers in the Western Highlands*

In my *History*, Mrs Annette Kok has written an Appendix entitled 'Early Scottish Highland Dyes'. Based on extensive practical research, her essay underlines the difficulties in neatly tabulating plant and mineral dyes involving 'the nature of the fibre to be dyed, the "hand", or individual temperament of the dyer and even the material of the dye vessel'. The variety of shades which emerge, and the impossibility of producing large quantities of wool dyed to the same shade, make nonsense of the idea that there was strict uniformity of colours in the eighteenth century.

The history of Scottish clothing is closely allied with the history of sheep in Scotland, and the Animal Breeding Research Organisation, Edinburgh, has produced some important information on this subject. Many of its findings are of particular interest to the student of prehistoric dress.

The brown Soay sheep which still survives on St Kilda is the most primitive sheep of Europe, and the remains of sheep from archaeological excavations of Iron Age sites in the Hebrides, and Roman forts in the southern Lowlands are of the small Soay type. In the National Museum of Antiquities of Scotland is a small terra-cotta model of a Roman wool bale found on the island of Skye. The fact that it has been painted green suggests that the wool had been dyed that colour. A fragment of cloth found close to the Antonine Wall at Falkirk is of a check pattern and has been given the rather romantic title of 'Falkirk tartan'.

Documentary evidence of the making of woollen cloth in Scotland dates back to the middle of the twelfth century, and Dr M. L. Ryder, whose research on Scottish sheep and wool is invaluable, points out that in the Border area Abbeys kept thousands of sheep in the thirteenth century. The Blackface was not introduced into the Highlands until the 1750s and there would, of course, be crossing with the native sheep.

The brown colour of the Soay sheep would have a considerable bearing on the clothing made from undyed wool and would also affect the shades obtained from the use of organic dyes. But up to the eighteenth century sheep throughout the Highlands and Islands had fleeces of a variety of colours. This must be borne in mind when we examine early textiles, and also when we carry out experiments with modern wool and vegetable dyes as described in dyeing recipes (*49*).

It is probably because of the hardness of the Highland wool that so many of the dyeing methods demand long processes; we read of recipes which involved several weeks of soaking. And before the dyeing began the natural grease was removed from the wool. This was done by washing it in human urine which had been allowed to become stale, but this obnoxious alkaline wash was later replaced by a brew made from soda ash obtained from burning sea-weed.

After the wool had been dried, teased and then combed or carded to produce the desired strength of thread it was ready for spinning. This was originally done with the distaff and spindle, or as they were sometimes called in Scotland, the rock and reel. The wool having been tied to the top of the distaff, some twisted fibres were teased from it and attached to the spindle, which was given a flick with the fingers and made to spin like a top. And so, spinning and dropping the spindle produced a thread which was wound on to it and the process continued (*50*).

Distaffs and spindles could be simply made from a stick and a lump of heavier wood, but frequently they were decorated and greatly cherished. They were a popular

50 *Spinning with the distaff and spindle. Engraving, 1780s*

betrothal gift and often had dates and initials carved on them. One distaff from Carluke in Lanarkshire bears the initials 'E.M.' and the date '1733'. This specimen can be seen in the National Museum of Antiquities of Scotland where there is another which was in use in West Calder, Midlothian, until presented to the Museum in 1855.

There was a practical reason why this simple piece of equipment continued in use into modern times. Life in the Highlands was hard, and if two essential activities could be carried out at the same time, so much the better. Using the distaff and spindle, a girl could tend the stock, or a woman could carry on her back the seaweed required to fertilise the fields.

One of the disadvantages of the spinning wheel, a development from the rock and reel, was its immobility. The great 'muckle' wheel could however produce the yarn much faster, although it was hard work. It had to be operated standing up, rotating the wheel with one hand whilst holding the wool in the other. As the yarn was formed, the spinner had to twist sideways whilst extending out the hand holding the wool.

This great wheel was in use in the British Isles from at least the sixteenth century. The actual wheel, about a yard in diameter, was mounted at one end of a three- or four-legged heavy wooden bench. The spindle, which often revolved in straw bearings, was mounted at the other. After a length of yarn was spun it was wound back on to this spindle. Despite the physical labour involved in operating the great, or spindle, or 'muckle' wheel it continued in use in Britain up to the beginning of the twentieth century.

The next advance in the evolution of the spinning wheel was the introduction of the 'flyers' and two whorls attached to the spindle. This allowed the spun yarn to be wound on at the same time as the spinning operation and, in conjunction with the foot treadle to power the wheel, revolutionised the whole process. A distaff was attached to the wheel and to this the roll of wool or flax was attached (51).

Several Scottish spinning wheels are described by Patricia Baines, who draws our attention to records of raiding Scots carrying off wheels from Ulster. Whilst specimens from the Western Isles, Harris, Benbecula and St Kilda are simple in design and heavily built, they are almost identical with those from Ireland.

Her comprehensive and deeply researched book contains much information of a Scottish nature, including the fact that a great many wheels bear the owners' initials and are dated. Some particularly fine wheels were in use in the Western Isles, including the smaller and comparatively rare horizontal specimens.

In the National Museum of Antiquities of Scotland there are several fine examples of spinning wheels. One vertical type has beautifully turned spokes and legs and an interesting feature incorporated in the distaff. It is surmounted by a little cage, the bars of which are laced through a wooden disc to produce an elegant 'waist'. This contrivance would make the attachment of the woollen fibres an easy matter. Also attached to the wheel is a small water pot used to dampen the flax fibres when spinning linen yarn. This was done to avoid giving the finished material a rough texture.

Another unusual spinning wheel from north-east Scotland, in the above-mentioned museum, is described and illustrated by Patricia Baines. It is built on a three-legged stool with cabriole legs, and she dates it to the nineteenth century. The supports of the small 39.5 cm diameter wheel are of a 'boomerang' shape, levelling out at the ends to support the flyer mechanism.

One type of wheel was known as the 'Castle', so-called because the driving wheel is above the flyers, and the very small rectangular base is supported by three unusually long tapered legs.

In the north-east of Scotland wheels with two flyers were in use and they were known as 'two-handed' wheels. They were intended to increase the production of linen yarn and help the poor to earn higher wages. With the same object of increasing output, a wheel with three flyers was designed. The central one was for spinning wool whilst the two outside were for spinning flax.

Some very elegant 'boudoir' spinning wheels were made for fashionable eighteenth-century ladies to amuse themselves with. In the National museum there is a lovely little example, the wheel of which is painted on one side and the wooden legs, spokes and spars are carved to imitate bamboo. It was made in Stirling.

In her 'Essays', Mrs Grant of Laggan tells us of an old lady whom she knew and who would suffer no such complicated machines as spinning wheels, but kept eight good old women in her house, 'spinning on as many orthodox distaffs to the last.' This old lady also repeats the saying that the year 1746 was when 'little wheels and red soldiers were introduced'.

The manufacture of linen played an important part in the history of Scottish costume, particularly in the region of the Lowlands between the Firth of Forth and Aberdeen. But it was at Peebles in May 1633 that the burgh council set up the first spinning school in Scotland. Here, 'bairnies' were to be 'bund for ane yeir to the small quheill in the house to be erectit to lerne the young anes to spyn'. In 1727, the board of Trustees for Manufactures set aside the sum of £40 per annum for the establishment of four spinning schools to teach the spinning of linen yarn in the Highlands. Wheels cost 5s 10d each. After the Forty-Five, the Commissioners of the Annexed Estates continued the establishment of spinning schools.

As a result of the manufacture of linen, early travellers saw and recorded the large number of bleach fields around most of the towns. In the 1730s agents collected clothes for transportation to the bleach fields where they were processed. The owners of the clothing were instructed to have their names sewn on in linen thread, but at least two customers no doubt regretted that they considered their initials were enough. In January 1746, ten Holland shirts ruffled at the wrists belonging to a gentleman who had marked them 'G.D.', and 12 women's shifts marked 'A.D.' were stolen from the bleach field near Heriot's Hospital, Edinburgh. If the culprit was caught he or she was liable to be transported to the colonies for 14 years, a sentence which was carried out for a like offence on a servant in Banffshire in 1766.

Scottish Lowland weavers of the eighteenth and early nineteenth century had many aspersions cast on them regarding their honesty, including the expression 'crooked as a weaver'. Also many allegations were made regarding short measure and inferior quality. Acts of Parliament were passed to prevent this in 1712, 1714 and 1720, the latter for 'ascertaining the breadths, and preventing frauds and abuses in manufacturing serges, pladdings, and fingrums and for regulating the manufactures of stockings. . . .' But the Weavers' Companies of the early nineteenth century embroidered on their Banners a warning to their members – 'Weave Truth with Trust'.

But we can end this account of the making of tartans and textiles on a happier note by returning to the Highland scene. Amongst the Gaels the whole process of the making of cloth was associated with folk-lore. There were many customs such as taking the driving band off the spinning wheel to prevent the little folk using it at night. Then there was the ceremony and blessing when the web was removed from the loom. Finally there were the lovely songs sung at the waulking, or felting process (52). Many of these Gaelic songs and incantations were collected by Alexander Carmichael and

51 *A Cailleath (old woman) spinning with the Saxony wheel, c. 1910*

published in his beautiful *Carmina Gadelica* which includes valuable notes on these customs. One of the Gaelic songs about clothing might be translated as follows:

> The wool is carded, washed and dyed,
>   And ready for the loom.
> The ember heat and reeking peat
>   Pervade and cense the house inside
> Wall shadows in the gloom.
>
> The threads' of yellow, blue and green,
>   The black, the red, the white,
> By fingers deft in warp and weft,
>   A criss-cross sett is laid between
> To form the cloth aright.
>
> The fulling at the waulking frame,
>   The maidens all a-row,
> On either side sit well supplied,
>   With love-songs ready to exclaim,
> In movement to and fro.

52 *Women waulking or fulling a web of cloth, c. 1770*

God bless the wheel, the spinning hand,
God bless the weaving through,
God bless the songs of rights and wrongs,
God bless the clothing of the land,
The maker, wearer too.

From the lovely island of Benbecula in the Outer Hebrides comes this poetic description of a tartan sett;

The black go by the white thread,
The white go by the black led,
The green go in between red,
The red between the black thread.

The black go in between red,
The red between the white thread,
The white between the green led,
The green between the white thread.

The white between the blue thread,
The blue between the bright red,
The blue, the scarlet hue thread,
The scarlet true the due thread.

The scarlet to the blue thread,
The blue to scarlet hue wed,
The scarlet to the black led,
The black unto the bright red.

A thread go to the threads two,
Of colours two, good and true,
The two the threads of black due,
The one the thread of white through.

Seven threads to five be,
And five be unto three,
Three to two, two to one,
In every border done.

This song would be difficult to memorise, and similar Gaelic 'tongue twisters' indicate that verses like these might have been memory games. Whereas the purpose of such songs as the Loom Blessing is clear, others are more difficult to classify. For instance, one song entitled 'The Highland Dress' is said to be associated with a Lewis funeral air, although the words would be well suited to a festive occasion;

Bonnet and feather with tartan and plaid,
Bonnet and feather with tartan and plaid,
Bonnet and feather with tartan and plaid,
The Clans of the Gael are swingingly clad.

See it and see it and see yet it cheers,
See it and see it and see yet it cheers,
See it and see yet its virtue appears,
The white and red ribbons round by thine ears.

In the Carmichael collection there is a waulking song called 'Prince Morag' which refers to Prince Charles Edward Stuart disguised as the woman Morag, and another song associated with the smoothing of the cloth invokes the blessing of the Trinity. There is also one which blesses the final folding of the cloth, which the singers hope will not turn out to be 'begging's wear'. This refers to the cloth begged by impoverished newly-weds from their more affluent friends.

The gentle whirl of the spinning wheel, the hypnotic clack of the weaver's shuttle, and the laughing girls singing their waulking gossip songs seem a far cry from the contentious arguments about the tartan today. The blessing of the cloth contrasts strongly with the controversies raging over what is the 'correct' sett of the clan tartan.

7

---❖---

The Ladies of Scotland

A SEARCH FOR truly Scottish characteristics in the costume of the Scottish ladies of the Lowlands is highly unrewarding. A study of pictoral evidence from earliest times will merely affirm that many of the portraits were painted outside of Scotland and most of them show fashions which can be found in other countries. Domestic and official documentary accounts are not much more helpful, although they do tell a little more about the economics of the lady's wardrobe, and in particular the extent of her wedding clothes.

The early writers of the sixteenth century were concerned with the morals of ladies costume rather than their modes. The peevish poet, Sir David Lyndsay of the Mount, complained that the ladies of the late 1530s wore their gowns far too long in an effort to imitate the Queen. As a result they became caked with mud and stirred up clouds of dust. His protest that women spent too much money on their clothes has been repeated for over four centuries. However, perhaps we can forgive his complaint and enjoy his pawky style:

> *I think it is ane verray scorne,*
> *That every lady of the land*
> *Suld have hir taill so syde trailland,*
> *Howbeit thay bene of hie estait*
> *The Quene thay suld nocht counterfait;*
> *Quhare ever thay go, it may be sene*
> *How kirk, and calsay thay soup clene.*

It was irritating to see the ladies of fashion with their tails trailing behind them and sweeping the causeway, but on the other hand he rather enjoyed the sight of a nun bearing 'hir taill abone hir bun' (*sic*).

An attempt to curb this extravagance inspired the passing of the Act of 1567, which decreed that 'it be lauchfull to na women to weir abone hir estait except howres'.

Plaids were in common use throughout Scotland by women of every social station, and this too brought up the question of morality. In late sixteenth-century Aberdeen, for instance, wives and daughters were warned that if they wore plaids out of doors they ran the risk of being suspected as loose women. They could suffer a heavy fine if their husbands or fathers were members of a Guild.

The clergy also threatened women-folk who might misuse the plaid in church by covering their heads as 'ane means to provoke sleep'. But the Scottish ladies were determined creatures and not easily persuaded. The Kirk Session of Monefieth in September 1643 gave the 'bedall, 5s to buy ane pynt of tar to put upon the women that held the plaid about the heir head in the church'.

Whereas the sixteenth-century Scotsmen were concerned with the economics and morality of their womenfolk's costume, the early visitors to the country had little to say about them. Admittedly Don Pedro de Ayala, Spanish Ambassador to James IV, considered them very graceful and handsome women, but his remark that he thought their head-dress 'the handsomest in the world' infers that he was speaking of the ladies of the Court.

After the ambassador's remark there is, according to my records, a silence lasting a century before another visitor says anything of interest about female costume. However, in the middle of the sixteenth century we are enlightened by two highly contrasting illustrations, although I would hesitate to place their value high.

Mention has already been made of the savage Highlander who appeared in the *Receuil de la Diversité des Habits*, published in Paris in 1562. Beside him is shown '*La Sauvage d'Ecosse*.' She is wrapped in a large cloak of sheepskins which hardly qualifies for the title of a costume. Indeed it has all the elements of having been drawn from the imagination. But, as too often happens in the history of costume, it was then taken by Speed as a source for the illustration of his 'Wild Irish Woman' on his map of Ireland, dated 1610.

Our other sixteenth-century illustration was drawn by Lucas de Heere, probably between 1567 and 1577. His drawing of a Scottish man has already been discussed, but another one shows two ladies and is entitled '*Schotsche edelvrouwe en burgervrouwe*.' They are unlike the drawings of Irish women which he also made, and conform to European styles. The noblewoman, however, wears a heart-shaped head-dress of the previous century and the citizen's wife wears an unusual type of turban. The rest of their clothing tells us little except that it is certainly long out of date.

When Fynes Moryson came to the Scottish Lowlands at the end of the century (1598), it was not the style of the women's costume that he found remarkable, it was the material of which it was made. 'The inferior sort of Citizen wives, and the women of the Countrey, did weare cloaks made of a course stuffe, of two or three colours in Checker worke, vulgarly called "Ploden"'.

John Taylor the Water Poet, who came to Scotland in 1618, does not appear to have had much of an eye for the ladies, but he does remind us how busy they were kept supplying the clothes for the family:

And I am sure, that in Scotland, beyond Edenborough, I have beene at houses like castles for building; the master of the house his beaver being his blue bonnet, one that will wear no other shirts but of the flaxe that growes on his owne ground, and of his wives, daughters, or servants spinning; that hath his stockings, hose, and jerkin of the woolle of his owne sheepes backs. . . .

In 1617, someone, probably Sir Anthony Weldon, visited Scotland and left to posterity one of the most unpleasant diatribes extant. Everything horrified him. The

53 *Early nineteenth-century engraving of the ancient custom of tramping washing*

ladies he found particularly offensive and he declared that they were of the opinion that 'Susanna could not be chaste, because she bathed so often.'

These early accounts depended almost entirely on the attitudes and opinions of the people who wrote them. For this reason it is important to discover as much as possible about the writer. There are so many conflicting reports at this period that by careful selection 'evidence' can be produced to demonstrate exact opposites. For instance, when Sir William Brereton the Puritan soldier, visited Edinburgh in 1636, he too remarked that the inhabitants were 'most sluttish, nasty, and slothful people'.

On one point Weldon and Brereton did not agree, namely the ladies' feet. The former considered them splayed and offensive whilst the latter described the ladies as 'only neat and handsome about the feet, which comes to pass by them often washing with their feet.' This custom of tucking up, or 'kilting' the skirts and then tramping the washing in large wooden tubs was quite ancient throughout Scotland. One observer of the rural laundresses of Inverness shortly after the battle of Culloden wrote: 'You'll see in a warm Morning, the River Edges lin'd with these Sort of Women that are Maid-servants, and frequently as many Soldiers admiring their Legs and Thighs, and particularly their motion in treading, which always put me in mind of the Negroes dancing.' (53).

Although the comments which Brereton made about the people of Edinburgh were highly uncomplimentary, he has left us the first extensive account of female costume, which includes some interesting observations on its various distinctions:

Touching the fashion of the citizens, the women here wear and use upon festival days six or seven several habits and fashions; some for distinction of widows, wives and maids, others apparalled according to their own humour and phantasy. Many wear (especially of the meaner sort) plaids, which is a garment of the same woollen stuff whereof saddlecloths in England are made, which is cast over their heads, and covers their faces on both sides, and would reach almost to the ground, but that they pluck them up, and wear them cast under their arms. Some ancient women and citizens wear satin straight-bodied gowns, short little cloaks with great capes, and a broad boun-grace – a shade in front of the bonnet to protect from the sun – coming over their brows, and going out with a corner behind their heads; and this boun-grace is, as it were, lined with a white stracht cambric suitable unto it. Young maids not married all are bare-headed; some with broad thin shag ruffs, which lie flat to their shoulders, and others with halfbands with wide necks, either much stiffened or set in wire, which comes only behind; and these shag ruffs some are more broad and thick than others.

By the end of the sixteenth century there are many accounts of women's dress and still many outbursts of annoyance at the 'uncivil habitte of women's wearing of plaids' and the 'impudencie of many of thame that they have continewit the foresaid barbarous habit.' Indeed, outside the Highlands there is no outstanding characteristic in women's dress which could make them recognisable as 'Scottish' apart from the plaids. Our first commentator to draw attention to this fact is Thomas Morer, whose very important account of Scotland was written about 1689:

Their habit is mostly English, saving that the meaner sort of men wear bonnets instead of hats, and pladds instead of cloaks; and those pladds the women also use in their ordinary dress when they go abroad, either to market or church. They cover head and body with 'em, and are so contrived as to be at once both a scarf and a hood. The quality go thus attired, when they would be disguised, and is a morning dress good enough when some hasty business calls them forth or when the weather disheartens 'em to trick themselves better.

Reading this one sees how very useful the plaid was and can realise how reluctant the women would be to abandon it. This would particularly apply to the Highlands and in fact its use was to continue through the centuries. William Sacheverell visited the island of Mull in 1688 and recorded that both sexes wore the plaid, but the women's were much finer and the colours more lively. This is just what one would expect, but it still impressed the visitors to such an extent that many of them describe it at length. When that keen and precise observer, Edward Burt, visited Inverness in the 1730s he wrote a letter to a friend in which he gives the following description:

The plaid is the undress of the ladies at Inverness and to a genteel woman who adjusts it with a good air, is a becoming veil. But as I am pretty sure you never saw one of them in England, I shall employ a few words to describe it to you. It is made of silk or fine worsted, chequered with various lively colours, two breadths wide, and three yards in length; it is brought over the head, and may hide or discover the face according to the wearer's fancy or occasion; it reaches to the waist behind; one corner as low as the ancle on one side; and the other part in folds, hanging down from the opposite arm.

The ordinary girls wear nothing upon their heads until they are married or get a child, except sometimes a fillet of red or blue coarse cloth of which they are very proud; but often their hair hangs down over the forehead, like that of a wild colt.

If they wear stockings, which is very rare, they lay them in plaits one above another from the ancle up to the calf, to make their legs appear, as near as they can, in the form of a cylinder: but I think I have seen something like this among the poor German refugee women and the Moorish men in London.

The indication of a women's marital status by the type of her head-covering is not uncommon in European folk costume. In the Highlands of Scotland this practice was taken seriously and in some cases the kertch or coif was the finest piece of attire in a poor woman's possession (54). The reason for this was largely the fact that it had a religious significance. Known in Gaelic as *Am Breid*, the young bride wore it on the morning after her wedding. She would have a number of kertches according to her means. Alexander Carmichael points out that the square of linen was folded into three angles symbolic of the Trinity, and its use signified the Holy blessing by which a woman could be protected throughout her life. Carmichael also quotes a number of Gaelic descriptions which include the white kertch, the hair kertch, the pinnacled kertch, the kertch on props, the shapely coif of the crowns and the shapely coif of the three crowns.

The distinction between a married woman and an unmarried woman was more clearly marked in the Highlands than in the Lowlands. Whereas the Lowland lass might go uncovered before her marriage, her Highland sister would almost certainly not do so. While the piece of cloth or ribbon worn in the southern lowlands was perhaps more of a status symbol, in the northern glens it had a deeper significance. In some instances the unmarried Highland lass seems to have worn a particular type of snood which indicated her maidenhood, but in most cases it would be little more than a ribband (55).

One of the many beautiful love songs in *Carmina Gadelica* describes the lover's wish to make his beloved his wife:

Her hair in coils, curled, curved,
And in clustered folds has my beloved,
And though beautiful it seems within the snood,
It would not look worse beneath the kertch.

Well becomes thee the white kertch,
Placed pinnacle-wise,
And cords of the fine silk
Binding it upon thee.

Even in the early twentieth century there were still old ladies living in the Highlands who always wore a fine lace cap.

One aspect of costume history which is particularly interesting is the manner in which people living in remote districts persist in wearing decorative items of dress regardless of the disadvantages of environment. Often, despite poverty and the physical demands of survival, men and particularly women, will devote much time – often with the most primitive equipment – to making artistic textiles, items of dress and ornaments.

The remote island of St Kilda, lying in the Atlantic over a hundred miles out from the Scottish mainland, was probably first occupied by prehistoric pastoral people living mainly on a diet of fish and sea-birds. But only two writers have given us descriptions of its early inhabitants. Martin Martin was the first and he visited the island in 1697. Many of the islanders were still wearing sheepskin, but also both men and women were wearing plaids which they fastened with the bone of that magnificent sea-bird the fulmar. Some of the men wore wide knee-length trousers. Both sexes wore coarse flannel shirts, and Martin Martin describes one odd feature whereby 'they thicken their cloaths upon *Flakes*, or mats of Hay twisted and woven together in small Ropes. . . .'

However, it is his description of the women's costume that shows that despite their geographical isolation the women went to considerable trouble to make their costume distinctive:

The Women wear upon their Heads a Linnen Dress, strait before, and drawing to a small point behind below the shoulders, a foot and a half in length, and a Lock of about sixty Hairs hanging down each cheek, to their Breasts with a large round Buckle of Brass in form of a Circle; the Buckles antiently worn by the Steward's Wives were of Silver, but the present Steward's Wife makes no use of either this Dress or Buckle.

The Reverend Kenneth Macaulay, the minister of Ardnamurchan, who visited St Kilda half-a-century after Martin Martin, has left us a much less attractive description. He found the adult population healthy, but their smell very offensive. The women, however, had they been properly dressed would 'be reckoned extraordinary beauties in the gay world.' He continues:

The cloathing of this people is quite coarse, and made for warmth; all the colours known among them, till of late, were black, white, grey, and brown, the natural colours of their sheep, and yellow was their only artificial one. . . .

54 *Old woman winding wool on jack-reel* c. *1910. She wears her best kertch*

55 *Engraving by David Allan (1786) showing the difference between the head-dress of married and unmarried women*

All the linen manufactured among them is a mere trifle and extremely coarse; One holiday shirt will satisfy the ambition of the most elegant or foppish person in *St Kilda*, what they wear next to their skin, upon ordinary occasions, is made of wool.

The wool of the St Kilda sheep having been plucked, not sheared, then the yarn oiled dyed and woven into a highly durable tweed became one of the islanders' valuable exports. In 1879, there were 36 spinning wheels on the island and nearly every family had a weaving loom.

In 1886, G. W. Wilson of Aberdeen made a photographic expedition to St Kilda and returned with a unique record of the costume of the islanders. The married women wear the kertch cap, and the plaid – now in the form of a shawl – and the minister stands severe in his large bell-top silk hat and black suit.

In contrast to the seventeenth-century women of the Highlands and Islands, the ladies of the Lowlands were spending very large sums of money on their bridal trousseaux. The Duke of Hamilton's account for the trousseau of Lady Margaret in 1687 included 22 ells of rich white satin at £9 per ell; for her gown, petticoat and lining, the very large sum of £198; and for black velvet for a gown, the even greater sum of £225. She also purchased crimson satin for a nightgown, and white satin and crimson velvet for petticoats, a hood, ribbons for garters and various trimmings, some fine holland for two smocks, 'silke stokens', and a pair of laced shoes.

Perhaps the earliest portrait in oils of a woman wearing what can be described as a definite Highland costume, is not that of a grand lady but is, in fact, one of the very few paintings we have of a humble Scottish servant. It is entitled 'The Hen Wife', dated 1706, and is one of the portraits painted by Richard Waitt for the series at Castle Grant (*56*). She does not wear any tartan, simply a plain red gown with long full sleeves and a blue apron. Over her head she wears a large piece of white cloth the long corners of which hang down below her waist. On her breast is a circular brass brooch. In her left hand she carries a large flat powder-horn from which she may be about to take snuff – snuff-taking was as popular with women as it was with men in the eighteenth century.

The earliest portrait of a lady wearing tartan which I have been able to trace is the half-length picture of Helen Balfour, signed and dated by William Mosman, 1742. Born in 1709, she was the wife of Gavin Hamilton, and this portrait is reproduced in *The Balfours of Pilrig*, published in 1907. It was on show at the Exhibition of Scottish Art, London, 1939.

Seven years later Mosman painted another portrait of an unknown lady now in the possession of the Earl of Home. The only Highland feature which is shared by both these portraits is the piece of tartan material which is draped around one shoulder and over the arms. This was probably made of silk or of fine wool; it might even have been of fine wool lined with silk, and it could have been called a plaid, a shawl or a screen. There was a great rage for tartan amongst the Edinburgh ladies shortly after the battle of Culloden. Some of them may have had Jacobite sympathies, some of them may have felt 'agin' the Government', but I suspect that most were just following the dictates of fashion. Ironically enough one of the most fashionable places to wear the tartan plaid at this period was in church. Sermons were shorter and the beadle with his pot of tar had joined his ancestors (*64*).

56 *The Hen Wife, Castle Grant, 1706, painted by Richard Waitt. She wears a long-sleeved red gown and blue apron*

The portrait by an unknown artist of Helen Murray of Ochtertyre was painted about 1745, and must still rank as the earliest picture known at present which illustrates a tartan dress. The pattern, which consists of a red ground colour with dark blue, green or black stripes and lines, is typical of the period in design and is, of course, pre-clan tartan. Her Jacobite sympathies are clearly indicated by the white rose which she holds in her extended hand (*57*).

In the Scottish National Portrait Gallery there are two fine portraits of Flora Macdonald. One is by Allan Ramsay, born in Edinburgh in 1713, who set up a studio

57 *Helen Murray of Octertyre. Artist unknown, c. 1745*

in London in 1739, and later another in Edinburgh (58). He soon became one of the lead-
ing portrait painters of the day, and he painted Flora Macdonald at the height of his
popularity. But here, it is the costume which interests us. At an early period of his career
Ramsay got a certain Joseph van Aken to paint the draperies of his sitters but is said to
have given up this practice in the 1760s. Well, in terms of costume evidence I do not
think it matters who painted Flora's costume as it does not have much significance in
the history of Highland dress. Apart from the usual tartan plaid attached to one
shoulder and draped over one arm, the only other indications of her sympathies are the
two white roses at her breast and the white rose in her hair. It is very much a stylised
portrait.

58 *Flora Macdonald, by Allan Ramsay. She wears a reddish tartan plaid and white Jacobite roses*

So too is the other portrait, by Richard Wilson, also undated. As far as the costume of this picture is concerned, I would be surprised if our heroine ever wore anything like it. Even the tartan is unconvincing (59).

We know that Flora was besieged by artists anxious to paint her, and that she sat for quite a number, many of whom have left us delightful studies. Not all, however, were from life, and the engravers produced some extraordinary efforts. I have one ridiculous mezzotint showing her as an Arcadian shepherdess, and there are others, including a mezzotint published in Paris about 1827 showing her in a feather bonnet, and an Italian print showing her in a costume of 1830.

As far as I know Clementina Walkinshaw, the Prince's mistress who gave him a son, was never shown in her pictures wearing any form of Highland costume, although her portrait by Philippe Mercier is of considerable interest to costume historians. Jenny Cameron, his reputed mistress, had, on the other hand, many engraved 'portraits' showing her in a variety of tartan costumes, including one published in Frankfurt in 1747, showing her on horseback, and carrying a large shield and a dart. Within two years after Culloden she had three 'Lives' published, and in 1746, a pantomine was produced in London entitled *Harlequin Incendiary or Colombine Cameron*, in which the 'Pretender' was played by Mr Blakes, and 'Colombine Cameron' by Mrs Clive. It would be interesting to know what the costumes looked like; perhaps the lady wore the costume in which, according to one of the 'Lives', Jenny met the Prince. She was then 'dressed in a Sea-Green Riding Habit, with a scarlet Lapel trimmed with Gold; her Hair tied behind in loose Buckles, with a velvet cap, and Scarlet Feather. She rode a Bay Gelding . . . and instead of a Whip, she carried a Naked Sword.'

Drummond-Norie repeated this description, although he still had considerable doubt about the whole Jenny Cameron story. According to his speculations she was a 'remarkable woman, who, like a second Joan of Arc, had come to fight for her king, sword in hand'. In his collection he had a print which he reproduces in *Loyal Lochaber*, and which was entitled 'Miss Jenny Cameron of Lochiel, one of the most numerous clans in the Highlands of Scotland' but which he goes on to admit that 'By some authorities this print is said to be a portrait of Flora MacDonald.' The only Scottish costume element in the print is the usual tartan plaid over one shoulder and one arm.

The story that Jenny had brought a party of female warriors with her to support the Jacobite cause has a counterpart. There is said to be a mysterious letter written in French, dated March 1746 and describing the entry of the Prince into Inverness. I can find nothing about it other than the fact that it was said to have been written by 'Lord B. . . .' and a translation of it was published by Charles Fraser-Mackintosh. He considered that it was fictitious and that it had been printed in Paris for distribution abroad to encourage the partisans of the Stuarts. This extract is interesting for its remarks about female Highland dress:

The whole nation has taken arms to defend their mountains and cliffs; the women of this part of Scotland, who dress so like men one can hardly distinguish them, have formed a company of

59 *Flora Macdonald. An undated portrait by Richard Wilson*

112 women, of whom the eldest is not over forty . . . I declare had I not been informed they were women, I should have been deceived. They wear a cap instead of the head-dress, and are dressed something like a running footman, except that the petticoat is longer, and they wear a half riding hood which comes down to the knees, instead of a cloak. They are armed with axes and swords, only fifty (those who are at the head) having guns and bayonettes.

At the Scottish Art Exhibition held in London in 1939 a most interesting 'Highland Lady's Marriage Costume' was exhibited. It consisted of a dress and shoulder plaid, or scarf, of hard home-spun tartan. The linen lining of the dress is said to have been made from lint grown and spun in the Aird district of Inverness-shire. Associated with the costume is a silver ring bearing the initials of the original owner, Isabella Fraser.

During the mid-eighteenth century most of the dress material being worn in the Highlands would be home-spun, but ladies of rank and wealth would, when the occasion demanded it, appear in the most expensive and showy materials. The accounts of such families as the Ramsays of Ochertyre show the expenditure of large sums for particular celebrations. It must be remembered, however, that these outfits served a lifetime and in some cases were used by two or three generations. By modern standards even the wardrobe of a great lady would not be very large, and the daughter of a moderately well-off country gentleman might only have one silk gown.

As far as millinery was concerned fly caps, morning caps and mob caps were worn according to social station and age. Materials, ribbons and lace were bought in considerable quantity from Inverness and Edinburgh, although it is said that there was only one milliner of note in Edinburgh in 1720. Unfortunately very little is known about a certain barber called Morison who, in the mid-eighteenth century, had been *valet de chambre* to Lord Perth, and who claimed to have introduced the French style of dressing ladies' hair.

Two costumes in the Royal Scottish Museum, Edinburgh, show the beautiful styles which could be seen on great occasions in Scotland. One is an embroidered silk dress of the 1740s which is said to have been worn by Margaret Oliphant of Gask at the celebration ball given at the Palace of Holyrood after the Battle of Prestonpans in 1745. The other, of a slightly later date, consists of a very beautiful open robe of white silk brocade which was worn by Margaret Colquhoun of Kenmore.

There were strict regulations as to what might or might not be worn at certain social occasions. The Edinburgh Assembly, for instance, insisted that no lady was to be admitted in a nightgown, and no gentleman in boots. Also 'No misses in skirts and jackets, robecoats nor stay-bodied gowns to be allowed to dance country dances but in a set by themselves.'

Fathers and brothers were becoming somewhat disapproving of the female fripperies of the 1760s. In a letter from Janet Dick of Prestonfield to her father, dated March 1760, she refers to her presence at Mr Lamole's ball: 'I was dressed in my green gown with gold trimmings and nothing about me but what you would have liked, except my train, which was a little troublesome, and if you don't like it when you come home I shall sacrifice it'.

Jacobite garters are sometimes referred to as 'bands', which is an incorrect and confusing description. Such garters were political emblems and are distinguished by the slogans embroidered on them. These include such sentiments as 'Come let us with one heart unite to bless the Prince for whom we fight' and 'The Glorious at Last Triumphant Prince Charles' which was rather optimistic, and 'God Bless P.C. and Down with the Rump'. Some of the garters are of considerable length, over four feet long, and most of them are of silk. In many cases the loyal inscription is embroidered on a tartan ribbon, but in some cases it is stamped on.

These garters were worn by men and women alike and often female garters were collected by young men as trophies. The 'naughty' garter has been in vogue for well over two centuries, and according to the *Colchester Journal* of 1739, great quantities inscribed 'No Search' were being bought up by the local ladies. One interesting Scottish inscription dated 1737 runs, 'My heart is Fixt I will not range. I like my Choyce too well to change'. This would allow the lady to deny any rebellious sentiments by claiming that it referred to the bonnie young laird.

The manufacture of stockings at this period was an important cottage industry, particularly in Aberdeenshire. Some of them were so fine that they took six months to knit and sold for five guineas a pair. When Thomas Pennant visited the city of Aberdeen in 1769, he found that the stocking trade was the principal export:

For this manufacture 20,800 pounds worth of wool is annually imported, and 1,600 pounds worth of oil. Of this wool is annually made 69,333 dozen pairs of stockings, worth, at an average, £1 10s per dozen. These are made by the country people in almost all parts of this great country, who get 4s per dozen for spinning, and 14s per dozen for knitting, so there is annually paid them £62,329 14s. And besides, there is about £2,000 value of stockings manufactured from the wool of the county, which encourages the breed of sheep much ... about 200 combers are also employed constantly. The thread manufacture is another considerable article, tho' trifling in comparison of the woollen.

Aberdeenshire women knitted incessantly as they went about their work, just as Highland women did until recent times.

It was customary, especially during the eighteenth century, to give servants a pair of stockings out of charity, but shoes were a recognised form of agreed payment. They were not, however, for everyday use. Many eighteenth-century visitors to Scotland were struck by the fact that most women wore neither shoes nor stockings. And although this habit did not in general apply to men, Doctor Johnson was surprised to find that the sons of gentlemen in the Western Isles could be found running about in their bare feet. Lord George Murray disapproved of bare-footed girls, and in 1745 admonished his daughter to be 'always neat, especially about the feet, for nothing is more becoming a young person like you than to wear stockings and shoes'. On the other hand, when Faujas de Saint-Fond visited Glasgow towards the end of the century, he found the bare feet of the young lassies very charming.

One Aberdeenshire clergyman wrote that shoes were formerly made from the hides of oxen, killed by the farmers and then tanned by the local shoemakers. But, by the early 1790s, they were chiefly made of English leather and none were tanned in the district. In one parish in Argyll (Kilfinan) there were, in 1793, 38 weavers, 22 tailors and 11 shoemakers.

Ready-made shoes were not always easily obtainable before the end of the eighteenth century in the Highlands and Islands, although some of the lairds were buying them from Inverness and Edinburgh. There was a strange custom, particularly amongst the shoemakers of Aberdeen, whereby shoes were sold by the inch and worked out on average about two or three shillings a pair.

The eighteenth-century shoes of the women of St Kilda were unique and described by Martin Martin:

The Women inhabiting this Isle wear no Shoes nor Stockings in the Summer-time; their ordinary and only shoes are made of the Necks of the *Solan* Geese, which they cut above the Eyes, the Crown of the Head serves for the Heel, the whole Skin being cut close at the Breast, which end being sowed, the foot enters into it, as into a piece of narrow Stocking; this shoe does not last above five days, and if the downy side be next the Ground, then not above three or four; however there are plenty of them. . . .

When the Reverend Kenneth Macaulay visited St Kilda in 1758, it was the unusual method of tanning leather which interested him:

All the leather of this island and those nearest to it, is tanned with the tormentil root, and done to great perfection. The St Kildians lay the leather, when sufficiently prepared for that purpose, in the warm infusion of this bark for two nights, and afterwards keep it in the hollow of a rock, which is under water at every full sea, with some of this root pounded about it, until it is sufficiently tanned.

Among the folk-lore tales of the Highlands is the story of the Silver Shoe of *Ailein nan Creach*. This Cameron chief was presented by some mysterious means with a magic silver shoe, which was to be put on the foot of every son born to the chief. It fitted them all with the exception of John Cameron 'whose conduct at Sheriffmuir was not in accordance with the traditions of the clan', according to Drummond-Norie who recorded that the shoe 'was lost when Ach-na-carry was burnt by the English soldiers in 1746.'

One highly amusing chronicler of late eighteenth century Scottish fashion was William Creech who, in his *Fugitive Pieces*, contrasts the Edinburgh styles of 1783 with those of 1763. Whereas in the former year there was no such profession known as a Haberdasher, 20 years later, the profession, 'which signifies a Jack of all trades, including the *Mercer*, the *Milliner*, the *Linen-draper*, the *Hatter*, the *Hosier*, the *Glover*, and many others, is nearly the most frequent in town'. Again, in contrast to their absence in 1763, by 1783 'Perfumers have splendid shops in every principal street; and some of them advertise the keeping of bears, to kill occasionally, for greasing ladies' and gentlemens' hair, as superior to any other animal fat.' And as for Hairdressers, whose busiest day was Sunday, not only were they numerous but there was even a 'Professor who advertises a Hair-dressing Academy, and lectures on that *noble and useful art*.'

William Creech wrote that in 1783 umbrellas were almost as frequently seen as shoes and stockings and that many 'umbrella warehouses' had opened. In fact he claims that an eminent Edinburgh surgeon introduced the umbrella to Edinburgh society. He 'had occasion to run about much in the course of business' and began to use one about the year 1780 and thereby started a craze for this useful article which had been introduced in England about 30 years before.

But Creech, publisher and Lord Provost of Edinburgh, described the lady of 1783's

silhouette in language superior to that of any Victorian music-hall master-of-
ceremonies: 'Spinal tenuity and mamillary exuberance have for some time been the
fashion with the fair, but a posterior rotundity, or a balance was wanting behind; and
you may now tell the country lasses if they wish to be fashionable, they must resemble
two blown bladders tied together at the necks.'

At this time most people were aware of the follies of fashion. In June 1785, a young
Edinburgh lady wrote to her friend in Glasgow describing the complexions of ladies of
fashion at the playhouse:

> *Ye ask me what beauties most touchingly strike –*
> *They are beauteous all, and all beauteous alike,*
> *With lovely complexions that time ne'er can tarnish,*
> *So thick they're laid o'er with a delicate varnish;*
> *Their bosoms and necks have a gloss and a burnish,*
> *And their cheeks with fresh roses from* Raeburn *they furnish.*

Scottish costume historians owe a considerable debt to John Kay, engraver,
portrait painter and, above all, caricaturist. Born in 1742 in Dalkeith and apprenticed
to a barber, he became a fully-fledged Surgeon-Barber in 1771 and moved to
Edinburgh. His profession gave him an excellent opportunity to observe his fellow men
and women, and from his small shop in Parliament Close in the centre of Edinburgh he
could view every walk of life. In the mid 1780s 'making likenesses' gradually and then
entirely supplanted barbering and for the next 40 years of his life he was to produce
many hundreds of drawings and etchings the rewards for which were to include
cudgelling and prosecution.

The compact and conservative nature of Edinburgh society is obvious in the status
costume of the civic dignitaries, soldiers, lawyers, doctors, professors and upper class
men and women of fashion – and unfashion. Few artists have shown how style and the
wearing of clothes can reveal the character, and in doing so Kay has emphasised one of
the most important aspects of the study of costume in relation to social history.

In contrast to pride and pomposity he portrays poverty, but frequently the poverty
is matched with humour. His beggars, fish-wives, porters, sweeps and chair-men are
authentic individuals as opposed to the idealised unreal common folk seen on the
'Romantic' prints and engravings of fellow artists.

Every single one of Kay's drawings is of importance to the costume historian and to
select a mere handful of them as good examples is nigh impossible. One of my favourites
is dated 1792, and shows Captain Billair walking out with his wife who wished to be the
tallest woman in the city. She wears a high Postillion hat and patterns in order to
achieve her ambition, but Kay has perched her inappropriate but fashionable hat on
top of a Mob Cap which could have been worn by a servant. And her polonaise is worn
in a highly unfashionable and inelegant way. In other words this is a very keen costume
satire which at the time would have created considerable mirth (*60*).

In 1787 Kay drew Captain Dalrymple and Miss Macdonald in what he described
as 'the fashions then prevailing in the *beau monde* (*61*). Despite the fact that the artist
described the Captain as one of the best and kindest landlords, and Miss Macdonald as

LEFT, ABOVE **60** *Captain Billair and his wife, who wished to be the tallest woman in Edinburgh. By John Kay, 1792*

ABOVE **61** *Captain Dalrymple and Miss Macdonald, a lady celebrated for her high fashion. By John Kay*

62 *Mrs Smith in the costume of 1795. By John Kay*

63 *Mr Pierie, Mr Maxwell and Three Graces. By John Kay, 1785*

'celebrated for her handsomeness of figure, her beauty and accomplishments' the couple were not amused. Consequently Kay printed another 'likeness' entitled 'Lovers', which he described as 'a retaliatory production, the artist's usual method of apologizing to those who happened to be offended by his choice of a subject.'

'Mrs Smith in the costume of 1795' is another amusing caricature of the 'somewhat ridiculous fashion prevailing towards the close of the last century' (*62*). She liked to walk in the Meadows and usually dressed rather well in the 'high' fashion. Her waistline has risen to her chest and disappeared under a billow of muslin and a broad sash. Her large fan might have been painted with a classical or biblical scene.

Mr Pierie and Mr Maxwell were two notorious bachelors who 'ate well, slept well and drank well' and for that reason Kay has depicted them in the company of Three Graces 'in the costume of 1785' (*63*). The ridiculous hats of the ladies are similar in style but slightly smaller in size to that worn by Miss Sibilla Hutton in another caricature. She kept a millinery establishment and was always 'at the head of the *ton*, and indeed generally so far in advance that few attempted to follow.' On one occasion her father, a Secession minister at Dalkeith, protested about her indescribable head-dress assuring her that she would never get to heaven if she wore it. She replied, 'I'm sure I'll make a better appearance there than you will do with that vile, old-fashioned black wig, which you have worn for these last twenty years!'

There is quite a lot of information on the question of old and new fashions in the first *Statistical Account*, which started publication in 1791. In most cases the parish ministers responded to Sir John Sinclair's appeal for information according to their interests, some wrote at length on the subject of fashion whilst others ignored it. One of the most informative writers on the subject of dress was the minister of Tongland, in the county of Kircudbright, who described the local styles in the 1720s:

They had no buckles in their shoes, but tied them with small leather thongs; had no metal buttons on their clothes, but large clumsy buttons of wood moulds, covered over with the same cloth as the coat . . . neither men nor women, in general, wore any shirts, and when they did, they were made of coarse woollen; in general, they changed their plaiding shirts twice in the year, at Whitsunday and Martinmas. It was long before linen shirts came into use among the vulgar. They wore no shoes in summer, nor winter, but in the time of severe frost and snow. Their children got no shoes till they were able to go to the kirk. The women wore coarse plaiding, or drugget gowns, made of the coarsest wool, and spun in the coarsest manner. The tenants wives wore toys of linen of the coarsest kind, upon their heads, when they went to church, fairs or market. At home, in their own houses, they wore toys of coarse plaiding. The young girls, linen mutches, with a few plaits in them above their foreheads, when they went abroad to the church, or to fairs or to market. At home they went bareheaded, with their hair snooded back on the crown of their head, with a woollen string in the form of a garter.

Many of the ministers refer to the increasing interest in fashion during the last quarter of the eighteenth century, and many of them are concerned about the amount of money spent by servants on their dress. Home-spun was no longer good enough as the minister of an Aberdeenshire parish wrote:

Within these twenty years, the whole clothing of the inhabitants was raised and manufactured in the district, or in the neighbourhood. Now at least one third is brought from England; and the difference between the value of the dress used now, and what was used fifty years ago, would nearly pay the rents of the two parishes. . . . Almost every servant has a coat of English cloth . . . while printed, cottons, or other showy, but unsubstantial articles of dress, are preferred by the young women, to the manufactures of the country.

Another Aberdonian, the minister of Cluny, wrote in much the same strain:

The dress of all the country people in the district was, some years ago, both for men and women of cloth made of their own sheep wool . . . . Now every servant lad almost, must have his Sunday's coat of English broad cloth. . . . The servant maids are dressed in poplins, muslins, lawns, and ribbons.

Meanwhile, further south in Mid Calder, the parish minister was disturbed by the fact that whereas the workers 'in days of labour . . . are clothed in a way more suitable to their various engagements', when they were 'in dress' they took to English materials and fashions. 'As to the higher ranks of both sexes, their dress is much the same as it is in the southern parts of the island, and the fashions of London soon find their way hither'.

Pointing out that at that time (1794), maidservants were earning from £2 to £3 per year, he continued:

The tartan (a well known Highland manufacture) or red plaids, close caps, with or without ribbons, gowns, petticoats and stockings of home manufacture, which 30 or 40 years ago, constituted the dress of women in the inferior condition of life, gradually gave way to clothes made of red or blue English cloth, and other approaches to an improved dress; and these in their turn are now yielding to the dress cap, the silk bonnet or beaver hat, printed or other cotton gowns, white petticoats, white thread or cotton stockings, and fine shoes or slippers. Formerly the best handkerchiefs for the neck were strong cambrick, but now they are of fine muslin, and sometimes there is an addition of a shawl, of 5s or 7s value.

This trend was very disturbing for the large number of local tradesmen and women who were employed in the clothing trade. In the parish of Galston, in the county of Ayr, there was a population of 1,013 in 1755. Of these there were 55 weavers, 11 stocking weavers, 11 tailors, 24 tambourers (girls who sew with the tambouring needle) and 21 shoemakers.

The changing styles and new materials that were becoming apparent in the costume of the country lasses, were matched by even more obvious changes in the dresses of the city ladies. This was illustrated in 1976, when the Costume Society of Scotland, in collaboration with the National Trust for Scotland, mounted an exhibition of costume covering the period 1790 to 1830, in the Georgian House, Edinburgh. The exhibits were arranged according to the function of the rooms in which they were displayed.

The costume of the ladies exemplified a very interesting point, namely that whereas the country girls and servants were dressing 'up', the city ladies of fashion were dressing 'down'. Pointing out that elegance was now becoming equated with simplicity, Mrs Barbara Acton in the Introduction to the catalogue wrote that 'Ideas of emancipation and of social equality spread from France and infected the mood of the time in England and Scotland so that no longer did the aristocrat set the tone with a way of dressing that distinguished his class from that of the bourgeoisie.'

Entering the dining-room of the Georgian House one was aware of the complexity of costume at this period. A blue-and-cream striped silk robe of an earlier period has been altered to suit the new costume line of the 1790s. A child wears a pink satin dress almost certainly passed on from an older sister, and another lady's robe and petticoat of cream silk damask, worn with paniers, might be out of date, but it was obviously much too valuable to discard.

In the bed-chamber was a delightful riding habit of fine beige cloth trimmed with military frogging in silk. It had a high waistline, typical of the new style, and an apron-front skirt. It was worn with a long matching stole. This costume belongs to Mrs Acton, who points out that the young lady is wearing it in the prevailing spirit of revolt. However, there is also the purposeful reason for wearing a riding habit indoors; it was 'not an uncommon fashion and was, in fact, an eminently practical way of keeping warm.'

Another riding habit of the early nineteenth century is described by Curtis in *Costume and Fashion* as the 'Glengarry Riding Habit'. This costume is said to have been designed by a dress-maker named Miss McDonald, who was inspired by feelings of patriotism. Made of the finest pale blue cloth, and richly ornamented with frogs and braiding, the habit 'slopes down on each side in a very novel style, and in such a manner as to define the figure to considerable advantage.' The sleeves were elaborately braided from the wrist to the elbow, as were the shoulders and epaulettes. The costume took its

Scottish title from the head-dress which was called a 'Glengarry Cap'. From the illustration, however, it appears to be a tall cylinder about 15 inches high, covered with a small checked material and described as 'composed of blue satin, and trimmed with plaited ribbon of various shades of blue, and a superb plume of feathers.'

The outstanding Highland lady of fashion of this period was undoubtedly Jane, Duchess of Gordon, who, according to one of the clan histories 'introduced tartan to Court in 1792; apparently using the plaid of the Black Watch, to which her son had just been appointed'. A contemporary caricature shows the 'Tartan Belle' in an enormous hat covered with tartan ribbons, a large tartan sash and even a tartan ribbon attached to her fan. There are also at least two oil paintings of the lady painted by anonymous artists in the 1830s or 1840s. She was born Jane Maxwell, 'a Lowlander of the Lowlanders'.

Robert Chambers, the Edinburgh author and publisher, has left us an important account of *Female Dress of Last Century* which he published in 1823, at the age of 21. Despite the inconvenient nature of the ladies' dresses he felt that they had the merit of dignity and grace:

'How fine it must have been to see, as an old gentleman told me he had seen, two hooped ladies moving along the Lawnmarket in a summer evening, and filling up the whole foot-way with their stately and voluminous persons!

Amongst female articles of attire in those days were calashes, bongraces, capuchins, negligees, stomachers, stays, hoops, lappets, pinners, plaids, fans, busks, rumple-knots, &c. all of them now forgotten.

The calash was a species of hood, constructed of silk upon a framework of cane, and was used as a protection to a cap or head-dress, in walking out or riding in a carriage. It could be folded back like the hood of a carriage, so as to lie gathered together behind the neck.

The bongrace was a bonnet of silk and cane, in shape somewhat like a modern bonnet.

The capuchin was a short cloak reaching not below the elbows. It was of silk, edged with lace or of velvet. Gentlemen also wore capuchins. The first Sir William Forbes frequently appeared at the Cross in one. A lady's *mode tippet* was nearly the same piece of dress.

The negligee was a gown, projecting in loose and ample folds from the back. It could only be worn with stays. It was entirely open in front, so as to show the stomacher, across which it was laced with flat silk cords, while below it opened more widely, and showed the petticoat. This latter, though shorter, was sometimes more splendid than the gown, and had a deep flounce. Ladies, in walking, generally carried the skirt of the gown over the arm, and exhibited the petticoat; but when they entered a room, they always came sailing in with the train sweeping full and majestically behind them.

The stomacher was a triangular piece of rich silk, one corner pointing downwards, and joining the fine black lace-bordered apron, while the other two angles pointed to the shoulders. Great pains were usually discovered in the adornment of this beautiful and most attractive piece of dress. Many wore jewels upon it; and a lady would have thought herself poor indeed, if she could not bedizen it with strings of bugles or tinsel.'

The wearing of tight stays by the lady of fashion at this period was essential and she would frequently hold her breath and the bedpost whilst her maid was lacing them. To be really fashionable, contours had to change according to the time of day and this was achieved by wearing a variety of hoops:

64 *A town lady,* c. *1745, drawn by James Basire. The tartan plaid is worn over the head and shoulders*

The hoop was contemporary with, and a necessary appendage of, the stays. There were different species of hoops, being of various shapes and uses. The pocket-hoop, worn in the morning, was like a pair of small panniers, such as one sees on an ass. The bell-hoop was a sort of petticoat, shaped like a bell, and made of cane or rope for frame-work. This was not quite full dress. There was also a straw petticoat, a species of hoop such as is so common in French prints. The full-sized evening hoop was so monstrous, that people saw one-half of it enter the room before the wearer. This was very inconvenient in the Old Town, where doorways and closes were narrow. In going down a close or a turnpike stair, ladies tilted them up, and carried them under their arms. In case of this happening, there was a *show petticoat* below; and such care was taken of appearances, that even the *garters* were worn fine, being either embroidered, or having gold and silver fringes and tassels.

The French silks worn during the last century were beautiful, the patterns were so well drawn, and the stuff of such excellent quality. The dearest common brocade was about a guinea a yard; if with gold and silver, considerably more.

The lappet was a piece of Brussels or point-lace, hanging in two pieces from the crown of the head, and streaming gracefully behind.

Pinners, such as the celebrated Egyptian Sphinx wears, were pinned down the stomacher.

Plaids were worn by ladies to cover their heads and muffle their faces when they went into the street. The council records of Edinburgh abound in edicts against the use of this piece of dress, which, they said, confounded decent women with those who were the contrary.

Chamber's account is particularly important because of his precise definitions and contemporary terms many of which cannot be found elsewhere. One can imagine that the use of such terminology in female conversation was regarded as an indication of a lady's knowledge of the latest mode:

The rumple-knot was a large bunch of ribbons worn at the peak of the waist behind. Knots of ribbons were then numerous over the whole body. There were the breast-knots, two hainch-knots (at which there were also buttons for looping up the gown behind), a knot at the tying of the beads behind the neck, one in front, and another at the back of the head-gear, and knots upon the shoes. It took about twelve yards or upwards to make a full set of ribbons. A gown then required ten yards of stuff.

Other minor articles of dress and adornment were the *befong* handkerchief (spelt at random), of a stuff similar to what is now called *net*, crossed upon the breast; paste earrings and necklace; broad black bracelets at the wrists; a *pong pong* – a jewel fixed to a wire with a long pin at the end, worn in front of the cap, and which shook as the wearer moved. It was generally stuck in the cushion, over which the hair was turned in front. Several were frequently worn at once. A song in the *Charmer*, 1751, alludes to this bijou:

'*Come all ye young ladies whose business and care*
Is contriving new dresses, and curling your hair;
Who flirt and coquet with each coxcomb who comes
To toy at your toilets, and strut in your rooms;
While you're placing a patch, or adjusting pong pong,
Ye may listen and learn by the truth of my song.'

Fly-caps, encircling the head, worn by young matrons, and mob-caps, falling down over the ears, used only by old ones; pockets of silk or satin, of which young girls wore one above their other attire; silk or linen stockings – never of cotton, which is a modern stuff – slashed with pieces of a colour in strong contrast with the rest, or gold or silver clocks, woven in. The silk stockings were very thick, and could not be washed on account of the gold or silver. They were frequently of scarlet silk, and (1733) worn both by ladies and gentlemen. High-heeled shoes, set off with fine lace or sewed work, and sharply pointed in front.'

In the Royal Scottish Museum there is a delightful costume of the 1820 period, consisting of a white embroidered muslin skirt, a blue silk high-waisted spencer, over one shoulder of which hangs a lovely Paisley shawl.

A great deal has been written on the subject of Paisley shawls, including authoritative accounts by Miss Dorothy A. Whyte. In the *Journal of the Costume Society of Scotland* (January 1970), she draws attention to the painting by David Allan, showing the family of the Earl of Mar in 1783, and in particular the eldest daughter who wears a long shawl. It is 'solid cream in colour, with fringed ends, bordered along its length with a narrow red band, the two ends decorated with a deep panel done in a design of red and blue shapes. . . .' But Miss White points out that the shawl presents an unsolved problem – was it an imported *indienne* or an early imitation of the Indian shawls?

The ancestor of the Paisley shawl came to Europe from Kashmir, and it was made of what was probably the most delicate wool in the world. Soon they were highly fashionable – the Empress Josephine is said to have had over 350 of them – and imitations quickly followed. The earliest British specimens were made in Edinburgh and Norwich. Made from wool, silk and cotton yarn they came in three principal shapes, the square shawl, the long shawl, and the stole. Some were printed whilst others were embroidered.

The *Glasgow Mercury* in 1785 reported that 'A Piece of Calico cloth containing 2 dozen of Chintz shawls' had been stolen from the Printfield of Dalquhurn. This must have been the time of their earliest appearance in Scotland, and by 1850 Paisley had captured the market in imitation Indian shawls. Although they were then essential to the Victorian lady, by the late 1870s the fashionable rage for Paisley shawls was over.

Margaret H. Swain, who carried out important research on shawls, published a short account of Ayrshire needlework in the *Journal of the Costume Society of Scotland* (October 1969). This industry was ancillary to the manufacture of muslin centered in the west of Scotland. In fact its contemporary name was 'sewed muslin' and it originated in an Edinburgh workshop set up in 1782. It was supplanted by the introduction of machine-made Swiss embroidery in the 1850s, so the fashion for the Paisley shawl and Ayrshire needlework covered about the same period.

Describing the extensive use of this type of embroidery, Margaret Swain reminds us that it was made in other parts of Scotland and was a significant accessory to costume of the period:

Ayrshire embroidery was used exclusively to decorate articles of costume. The only known exceptions are two large bedspreads presented to the Countess of Eglinton, who helped to foster the industry. Baby robes and caps, men's shirt ruffles, women's dresses, sleeves, cap frills, pelerines, collars and cuffs, shawls and handkerchiefs, were all decorated with this type of white needlework on cotton muslin.

Another popular type of shawl was made by the women of Shetland, said to be the finest knitters in the world. The wool from the small island sheep was fine and delicate to the touch once it had been prepared. The Norsemen, who had settled in the islands many centuries before, probably brought these sheep with them, and they have an interesting affinity with the primitive small brown Soay sheep of St Kilda.

Different districts specialised in different articles such as stockings, underwear or gloves, in addition to the shawls. The island of Unst produced such fine shawls that they could be passed through a wedding ring. Lace shawls were also knitted in sections which were then sewn together to form an area about two yards square.

The demand for Shetland 'lace', or openwork knitting, reached its zenith in the mid-nineteenth century when the best examples were made from fine single-ply white wool. But it was after the knitting was complete that the crucial process took place. The shawls then had to be delicately washed and stretched on light-weight wooden frames then placed outdoors in a careful manner when the weather conditions were right.

These fine Shetland shawls were highly popular with the elderly ladies of Edinburgh. Several writers have recorded their impressive appearance in their white caps, usually worn beneath black bonnets, and their beautiful shawls.

Lord Cockburn describes this 'singular race of excellent Scotch old ladies . . . embodied in curious outsides; for they all dressed, and spoke, and did, exactly as they chose; their language like their habits entirely Scotch. . . .'

One particular lady of character who caught his attention was Sophia Johnston, who could shoe a horse quicker than a blacksmith. Indoors and outdoors she wore a man's hat and greatcoat, worsted stockings and heavy shoes with large brass clasps. In this costume 'she sat in any drawing-room, and at any table, amidst all the fashion and aristocracy of the land.'

But other Scottish ladies of this period were much more fashion conscious, particularly one Highland lady, Elizabeth Grant of Rothiemurcus, who has left us a splendid autobiography. In 1809, her father was a Lieutenant-Colonel in the local Volunteers and her mother 'rode to the ground with him dressed in a tartan petticoat, red jacket gaudily laced, and just such a bonnet and feathers as he wore himself'.

Elizabeth refers to an aunt who, in 1808, had been 'rusticating' for four months in England and whose wardrobe was out of date; therefore 'as there was always a great deal of company in the Highlands during the shooting season, it was necessary for her to add considerably to it'. On the other hand, when Elizabeth and her sisters were in England they wore cloth wraps in pelisse form, with beaver bonnets which they could still wear on their return North. But the pelisse wraps were put away when outworn, and replaced with hooded cloaks made of tartan.

One of the greatest social events for the Highland lady of fashion was the series of balls held during the Northern Meeting at Inverness. For these Elizabeth had three outfits, white muslin with blue trimmings, white gauze and pearl grey gauze.

In the opinion of Elizabeth Grant, the excessive display of tartan during the visit of King George IV to Edinburgh in 1822 was a great mistake and 'offended all the southern Scots.' However, an examination of the contemporary accounts of the costumes worn by the ladies at the various social occasions show very little tartan being worn by them. Even the caricaturists did not show any tartan dresses and one can safely presume that they would not have overlooked such excellent targets for their satires. They certainly did not show the Scottish ladies as beauties.

65 *An Edwardian lady piper photographed by William Skeoch Cumming*

66 *An Edwardian lady complete with tartan bowler hat and staghorn hunting knife*

The Eglinton tournament of 1839 caused a revival in the use of tartan in ladies' costume, particularly for formal occasions. Although the principal guests were required to dress in medieval style, many of the thousands of spectators decided to make their costumes 'Romantic'. In order to meet this demand some of the dress-makers and milliners solved the problem with a few yards of tartan. Many fancy tartans were used including a fashionable mixture of a woollen material with the fine lines woven in silk. The 'Montgomery' sett was also worn as a compliment to the Earl of Eglinton's Lowland family.

During the Victorian period tartan was a popular material for use in ladies' dress material, scarves, shawls, ribbons and trimmings throughout Britain and France. There was, however, no attempt at that time to devise a female Scottish costume as a fashion.

In the Edwardian era one Edinburgh lady caused a sensation by not only learning how to play the bagpipes but also dressing herself up in a Highland costume (*65*). One wonders what her reaction would have been to the modern mini-skirted girl piper.

8

◆

Scottish Tweed

THE ORIGIN OF the word 'tweed' is usually given as follows. Early in the nineteenth century a consignment of cloth was sent by a manufacturer in Hawick to a London merchant. It was described as 'tweel' but, owing to a misreading on the part of a clerk, it was recorded as 'tweed'. Because of its association with the River Tweed the name stuck.

However, W. F. H. Nicolaisen, the eminent Scottish philologist, cautions that this explanation may be too plausible. In 1541, there is a reference to 'ane sack of small twedlyne' in Aberdeen, and this word continues in use thereafter. Nicolaisen considers that just as tweel is a parallel form to twill, twilling is paralleled by tweeling or tweedling, therefore as tweel stands beside tweeling so could tweed stand beside tweedling. As far as the association of the name of the river is concerned, if that assumption is correct then the material called Harris tweed presents a puzzle.

The complexities of the seventeenth and eighteenth century Scottish wool textile industry have been ably described by Clifford Gulvin, to whom I am indebted for much of the following information.

In the seventeenth century the industry produced coarse cloth made of local wool by native labour which served the majority of the population. In the early years of the century 'plaiding and cloth were said to be among the most important of Scottish exports.' But, by the late 1680s the coarse woollen trade declined due to economic and political reasons. Scottish society began to disdain home-produced goods and wore English or French cloths. In an attempt to encourage the home manufacture of finer quality cloths skilled foreign instructors were brought into the country, but without success.

Gulvin describes the period 1770 to 1830 as the 'Formative Years' when the Border woollen industry developed rapidly and eventually emerged as the principal seat of wool-manufacturing in Scotland. He suggests the end of this period as the time which 'witnessed the introduction to the London market of the products to be known later as tweeds, which were to give the Scottish woollen industry its main claim to fame.' The 'fancy trade on which the name of the industry was built during the nineteenth century was rooted in the products of the pre-tweed era, and in one product in particular – the black and white checked plaid used by Border shepherds.' This was a rectangular piece of woollen material about four yards long by a yard and a half wide, usually woven from local undyed wool (25).

Variations of these Border checks became highly popular and Sir Walter Scott increased the vogue by adopting them for his trousers and jackets. At the same time the

67 '*The Ettrick Shepherd*' *by Watson Gordon, c. 1827, showing the large Border shoulder plaid*

popularity of the 'clan' tartan idea was applied to 'District Checks' in tweed for use by the ghillies, stalkers and estate employees of the new lairds of sporting estates. The final accolade was given by the Prince of Wales when, in 1867, he appeared wearing a complete suit made of Scottish tweed.

Scottish district checks have been well described and illustrated by E. S. Harrison. Apart from their widespread use on estates, which included Balmoral, many patterns were designed for the Scottish regiments and worn by officers whilst in civilian dress.

The shepherds' check was 'the traditional pattern of the shawls or plaids worn by the Border shepherds and introduced to the Highlands along with the sheep late in the eighteenth century.' These small-checked plaids became closely associated with the Scottish shepherd when described by the poet or painted by the artist. When James Hogg, the poet known as 'The Ettrick Shepherd', was painted about 1827 by Watson Gordon, his large plaid was conspicuously shown draped over his shoulder (*67*).

Such plaids served two purposes, to protect the shepherd in bad weather, and to carry new-born lambs. They were nearly always rectangular in shape and often fringed at the ends. There was also a certain type known as the 'Poke Plaid', the ends of which were sewn up to form large pockets for carrying lambs.

William Wilson of Bannockburn manufactured material for shepherds' plaids in large quantities and in a wide variety of colours. These had either numbers or fancy names, one of the popular patterns being known as 'Indiana'. Several Border weavers tried to undercut Wilson's prices and in a letter dated October 1831, John Clapperton & Company of Edinburgh wrote that a Jedburgh weaver had offered them 'Shepherd's Plaids' at a half pence a yard lower than the price quoted by Wilson.

In April 1823, James Helliwell of Liverpool wrote to Wilson to say that he had invented a process to make these plaids waterproof 'in the severest Storms of Rain'. Despite the fact that the ingredients for this process were not to cost more than a farthing a yard, Wilson does not appear to have taken up the offer.

Some of these plaids were of 'Hodden Grey', but this colour was not popular with the Highlanders. It was regarded by them as the colour 'appropriate to the churl', and it was also believed to be the personification of ghostly ideas and associated with phantoms and demons. The Devil himself was known as *Mac-an-Riochda* – 'The Son of the Grey'.

Black, green and red checks on a white or cream ground were very popular, and they became fashionable in a light-weight material for ladies' wear in the 1840s. Miss Balfour of Glen Feshie, 'being troubled because she had no right to any tartan' adopted the 'Shepherd's check with a bold scarlet overcheck'. It was also about this time that the Glenurquhart design was introduced as the Countess of Seafield's estate check.

Gulvin's book includes a glossary of technical terms of which the following are of particular interest to the student of Scottish costume.

Bays (*or Baize*) A cheap lightweight woollen cloth. Probably one of the 'new draperies' of the seventeenth century.

Cheviot Originally this term was applied exclusively to cloths made from the wool of the Cheviot sheep but, for the sake of convenience, it came to denote any cloth in a particular quality range whatever wool was employed in its manufacture.

Drab A thick yellow/brown woollen cloth.

Drugget A coarse stuff, often undyed and unmilled, used by the peasantry for everyday clothing till the last century.

Duffle A coarse milled cloth similar to that used in duffle coats today.

Fingram A coarse serge made in Aberdeenshire in the seventeeth century and earlier.

Kersey A coarse but smooth-faced woollen cloth.

Plaiding A long piece of coarse woollen cloth usually worn over the shoulder. In Highland areas it was normally a tartan and in the Lowlands a check. Worn by all sexes a plaid could be used as an overcoat, a blanket or a bed-pallet. Sometimes it was drawn up between the legs to form a kind of skirt.

Serge A twilled cloth, sometimes with a worsted warp and a woollen weft, but usually all worsted.

Shalloons A twilled worsted cloth of a coarse variety, often used for undergarments.

Wincey In Scotland this was a cloth that had a linen or cotton warp and woollen weft.

Originally termed a 'linsey-woolsey', it was mainly made in the Glasgow area, and also for a while in Aberdeen.

Woollens Strictly, cloth made of yarn that has been carded not combed, i.e. cloth made from short wool and from noils. Noils are short fibres of wool that are combed out in the worsted process.

Worsteds Fabrics made from longer wool that has been combed, i.e. the fibres have been straightened and laid parallel to each other.

The Harris tweed industry may not be very ancient but it has been highly successful. In 1844, the Earl of Dunmore, who owned the island, had a pattern of the Murray tartan copied in local tweed. This venture proved so successful that his Countess organised and improved the texture and introduced new patterns. She also encouraged the use of local dyes, and soon the spinning wheels were whirling and the hand looms clattering throughout the island. Before her death in 1886, the industry had spread over the whole of the Outer Hebrides.

9

The Scottish Bonnet

'WE'LL HAE NANE but Highland bonnets here' declared Sir Colin Campbell at the battle of the Alma in 1854. This rousing cry from the Commander of the Highland Brigade typifies the symbolism of a very ordinary form of head-dress. It had been worn in most European countries since medieval times but nowhere had it become associated as a national emblem except in Scotland.

The term 'bonnet' was originally applied to the material used in the making of this type of head-gear; however the word disappeared in its original form, and for centuries has been used to describe any head-dress other than a hat.

The great costume historian, J. R. Planché, states that the hardy Celtic tribes had, in the past, cared little for head coverings, although the chiefs occasionally wore a cap or bonnet 'as much perhaps for distinction as for defence.' He did not consider that the flat cloth Scottish bonnet had formed part of their primitive costume, but if it was an ancient head covering it was of 'Saxon, Norman or Danish introduction'.

Almost certainly the Scottish knitted bonnet with its flat crown and double-sided head-band or brim had its origin in the sixteenth-century cloth bonnets or caps worn in western Europe. And yet this form of head covering was given a particular Scottish context by 1540, when coins made of native gold were known as 'bonnet pieces'. This was because on their obverse side they showed a bust of King James V wearing one.

The Oxford English Dictionary states that the bonnet was replaced by the cap in England but retained in Scotland, hence occasionally it was known as the 'Scotch cap'. I find this comparison between the words 'bonnet' and 'cap' rather confusing.

The word 'bonet' was often applied to a defensive helmet in Scotland. In 1541, an Edinburgh armourer made a 'stele bonet to the King's grace', and there are a number of similar references in Guild records of that period. Up to the time of the eighteenth century the Border raiders were known as the 'Steel Bonnets'.

The only item of male costume which could be said to be characteristic of the Scots, and which was noticed by an anonymous English soldier who visited the country in 1650, was the bonnet. He wrote that 'men generally wear blew bonnets. . . .' Twelve years later, John Ray recorded that 'the Scots generally (that is, the poorer sort) wear, the men blue bonnets on their heads, and some russet. . . .'

Certainly by the mid-seventeenth century the blue bonnet had become the symbol of a Scot. During the wars of the Covenant a number of English freebooters disguised themselves as Scots by wearing blue bonnets in order to plunder.

The social implications of this head-dress had also become established by this period. Amongst the 'unciwill kynd of cloithes' of which Sir Robert Gordon disapproved in 1620, were included 'blew bonnets'. Likewise the Church Synod of Moray declared them as 'ucomly' in 1624. The seventeeth-century Merchant Guild of Stirling took a stronger line with its members and fined them if they wore blue bonnets in church.

The bonnet was being worn in both wide and close-fitting form under the description of 'bonet' and 'cap' throughout Scotland at the end of the sixteenth century. Fynes Morison visited Scotland from Cambridge in 1598 and remarked on the 'flat blew caps' being worn by the Lowlanders. Taylor wrote of the 'blue caps' being worn in the Highlands in 1618.

The Highlanders depicted as supporters to Blaeu's map of *Scotia Antiqua*, 1643, are wearing large bonnets of the type which a century later were to be known as 'Lowland'. They are almost identical to the bonnet being worn by the central figure in a picture entitled 'Lowland Wedding' painted by Jacob de Wet, who came to Scotland in 1673. The portrait of a 'Chieftain' painted by Michael Wright about 1660 shows a particularly large bonnet with a splendid plume adorning it, whilst the henchman in the background wears an equally large bonnet but with no plume (*colour plate 1*).

When William Cleland described the Highland Host of 1678 in his satirical poem, he drew attention to the fact that whereas the rank-and-file were bare-headed, the officers appeared:

With good blew bonnets on their heads,
Which on the one side had a flipe,
Adorn'd with a tobacco pipe.

Not all bonnets at this time were blue. Martin Martin describes the men of the Western Islands wearing 'Bonnets made of thick cloth, some blew, some black and some grey.'

This reference to cloth bonnets is interesting as it would appear that in the seventeenth and early eighteenth centuries most of the bonnets were knitted. In order to make them fit tightly they would be made twice the size of the finished article and then shrunk. During this process they became closely felted which would make them almost waterproof.

Three early Scottish caps can be seen in the National Museum of Antiquities of Scotland. The first came from Dara Moor in Morayshire and is knitted, and an unusual feature is the two strings, one on each side, which were tied under the chin. The second cap, or bonnet, was dug up in Tarvie in Ross-shire and it too is knitted, in this case in green wool. It has two little slits just below the edge of the crown into which a brooch could have been fitted.

The third specimen, excavated at Barrock, in Caithness, is made of dark brown cloth. This one has a small triangular vent in the head-band at the back which has been overlapped to fit the wearer and then stitched up (5).

Obviously the smaller the bonnet and the better the fit, the more easily would it be kept on the head whilst working in the almost constant winds of the Western Highlands and Islands. But this does not seem to have prevented large bonnets being worn fairly widely. The ribbons worn at the back of the modern bonnet are, of course, a relic of the days when they were actually used to tighten the fit. A small piece of the brim was cut out at the back and a short ribbon attached to either side of the gap. Another vestige of this simple method has survived in the small bow of ribbon inside a top-hat.

Amongst the items of clothing belonging to a young man who had died in the early eighteenth century, and whose body was excavated on the Isle of Lewis, was his bonnet. It had been knitted with several needles in order to achieve its circular form, then shrunk and felted. Having been dyed with indigo, it was probably dark blue originally, and the head-band was decorated with little knots of red wool.

In her report of the clothing (1975), Helen Bennett points out that this bonnet was helpful in establishing a date. Similar bonnets covering a period from possibly the late sixteenth century to the eighteenth provided comparisons, particularly in the type of decoration. The knots of red wool, which occur approximately every two stitches on the head-band of the Lewis bonnet, do not appear on any of the other finds. However, this form of decoration does occur on a bonnet associated with Prince Charles Edward Stuart in the Oliphant of Gask collection, and in the portrait of Alastair Grant painted by Richard Waitt in 1714 (*15*).

Another interesting point about the Lewis bonnet is that the knotted decoration might have some association with the diced pattern on the head-band of later bonnets. These appear to have come into use some time after the late 1750s.

The first *Statistical Account of Scotland* provides a great deal of information about the manufacture and use of bonnets in Scotland. For instance, with reference to the parish of Tongland in Kirkcudbright, we read about a bonnet ritual:

At the above period (1720s) there was not a hat to be seen in the whole congregation upon a Sunday. They wore Kilmarnock bonnets or caps of different colours. In church they kept on

68 *Fishwife and young man wearing a deep bonnet. Drawn from life by Walter Geikie, c. 1830*

their bonnets or caps during the lecture and sermon, and took them off only during the prayer, the singing of psalms, and the pronouncing the blessing.

The Statistical Account report of the industries in the parish of Kilmarnock, in Ayrshire, states that there were, in 1700, 'five incorporated trades; the bonnet makers, skinners, taylors, shoemakers and weavers; of which, the bonnet makers, incorporated in 1646, is the most ancient.'

It was in the south-west of Scotland, particularly in the county of Ayrshire, that the bonnet trade flourished. Originally a cottage craft, it became, by the end of the eighteenth century, a major industry. The small village of Stewarton, north of Kilmarnock, eventually became known as the 'Bonnet Town'. In 1650, Sir Alexander Cunningham, Laird of nearby Corsehill, regularised the bonnet making, under the authority of the Bonnet Court of Corsehill. He signed a 'Great Agreement' with the Deacon of the 'Incorporation of Bonnetmakers and dyers of Glasgow' in which he gave his bond that the bonnets sent to Glasgow for sale would be of a high quality, and he fined any bonnet-maker trying to sell an inferior article.

Illustrations of bonnets abound, showing that they range in style from the elegant blue bonnets in Sir David Wilkie's genre picture of Pitlessie Fair, painted about 1804, to the large flat examples worn by Edinburgh chimney sweeps, and drawn by John Kay about the same time. One charming drawing by Walter Geikie made in the 1830s, shows a young man wearing a deep bonnet with a small crown and a large brim checked in the two colours (*1, 68, 69*).

The bonnet was very popular with 'characters' in the Highlands and Lowlands. At

69 *The boy in this drawing by Walter Geikie, c. 1830, wears a bonnet with a thistle motif, a very popular style at the time*

the end of the nineteenth century there was a famous Dundee individual called 'Tea Pot Tam' who wore an outsize Tam o' Shanter with a large red 'toorie', or woollen ball, on the top. Whenever a tourist appeared, he bent his right arm forward in the shape of a tea-pot spout and requested that a penny be put in 'the mouth of the spout' for good luck. The same city's greatest character, the poet William MacGonagall, was also famous for his bonnets.

There are a number of 'historic' bonnets including some associated with the cronies of Robert Burns. Another is said to have been worn by the Duchess of Gordon when raising her husband's regiment in 1794, and there is at least one bonnet claimed with good evidence to have belonged to Prince Charles Edward Stuart.

One item closely associated with the Scottish bonnet is the highly romanticised 'White Cockade' about which many songs, poems and stories have been written.

The history of cockades in general and the white cockade in particular has been fully investigated by W. A. Thorburn who attributes their origin to the lengths of black ribbon issued to the British army in 1700, to 'cock' or hold up, the brims of the plain black military hats of that period. When these ribbons were neatly tied up they formed cockades which had nothing to do with Hanoverian badges. They were not even unique to Britain, being worn by several European armies without any political significance.

The origin of the white cockade as a significant Jacobite symbol requires explanation as it was not a Stewart emblem when the Stewarts were on the throne nor was it ever worn then by their troops.

It was Louis XIV who decreed that the national colour of France would be white, and Thorburn points out that the French army was the only one to use white cockades as a uniform feature. He concludes that: 'Because of the strong connection with France, it seems very likely that the "white cockade" worn by the Jacobite rebels was the emblem of France.'

70 *A mixture of broad bonnet and feather bonnet with two eagle feathers of a chieftain. From the* Book of the Club of True Highlanders, *1881*

But there is no doubt that the white cockade was associated with the Jacobite cause. The earliest portrait of the Prince used for propaganda purposes had a bonnet and a white cockade added to it. It also appears on portraits of eminent Jacobites and Morier's picture of the battle of Culloden (*colour plate 3*).

There is a unique contemporary account of the significance of the white cockade written by James Ray of Whitehaven who fought as a Volunteer in Cumberland's army. After the battle of Culloden he came upon a young Highlander who declared that he was a Campbell, to which Ray replied:

'Where is your bonnet?' He replied 'Somebody hath snatched it off my head.' I only mention this to shew how we distinguished our loyal clans from the Rebels, they being dress'd and equipp'd all in one Way, except the bonnet – ours having a Red or Yellow Cross or Ribbon, theirs a white Cockade. He having neither of these distinctions, I desired him, if he was a Campbell, to follow me. . . .'

The wearing of plant badges on the bonnet is an interesting custom about which little is known. Lists have been published giving the names of a number of clans with their appropriate plants but who the originators of such lists were is not entirely clear. The use of crested cap badges is widespread today and they should consist of the badge of the clan Chief within a belt and buckle, the belt being inscribed with the clan motto. There is no such thing as a 'clan crest' and the cap badge described above is worn by a clansman as an expression of loyalty. The crest is the personal property of the Chief, and when he wears it he surmounts it with three small silver feathers. If he is a peer then he surmounts the crest with his coronet. Only a chief is entitled to wear three eagle's feathers in his bonnet whilst a chieftain wears two, and a gentleman, or *Duine-uasail*, one (*70*).

10

♦

Fisher Folk

RURAL occupational costumes can nearly always be divided into two distinct categories: the functional every-day working clothes, and 'best' costume. These distinctions apply to the two main forms of Scottish dress associated with sea fishing, namely the woollen knitted garments of the jersey type and the costume of the Newhaven Fishwife.

It has been said that the fisher folk who lived in the village of Newhaven, on the outskirts of Edinburgh, were descended from Flemish immigrants. This is probably an over-simplification although there was close association between the two countries. In the fourteenth century the Firth of Forth was crowded with Flemish and Dutch fishing vessels.

The costume of the Newhaven fishermen had a few interesting features, but it was the womenfolk whose appearance was distinctive. Although the men caught the fish, it was the wife who was the head of the house and who controlled the sale of the catch and all the family finances.

The unmistakable dress of the Newhaven fishwife was of as much importance to the advertisement of her wears as was her distinctive cry in the streets of Edinburgh, which inspired Lady Nairne to write the words of the song 'Caller Herrin''.

Probably the earliest illustration of a fishwife is the engraved plate entitled 'Wha'l O Caller Oysters' in John Kay's *Portraits*, signed and dated 1812. The description of the engraving includes an account from *Chamber's Edinburgh Journal*;

A cap of cotton or linen, surmounted by a stout napkin tied below the chin, composes the investiture of the head; the more showy structure wherewith other females are adorned being inadmissable from the broad belt which supports the 'creel', that is, fishbasket, crossing the forehead. A sort of woollen pea-jacket, of vast amplitude of skirt, conceals the upper part of the person, relieved at the throat by a liberal display of handkerchief. The under part of the figure is invested with a voluminous quantity of petticoat, of substantial material and gaudy colour, generally yellow with stripes, so made as to admit of a very free inspection of the ancle, and worn in such immense numbers, that the bare mention of them would be enough to make a fine lady faint. One-half of these ample garments is gathered up over the haunches, puffing out the figure in an unusual and uncouth manner. White worsted stockings and stout shoes complete the picture.

The style of this costume is interesting because it is obviously governed by function. The small spotted handkerchief tied securely under the chin would hold the fishwife's white cap in place, especially as she would be constantly lifting the strap of the creel

71 *Advertisement for 'Fishwife Flannel' suitable for 'Ladies' and children's costumes'*

WILLIAM JEFFREY & SON'S

NEWHAVEN FISHWIVES. 218.

"FISHWIFE FLANNEL."

The Most Durable Material for Ladies' and Children's Costumes.

WRITE FOR PATTERNS TO

MARKET HOUSE, LEITH.

ESTABLISHED 1842.

over her head. So too would the 'voluminous quantity of petticoat' be very necessary owing to the cold conditions under which she worked. As for the display of 'ancle', this would certainly not be for reasons of coyness but rather for the practicality of preserving her skirts. As might be expected, the whole costume was made of good hardwearing material, and in 1842, William Jeffrey & Sons were advertising 'Fishwife Flannel' available from 'Market House, Leith'. A few years later, although their advertisements consisted of photographs of fishwives, they described the flannel as 'The most Durable Material for Ladies' and Children's Costumes.' (71).

One of the great status achievements of the costume occurred in the year 1844, when Ackermann and Company of London published a coloured engraving after a painting by T. Bonnar entitled 'Newhaven Fisherwomen'. It is subtitled 'Strangers visiting the Scottish Metropolis much admire the cleanly and peculiar appearance of this hardy class of females; and their picturesque and novel costume particularly attracted the attention of Her Majesty during her recent visit to Scotland.' The print shows two attractive lassies in Gala dress standing at the entrance to Newhaven harbour (74).

The arrival of the photographic era meant there was ample pictoral evidence of the

72 *Two Newhaven fishermen, one wearing the hard tarred hat. D. O. Hill photograph, c. 1840*

73 *Newhaven fishwife photographed by D. O. Hill, c. 1845*

74 *Newhaven fishwomen. Ackerman print of 1844*

costume of the fishwives, their husbands and children. In the mid 1840s, D. O. Hill and
Robert Adamson produced their fine collection of calotypes of these people. It is
possible that some of the photographs were intended to be sold in aid of a Newhaven
fisher folk fund; certainly many of them are posed in a manner which would appeal to
romantic sentiments (*73*).

But by this period a definite 'gala' dress had evolved with lighter colours, white
aprons, kilted and carefully arranged skirts, finer shawls and careful hair styles. Two
famous Royal visits had greatly helped to formalise this costume. When George IV
came to Edinburgh in 1822, the 'Newhaven Fishwives' had taken part in the parades.
And in 1842, after Queen Victoria had passed through Leith on her first visit to
Scotland, she recorded in her *Journal*;

> The Porters, all mounted, with curious Scotch caps, and their horses decorated with flowers,
> had a very singular effect; but the fishwomen are the most striking-looking people, and are
> generally young and pretty women – very clean, and very Dutch-looking, with their white caps
> and bright-coloured petticoats. They never marry out of their class.

Not all the Hill and Adamson studies show formal costume, although some of the
children are obviously posed to give a romantic appeal. For instance one photograph of
a small boy wearing his father's clothes is entitled 'The Fisher King' or 'In his Feyther's
Breeks'.

There are some interesting pictures of the fishermen standing in groups beside their boats. Some of them wear the round tarred hats which served a functional purpose as protection against head injuries from spars or heavy rigging blocks. The skipper usually changed into a tall top hat on entering harbour, but most of them wore the round hats at sea (*72*).

Present-day fishwives treasure their old family costumes as heirlooms and it is easier to replace the more expensive shawls and blouse material than the older druggets and flannels. The Newhaven Fishwives Choir has made the costume famous throughout the world and it is also seen in its full splendour at the annual Fishermen's Walk when rules of 'correct' costume are carefully observed.

The working clothes of the thousands of fishermen who toiled around the Scottish coast might appear uniform to the casual observer. But to the fisherfolk themselves, tiny details would often identify the district to which the wearer belonged.

Mary Murray has given us an excellent description of the clothing worn by the fishermen of the East Neuk of Fife, but which could well apply to the dress of the Scottish fishermen in general during the early years of this century. I am indebted to her for the following details.

Over a grey flannel shirt, the collarless neck of which was traditionally bound with a twilled material called 'Turkey Red', a long sleeved dark wincey shirt was worn. This was usually lined with smooth white cotton. The hand-knitted long drawers were almost invariably of a colour known as 'Shetland Grey', although the wool was not Shetland. But some of the older men wore drawers made of plaiding material which were fastened below the knee with tapes.

Dark brown woollen cloth Kersey breeks were normally worn as working trousers and made by local tailors.

The most distinctive garment in the fisherman's everyday wear, the Guernsey, Mary Murray describes as follows:

Until the beginning of the Second World War the guernsey was always navy blue in colour, and almost invariably knitted from Seafield wool which kept its colour in spite of sea water and many washings, for a guernsey could last for years, going down the scale from a Saturday Nicht guernsey to a through-the-week guernsey and finally to a sea guernsey, by which time it had probably been half sleeved, had its neck reknitted and its lower edge replaced.

The patterned shoulder-bar on these strong close-knitted garments was a feature of the Fife guernseys, and there were many traditional patterns of 'Marriage Lines' and 'Tree of Life' in addition to ropes, anchors and diamonds. New designs were frequently introduced but the guernsey patterns were 'chief among the indications of a man's home port, not so much because of some inherent tradition as because the women of the different ports had their own favourite patterns as a matter of choice and local taste.'

A touch of style was added by the muffler, or 'neepyin' which was worn round the neck, just showing above the guernsey. Made of pure silk, it was either plain black or a small check pattern.

At sea, a short canvas pull-over was worn. It took its name, 'Barket Jumper', from its bark-like colour. But whilst working with the fish, a heavy yellow oilskin over-garment reaching down to the calf was the main protection. It was known as a 'Dauper'.

The 'Sea Hat' was similar in shape to a pith sun-helmet, but it was made from heavy tarred oilskin and the brim extended a considerable distance behind the neck. The headdress which we know as a 'Sou' Western' was a soft oilskin hat with ear-flaps to which were attached cords for fastening under the chin, and it was particularly useful in a gale.

It has been said that the body of a drowned fisherman could often be more readily identified by the pattern of his knitted guernsey or 'gansey', than by his face. It has also been suggested that the type of local sea-shore had some influence on the ornamentation of these garments. Where the boats had to be carried down open beaches there tended to be heavier ornamentation on the shoulders. This protection was not required by fishermen working from harbours.

Young women sometimes knitted special guernseys for their future husbands, but this was more usually the case in the making of jerseys. The latter were finer, thinner and more closely knitted.

The remote island of Fair Isle, lying between the North Sea and the Atlantic has given its name to knitting patterns which are famous throughout the world. The origins of these highly individual designs have been suggested as Indian or even ancient Egyptian. But the most popular theory is that they were introduced to the island by Spanish sailors from *El Gran Griffon*, an Armada ship wrecked there in 1588. I find this difficult to accept and prefer the suggestion that the Fair Isle patterns were introduced by the Norsemen.

There are said to be over 150 designs including 'ancient religious and national symbols intertwined with various bands of delicate patterning'. It is frequently stated that Fair Isle's highly distinctive form of multicoloured knitting is based on a style known as the 'Armada Cross', in contrast to the Scandinavian styles of Orkney and Shetland. The latter are also said to have been originally knitted from natural-coloured wool.

The wool of these northern island jerseys was particularly fine and was advertised as the 'softest sheep's wool in the world'. In the early days it was teased out and then oiled with fish-oil before spinning.

The island of Fair Isle was fortunate in having a variety of flowers and lichens from which organic dyes could be made and which produced many soft and pleasing shades. This also applied to the Shetland Islands where the standard of knitting was particularly fine. Many lace-knitted shawls and christening robes are now regarded as family heirlooms, and some very fine specimens are exhibited in Scottish museums. It might be said that many of these most delicately knitted garments were the result of skills originally acquired by the young women who made woollens for their fishermen families and sweethearts.

The development of this craft to a cottage industry selling its products outside the islands quickly brought prosperity to people who had known great poverty for centuries. By the middle of the nineteenth century the influx of tourists into the Highlands was increasing rapidly and the exclusive knitwear of the islands was fetching high prices. By the end of the century Fair Isle jerseys, jumpers and cardigans were highly fashionable, and when the Prince of Wales began to wear them in the 1920s, they became a 'rage' and the patterns were widely imitated. Their popularity has continued ever since.

Salmon fishing in Scotland has been of major importance since prehistoric times, much of it being carried out in estuaries and rivers by net fishermen without the use of boats. The long wading boots which they had to wear in these cold waters were adopted by sporting anglers in the early nineteenth century and one particular pair became a little-known item in the history of Scottish costume.

On 28 September 1837, Sir Walter Scott wrote a letter to John Younger, poet and shoemaker and renowned Tweed angler, thus:

Sir Walter Scott wishes to have a pair of strong Fishing Boots made, to come half way up the thigh – hob nails at the bottom – the sole of Sir W. Scott's boots and they are *very large ones* measure twelve inches in length and 3 and $\frac{3}{4}$ in width – Sir W. S. being upwards of 6 feet they must be made very long. If Mr Y. can make without further measurements so much the better.

In his reply, Younger pointed out that there were long straps inside the boots which were fastened around the knees and that the leather used throughout had been thoroughly greased with sheepsuet and beeswax. No specimens of these early waders seem to have survived.

11

◆

Medieval Highland Warriors

O<small>N THE</small> mainland and islands of the west of Scotland there is a fine collection of effigial monuments bearing over 150 human figures, many of them wearing fourteenth- to sixteenth-century armour and carrying arms. Unfortunately the valuable information which they provide has been misinterpreted in the past, mainly by writers seeking to support their theories regarding the antiquity of 'Highland dress'.

But this wishful thinking had also been applied to an even earlier period. In the section of his book headed 'The Féileadh Beag' – the little kilt – J. G. Mackay wrote:

> The sculptured stones of Scotland give clear and decided evidence of the great antiquity of the dress, and their period may be said to extend from the sixth to the ninth century. There is one at Dupplin, in Perthshire, Forres in Morayshire, and Nigg in Ross-shire, each representing figures in the Highland dress.

It takes a great deal of imagination to describe the costume of the Picts as the kilt.

Mackay may have copied the opinion of W. F. Skene who wrote that the date of the Dupplin Cross could 'be fixed to have been towards the end of the ninth century', and stated that on it there were 'a number of figures represented in the Highland garb. . . .' So even the Historiographer Royal for Scotland saw spear-carrying Picts as significant figures in the history of Scottish national dress.

The ninth-century carved slab from Dull in Perthshire, now in the National Museum of Antiquities of Scotland, shows three Pictish foot soldiers and two horsemen in the normal dress of the period portrayed on many such stones. But to J. G. Mackay it 'represents several figures in the Highland dress'.

James A. Robertson had little doubt about his opinions and entitled his book *Concise Historical Proofs respecting the Gael of Alban*, published in 1866. He embellished the binding with what he described as 'the most faithful representation of the ancient Highlander's dress that can be given to the reader.' His source is the Pictish stone from Dull and his 'faithful representation' he assures us is 'a fac-simile of the countenance, bonnet, and shield of one of the figures thereon.' Both the stone and Robertson's book can be examined in the National Museum and it will be seen that there is little evidence of a 'fac-simile'.

This wish to see the Scottish costume of the Dark Ages as 'Highland dress' met with

168

the approval of those who thought of the subject as 'romantic'. And the same attitude was applied by some of the popular writers when they described the dress and armour to be seen on the medieval monumental sculptures of the Western Highlands and Islands.

One of McIan's popular but highly fanciful pictures purports to show MacDonald of the Isles in the costume of a medieval Highland warrior. It is described by James Logan as a 'habergeon, or shirt of mail . . . the usual defensive armour of the Highlanders, who continued its use until a late period. . . .' Underneath this he wears a 'leather doublet' and as a foundation garment, a pair of combinations in MacDonald tartan!

Several other writers have described the defensive armour of these medieval sculptured figures as 'Highland dress'. This is almost certainly because they imagined them wearing some sort of kilt. The fact is that they wear a long padded sleeved coat, common to most fighting men during the middle ages. It is, however, because it is padded with vertical quilting that in some cases it has the appearance of a pleated kilt below the waist.

This simple protective coat was known as an acton or aketon, and it was worn in conjunction with a tippet or camail or pisane which was a mantle of mail protecting the neck and shoulders. On their heads they wear the bascinet or conical helmet. This battle dress is clearly seen on an effigy at Kilmory in Argyll (75).

75 *Monumental effigies of medieval warriors wearing pisane, action and bascinet. Kilmory, Argyll*

The warrior's costume varied in quality and decoration, and Miss M. E. M. Donaldson gives a condensed account of that worn by John, last Lord of the Isles, who died in 1498. It is taken from the *Red Book of Clanranald*:

First, Lord John wore a 'fine tunic, beautifully embroidered', then a 'silk jerkin, well fitting, highly embroidered, gusseted, corded, put on to guard him against dangers', next, a coat of mail, 'well meshed, light, of substantial steel, beautifully wrought, gold ornamented, with brilliant Danish gems.' Over this 'battle mail coat' was worn 'an encircling belt with good clasps made of bronze', and there was put over that 'an angular cape of fine material, pointed, buckled.' The crested helmet follows, with a long sword, and 'full military gloves, that they should be a protection to his hands against the impression of the white ivory hilt made by the force of many blows.' Last of all an axe is named.

There is a fine grave slab of the fourteenth century on Iona on which is sculptured a MacKinnon warrior wearing the pisane, acton and basinet. On his left arm he carries his heraldic shield and in his waist-belt a long sword with a lobated pommel. Also on Iona, at Abbey Kirk, is a delightful carving of two men carrying off a cow, followed by the protesting guidwife and her husband. The costume is interesting because it shows a quilted tunic possibly worn with trunks similar to the costume on the Macmillan Cross at Kilmory, Argyll, and the MacLeod monument in Harris. Steer and Bannerman describe this MacLeod chief as wearing 'a bascinet, an aventail and hauberk of mail, and two long undergarments, the lower of which reaches to the ankles'.

The historical importance of the study of costume is evident when we turn our attention to very similar medieval stone figure sculptures in Ireland. There are some 150, of which over a third show knights in armour. Of these, a small group are of particular importance to the history of Scottish dress in war. By their appearance, almost identical to the warriors of Argyll, they confirm the presence of the mercenaries from Scotland who played a major role in the resurgence of the native Irish element in the fourteenth century. Known as 'gallowglasses', they enabled north-west Ulster to remain independent until the mid-sixteenth century.

The contemporary sculptures of these Scottish warriors provide evidence of the stage of armour evolution which had been reached by the two countries concerned. Sir James Mann, former Keeper of the Tower of London Armouries, considered that these knights and squires of the sixteenth century were clad in a manner more akin to the fourteenth, with their pointed bascinets, aventails and habergeons of mail. In other words the defensive armour of the fighting men of Scotland and Ireland was archaic and therefore indicated the ancient modes of warfare prevalent in both countries.

At Roscommon Abbey in County Roscommon there is the late fifteenth-century tomb of Felim O'Connor, along the front of which are the carved figures of eight gallowglasses. They wear high pointed bascinets and their necks and shoulders are protected with pisanes. The main body defence is the mail habergeon with short sleeves and knee-length skirts split in front. Beneath this they wear the acton pleated longitudinally.

The swords which these warriors carry bear strong similarities to the Highland claymore. They have round or disc pommels beyond which the tang of the blade protrudes, down-sloping cross-guards terminating in finials of the Scottish quatrefoil

76 *Effigy of an Irish medieval warrior (County Galway). Under his coat of mail he wears the pleated acton often misinterpreted as an early form of kilt*

type. One of the figures is armed with an axe, the favourite weapon of the ancient Irish, perhaps owing its origin to the Vikings. Although generally referred to by the Irish as a 'sparth', it later became known as a 'gallowglass axe'.

At Dungiven in County Derry there is another group of gallowglasses carved on a late fifteenth-century tomb front. They are wearing 'jacks', or what have been described as 'cotes of fence', quilted vertically like the acton. But again we find a link with Scotland as these coats were deeply skirted and, for that reason, were known as 'side Jacks', and in Irish *cotúns*. This style of acton worn by the Scots had nothing whatever to do with the plaid or the kilt, but some latter-day writers could not resist referring to it as 'kilt-like' (*76*).

12

◆

Scottish Military Uniform

Scotland is fortunate in having a fine United Services Museum with an extensive collection of uniforms and a comprehensive library. The history of Scottish military uniforms can also be found described in a number of books on the subject and in regimental histories. My intention here is merely to describe certain aspects of military dress which are appropriate to the history of Scottish costume in general.

The close association between the civilian and military styles of Highland dress is such that a study of both is essential to an understanding of either. Several authorities on the subject have claimed that the Highland costume would not have survived in civilian form had the Highland regiments not been raised and uniformed in elements of their native dress. Certainly during the time when the costume was proscribed, from 1746 until 1783, the only legal form in which it could be seen was when it was worn by the armed forces.

In 1725, six Independent Companies were raised in the Highlands, and then in 1739 formed into a regiment which became the Royal Highland Regiment or Black Watch. They were dressed in the belted plaid, but in order to conform with the other regiments of the British Army, they wore a red coat cut away at the skirts to allow for the voluminous folds of the belted plaid. The other distinctive Highland features of the uniform were the small round blue bonnet, cloth hose and the small leather purse or sporran (77).

The regimental tartan was known as the 'Black Watch', 'Government', or even just 'military' sett or pattern. When other regiments were raised they distinguished their tartans by adding a line of a different colour to the basic dark green and blue military sett.

In 1743, G. Bickham published a print entitled 'The Scottish Highlander' which shows a private soldier of the Blach Watch wearing the Highland bonnet, belted plaid, sporran, tartan hose and Highland weapons. Hundreds of prints showing the dress of the Highland regiments were published from then on, and an examination of these clearly illustrates the way in which civilian costume followed the changing styles of the army uniforms (78–81).

By about 1810 the great belted plaid had been replaced in the army by the little kilt. This meant that the red coat no longer had to be altered to allow for the bulk of the plaid material and the standard jacket worn by other regiments was adopted.

One of the most amusing episodes in the history of Highland military uniform happened in 1815 when the Allies occupied Paris after the victory of Waterloo. The French were fascinated by the appearance of the Highlanders strolling along the boulevards and soon the print and caricature sellers were doing a tremendous trade in comic and serious illustrations of the kilted troops. Amongst the Scotsmen who were visiting Paris at the time was the Edinburgh advocate, James Simpson, who describes a visit to the Opera:

In one general dance four of the performers were elegantly dressed as Highland soldiers: the latter much excited the Parisians. Their entré was loudly applauded, and the exact imitation of their dress occasioned much mirth. '*Vive les Écossais!*' was the cry. It is pleasing to see how much these brave men make friends even of their enemies.

77 *Highland soldier of the 42nd Regiment, 1742, wearing a belted plaid*

OPPOSITE **78** *Engraving by Van der Gucht, c. 1743, showing Highland military uniform at that time*

79 *'Highland Soldiers' from Francis Grose's* Military Antiquities, *1801. Copied from one of Van der Gucht's series of prints (c. 1743)*

80 *A Highland piper, soldier and drummer of the early 1740s, drawn by J. S. Miller, but based on earlier British prints*

Lieutenant. *Lieute nant.* *Schottische Officiers Frau.* *Femme d'un Offici er Ecossois.* *Provian Valet des P*

81 *Highland Lieutenant with his wife and 'valet' from a set of German engravings dated 1743. Highland troops fought in the British Army during the War of Austrian succession*

The French ladies saw in the Highland dress an opportunity to introduce a new style in their fashionable costume. Tartan dresses and even feather bonnets soon became the rage *(82)*.

The French military prints of the occupying troops illustrate an interesting aspect of costume evidence. They tell us very clearly what the attitudes of the conquered were to the various nationalities of their conquerors. Whereas the troops of almost all the other nations serving in the Allied Army are scathingly caricatured, the Highlanders are portrayed in an amusing or natural manner *(83)*.

During the period between the battle of Waterloo and the outbreak of the Crimean War, the uniforms of the Highland regiments became so cumbersome and ornate that they must have been highly uncomfortable *(84)*. And it was at this time that the civilian Highland dress – now a national costume – copied the military style and reached a peak of romantic elaboration.

Two particular items of wear became particularly ostentatious – the sporran and the dirk. The early uniform of the Black Watch included the small practical leather sporran worn during the first half of the eighteenth century. But by the 1790s the function of the sporran was beginning to disappear and it became more and more a

82 *Print published in Paris during the British occupation after Waterloo and illustrating the effect of Highland dress on Paris fashions of 1815*

decoration. By the 1820s it had become a large hairy affair embellished with gold bullion tassels and a top decorated with regimental badges, thistles, scrolls, etc. During the uniform peak period of the 1840s and 1850s, the sporran sometimes had an animal's head as a flap and had become so large that it extended from the waist-belt down to below the front edge of the kilt apron. The post-Crimean tunic worn by the Highland regiments had to have a space between the two front flaps in order to show the large sporran.

The dirk with its strong all-purpose blade was originally an essential weapon, but at a very early stage in the formation of the Highland corps it assumed a regimental pattern. By the 1820s it was highly decorated with cairngorms, silver or gilt devices and slung in an excessively decorated scabbard. Even the dirk blades became engraved with regimental badges and battle honours.

This decline from well designed functional sporrans and dirks to over-decorated ornaments in the army was matched closely in the evolution of the same items carried by civilians as part of their Highland dress. But one important Scottish item broke this rule of imitation – the bonnet.

Until about 1790 the small circular bonnets worn by civilians and soldiers were

83 *The judge points out a bill ordering the Scots to 'Porter les culottes', but Donald replies that he and his friends do so. Print published in Paris, 1815*

almost identical. Originally of plain blue cloth, they later had red, green and white dicing. But at this stage, whereas the military head-dress developed in an extraordinary way, the civilians continued to wear the small simple form.

The dicing of the military bonnet has been the subject of much argument. One school of thought insisted that it represented the 'fesse-chequey' in the arms of the House of Stewart, whilst their opponents argued that the origin was much more practical. They claimed that the pattern was the result of lacing a ribbon through vertical slits in the head-band and tightening it so that the bonnet was a close fit. I have never seen a bonnet with these multiple slits, and I describe the method of tightening in the chapter dealing with civilian bonnets.

The dicing of the bonnet was woven in a variety of colours and an interesting survival is the small red and white pattern worn by the Argyll and Sutherland Highlanders up to modern times. This is probably derived from the similar dicing worn by the Sutherland Fencibles, the predecessors of the regiment, in 1799.

A water-colour drawing by Edward Dayes showing a Highland officer of 1790 provides the clue to the development from the small bonnet to the huge mass of

84 *Photograph of Quarter Master Sergeant Gardiner, 42nd Highlanders, taken in 1856. In 1858 he received the Victoria Cross*

feathers worn by the regiments 50 years later. On the left-hand side of the 1790 bonnet we see a large bunch of black feathers fastened to the broad diced band with a black cockade having a button in the centre. All regiments did not, however, wear ostrich feathers; some adopted a tuft of bearskin, probably as it was more economical. One regiment, raised in 1794, used an imitation of feathers made of worsted which their colonel declared was cheaper and 'much superior in richness and appearance to real feathers, much more durable, and easily kept in order.'

Hackle plumes in different colours to display regimental and company distinctions were then worn above the cockade, and finally a bonnet badge was added. The feathers increased in size and number until by the time of the Napoleonic Campaigns the bonnet had disappeared beneath them. In the 1840s the bonnet was 16 inches high.

The so-called 'fox-tails' which hung down over the right ear differed in number. Most regiments wore five, but the Black Watch wore four and the Argyll and Sutherland Highlanders six. During the Peninsular and Waterloo periods a detachable peak was worn, and for a number of years troops carried an oilskin cover which could be fitted over the bonnet in bad weather.

Despite what romantic writers had to say, the feathered bonnet was not particularly popular with all ranks. Admittedly it was a favourite place for keeping the fragile clay pipe, and the space behind the tails was used for keeping small items to such an extent that it was known as the 'Craw's Nest'.

When the Government suggested the abolition of the feathered bonnet in the winter of 1883, an outcry was raised by senior officers. In January 1884, the *Standard* published a letter describing it as light, comfortable and easy to wear, but its main advantage was that it gave height to the figure 'which the kilt in nine cases out of ten tends to dwarf and broaden'.

On 9 February, the same paper published a letter from a 'Lieutenant-Colonel, late 93rd Highlanders', who declared that 'the feather bonnet is *a most useful* head-dress . . . and *the most economical* head-dress in the army'. This was followed by a letter signed 'Highlander' who gave a graphic account of the large number of feathered bonnets swept by the great gale of 1850 into the ditches around the heights of Balaclava. However he 'saw those bonnets shortly afterwards recovered, rinsed and dried and restored completely to their normal condition'.

The opposite point of view was published in 1905, when it was reported that the Glasgow Volunteer regiment were to wear flat bonnets instead of the feathered bonnets of the regular Highland regiments. The anonymous writer described the 'funeral plumes' as:

. . . the most extraordinary and uncomfortable military 'confection' that has come down to us from the hand of last century military milliners. They thought poor dears! they had discovered a Highland bonnet, instead of which they produced a bird-cage whose cost and inconvenience are only its most obvious defects.

There was a great variety of bonnets worn by the Scottish regiments including Hummle Bonnets, Kilmarnock Bonnets, Tam o' Shanters, Glengarries, etc., but details of these can be found in regimental records. What is not generally known is the problem of meeting the demand faced by the suppliers. The following extracts from the

85 *A fine coloured drawing by J. Ferguson showing the uniform of the Highland regiments in 1866*

manuscripts in my collection may therefore be of interest. They are all from the correspondence of William Wilson & Sons of Bannockburn, who had the bonnets made by James McLean of Kilmarnock and then supplied them to the regiments.

In June 1795 Wilson ordered 'Two Hundred dozen Blue Caps' but McLean wrote that they were very scarce 'owing to so many Highland Bonnets being wanted at present'. He was trying to buy some in at seven shillings a dozen.

In June 1800 McLean acknowledged an order for 67 bonnets for Volunteers, but wrote to Wilson that he was 'at a loss to know the Colour that is wanted in the dice' but that he would send them 'of the Common dice, say red, green & White.'

Between September 1799 and April 1800 Wilson purchased over 300 dozen bonnets. They also purchased large quantities of cockades from 'Isiah Maxton' of Edinburgh.

There are also a large number of letters regarding the supply of bonnets to regiments overseas – including complaints. On 10 January 1810, Major Dale of the 93rd wrote from the Cape of Good Hope; 'The bonnets sent last are not the Regimental Pattern . . . the 93 Regl Bonnets are Three Rows of plain Red & White dice *without any green* whatever'. Wilson also sent out hose and garters to the regiment.

In 1813, Officers' red and white diced bonnets cost 38/- a dozen, Sergeants 28/- a dozen, and Privates 21/- a dozen.

In 1829 the Colonel of the 92nd Highland Regiment wrote that the feathered bonnet was 'undoubtedly the most becoming soldier's head-dress in Europe and consequently requiring great attention on the part of the wearers'. Apart from appearance there was a very practical reason why the bonnet should be correctly worn, and this was explained in a Regimental Order of the Gordon Highlanders dated 1829:

> The centre ostrich fox-tail feathers to hang over the right ear, two to the front and two to the rear of them, none to hang lower than the line of the right eye, so that the soldier can take aim without having his feathers burnt by the priming, or his vision disturbed by their fluttering in his eyes.

The other main item of Scottish costume worn by soldier and civilian alike was the tartan trousers or 'trews'. Sir John Sinclair's Fencibles wore tartan trousers in imitation of the old genuine trews which covered the feet as well as the legs, and this footless style was to be continued by the military.

The uniforms of the Scottish corps were very inconsistent throughout their history and some of the regiments, despite the fact that they were 'Highland', wore ordinary infantry uniform for part of their career. Three Highland regiments were dressed in the 'trews', as they were now officially known, between 1824 and 1864 (*85, 86*).

Sir Herbert Maxwell, writing in 1918, considered that the uniform of the Lowland Scottish infantry regiments was entirely unsatisfactory both in the historic and aesthetic senses. In 1881 they were all, except the Scots Guards, dressed in Highland doublets and tartan trews. But Maxwell, who had served as Honorary Lieutenant-Colonel of the 3rd Royal Scots Fusiliers, felt that if the change to a form of Highland uniform had to be made, then the decision should have been to go the whole way and adopt the kilt. Both trews and kilt were inappropriate to Lowland regiments, but there they were and the plain course seemed to be 'to carry the change a step further, acknowledging the Highland dress as the national military costume, and making it the uniform of all the Lowland regiments. . . .' These Lowland regiments stood at a disadvantage in relation to the Highland regiments 'owing entirely to the superior picturesqueness, and subsequent popularity of the kilt.'

The military 'reforms' of 1881 aroused a highly emotive reaction from Scottish civilians and help to underline the particular agitation which resulted from any tampering with the tartan. Such was the change in significance which had taken place within a century from a localised costume to a national emblem. Writing in 1881, McIntyre North described the tartans worn by the Highland regiments as 'sanctified in the life's blood of their gallent wearers'. The proposed reforms were an insult 'worthy of the most contemptible conglomeration of cheese-paring negatives that ever the madness of a nation dignified with the *name* of Government.'

Perhaps the most widespread conception of Scottish national dress is the result of the appearance of pipers and pipe bands throughout the world. The sight and sound of the pipes and drums of a Highland regiment is something not easily forgotten. And yet, although pipers played on the field of battle long before the regular regiments were raised, it was not until 1854 that pipers became official members of the Highland regiments. Until then, the Colonel of the regiment normally paid for his pipers, or they were chosen on the muster roll as 'drummers'.

The armies of many nations have dressed their bands in highly colourful uniforms

86 *Sergeant, private and officer, 72nd Highlanders, 1825, in Review Order, wearing tartan trousers*

and the Scottish regiments were no exception. The earliest distinction was probably the adoption of a brighter tartan and particularly one having a considerable amount of red in its pattern.

The uniform of the piper changed constantly throughout the life of the regiment, as described by Major MacKay Scobie. His regiment, the 1st Battalion Seaforth Highlanders (old 72nd) was raised in 1778 with ten companies each having a piper paid for by the company commander. These pipers wore the same uniform as the rank and file, but when the regiment adopted the trews in 1824, the pipers were dressed in the kilt. And then, in 1850, a green doublet and blue Glengarry bonnet were taken into wear. In 1882 the tartan was changed from Stuart to Mackenzie. During this period further distinction was given to the pipers by the use of larger belts, badges and buckles, different coloured hackle plumes and elaborate dirks.

Centenaries were sometimes marked by changing the tartan of the pipers. In 1933 the Royal Scots were granted the right to use the Royal Stuart tartan for their pipers in honour of their Tercentenary. In 1928 the Royal Scots Fusiliers pipers were granted the Dress Erskine tartan to commemorate their 250th anniversary.

The history of regimental tartans starts off with an argument as to what tartan was worn by the Independent Companies of 1725. Whatever the truth of the matter is, when these Companies were regimented as the 'Black Watch' in 1739, they wore the 'Universal', 'Government' or 'Black Watch' tartan. This was a dark blue and green sett which was also used by many of the other Highland corps raised at this period. In certain cases a narrow line or lines of a different colour, that of the facings of the jacket, were superimposed on the Government pattern by the regiment.

When the 4th Duke of Gordon raised a regiment in 1793, he had no clan tartan, being a member of a Lowland family. The Duchess, however, took a considerable interest in tartans and did not wish to see her husband's fencibles dressed in the Government pattern. She therefore requested William Forsyth, a clothing agent in Huntly to supply patterns for a new tartan. Forsyth applied to William Wilson of Bannockburn, who merely added a yellow line to the Government sett and this was adopted for the regiment and later became the Gordon clan tartan.

The Mackenzie tartan had a somewhat similar origin. In 1778, John Mackenzie, Lord Macleod, raised a regiment which adopted the Government pattern with red and buff lines superimposed on it, but these were later changed to red and white lines. When this tartan was supplied to the regiment by William Wilson, it was referred to by the regiment's number, 'The 78th Regimental Tartan'. But the same sett was used by the 71st Regiment, and when William Wilson supplied it to them it was called 'The 71st Tartan'. It soon became popular with civilians and was sold to them by Wilson as 'The Mackenzie Tartan'.

The correspondence of William Wilson and Son shows that they had great difficulties in supplying the Highland regiments, particularly when they were abroad on active service. Tartans often arrived damaged by sea-water and there were many complaints about faulty colours and poor quality cloth. This was particularly the case during the great build up of regiments in the early 1800s when the demand was so great that Wilson had to extend his premises with a large building to be known later as the 'Waterloo Mill'.

The regiments were constantly in arrears and in 1808 Wilson wrote in desperation to 'Brigr. Genl. Craufurd of the 91st Regt. Lord Wellingtons Army Portugal' asking if he could be of any service in having the account settled. In January there was outstanding a payment for 2,058 yards of 'Hose Tartan'.

During the war in the Crimea the demand for tartan was again very great. In addition to supplying the regiments abroad, Wilson had to provide for the large numbers of recruits needing clothing. In December 1854, the Quartermaster of the 72nd Regiment Depot at Limerick wrote in desperation for 700 yards of calico to line the trews and 1,00 yards of tartan: 'I must also beg to inform you that recruits are coming up very fast and our tartan is very nearly done, in fact we have only in store what would make about 54 pairs of Trews'.

Because of the demand at this period a lot of incorrect tartan was manufactured. In November 1855, two faulty specimens were returned to Wilson from the 72nd with the complaint that 'in one you will see that the pattern or dice is misplaced, in the other that the stripes are of such different distances apart, that it is impossible to cut the trews as they ought to be, i.e. with all the stripes running all ways exactly to match.' Wilson replied admitting 'that there are irregularities with weaving', but agreed that it was the fault of his workmen.

It has been said that up to 1872 all the tartan issued to the rank and file of the Highland regiments was of the old 'hard' material which often cut the men's thighs and knees, especially in cold or wet weather. In that year, Queen Victoria is believed to have noticed this plight whilst inspecting a Guard of Honour in the Highlands, and as a result the army were issued with soft tartan material thereafter. The Wilson correspondence shows that this is not so. In May 1853, the officer commanding the depot of the 72nd Highlanders ordered from them '1,100 yards Privates Soft Tartans and 80 yards Serjeants Soft Tatran', and there are several other orders for 'Soft Tartan' to be supplied to a number of Highland regiments at that time.

The association between military and civilian Highland dress can still be seen in certain styles of evening dress jackets worn today. Shoulder straps or cords, military style buttons and cuffs have all been adopted for doublets and coatees. So too, but to a lesser extent, can they be seen incorporated in day wear. Unlike the military uniforms, there are no regulations which govern civilian Highland dress which should be worn according to the dictates of good taste.

There is one interesting episode in the history of Scottish military uniform which illustrates certain attitudes towards Highland and Lowland traditional costume. This was the attempt by the Duke of Kent, Queen Victoria's father, to 'tartan' the oldest regiment of the British line – the Royal Scots.

In 1801, he was appointed Colonel of the Regiment and immediately displayed a keen concern in the dress of his corps. His first effort was to have the Highland dress adopted and the 'Strathearn' tartan worn, but he received a reply from the Commander-in-Chief observing that as the Royals were always a Lowland regiment he could not conceive that it would be advisable for them to adopt the dress and appointments of a Highland one.

During 1810, the Duke again made an attempt to introduce tartan. This time he applied to have a diced or tartan band, worn round the chaco head-dress. The C-in-C

87 *The Atholl Highlanders on parade at Blair Castle, 1890. From a painting by W. Skeoch Cumming*

turned down the proposal as he 'could not recommend any alteration in the present dress of so distinguished a regiment'.

Finally in 1813 he submitted a pattern tartan plaid which he proposed should be worn by the Royal Scots, but once more his proposal was rejected.

13

◆

The Royal Company of Archers

'THE ROYAL COMPANY OF ARCHERS' was formally founded in 1676, and in 1822 became 'The King's Body Guard for Scotland'. Their highly original and picturesque uniforms are a particular feature of the Royal Visits to Scotland and other great events which are held in the capital (*88*).

The historical evidence of their dress is preserved in a very fine collection of portraits, medals and costume in the headquarters at Archers' Hall, Edinburgh. The portraits are particularly well described by Haswell Miller in Ian Hay's *History* of the Royal Company.

Their first Captain-General was a Highlander, the Marquis of Atholl, and from an early date tartan was a conspicuous element of the dress. Although their original distinguishing feature was merely the 'Company's Seal and Arms on their Hatts or Bonnets', the Company's Council decreed that the 'Theasaurer Shall provide him a Coat of green colour, with a sash to wear about his weast, and a buss of white Ribbons on his shoulder'. Green breeches and a white vest were approved about this time but there is no mention of any form of regulation dress.

By the beginning of the eighteenth century extremely striking costumes – even by the standards of that period – were being worn. The Archers do not seem to have been controlled by strict dress regulations, and even a certain amount of individual initiative appears to have been encouraged. The Council's records of 1713 describe the dress as follows:

Stuart tartan coat lined with fine white shalloon; white stockings, white linen bow-case, with green worsted bob; and a blue bonnet, with a St. Andrew and a coque of white and green ribbons.

Officers to be allowed to trim or adorn their habits as they think proper, according to their ranks.

This description agrees fairly closely with the earliest portrait painted about 1700 by John de Ryck (1640–1702). It shows an unidentified officer wearing a tartan coat of a small reddish sett, with a black collar and cuffs edged with wide bands of silver lace. The widely slashed sleeves are similarly edged on the seams. His blue velvet bonnet is ornamented with a silver tassel and a silver and gold badge below a black and white cockade. It has been suggested that the substitution of black for the proper green may imply a sympathy for the House of Hanover, but I doubt this. It could be easily explained as an error on the part of the artist about whom we know very little, although this waist-length portrait is painted with great care.

It is interesting to compare the portrait with another which is signed and dated 1715, and which Haswell Miller describes as the 'more or less contemporary and oddly mannered picture by R. Waitt'. The subject of this full-length portrait is Archibald Burnet of Carlops, who was admitted to the Royal Company in 1708. He wears a blue bonnet with badge, and the green and white cockade. His long tartan coat has a collar and cuffs also of tartan, in contrast to the black velvet shown in the Ryck portrait. He also wears short tartan breeches over white hose which come to above the knee.

Although the tartan of the 1713 uniform is described by the Council as 'Stuart', an examination of both the Ryck and the Waitt rendering of it shows considerable differences in the sett. Nor do they agree with the sett of two actual costumes of the period, one of which is preserved in Archers' Hall, and the other at Wemyss Castle.

This latter costume is very similar to that of the splendid portrait in Archers' Hall believed to show James Wemyss, 5th Earl of Wemyss, who was Captain-General of the Royal Company from 1743 to 1756. The painting has been attributed to Allan Ramsay (*colour plate 4*). Although a date of c. 1715 is suggested it probably belongs to the 1740s.

This is undoubtedly one of the finest portrayals of Scottish costume and it consists of a large blue bonnet with the St Andrew badge over the cockade surmounted by three ostrich feathers, a tartan coat copiously embellished with silver lace and heavy fringe, and tartan breeches.

Here then we have three portraits and two costumes all with tartan of a similar nature, and a description (1713) which describes it as 'Stuart'. The Earl of Wemyss was a confirmed Jacobite as were other members of the Royal Company, which however, as a body, never displayed political sympathy and eventually expressed complete loyalty to the Crown. Ian Hay rightly points out that the Royal Company 'maintained a discreet impassivity in the matter, going so far in 1716 as to cancel the shooting fixtures for the Edinburgh and Musselburgh Arrows.'

Another, and highly surprising illustration of Archers' costume adds to the enigma of Scottish costume during the Jacobite period. This is a portrait of none other than the future King George the Third, painted in 1746, by Barthélémy du Pan. The Hanoverian prince holds a bow and arrow and wears an elaborate blue bonnet with the Archers' badge prominently shown, a long tartan coat with silver lace and fringes, and tartan breeches.

Here then is a picture painted at the command of Frederick, Prince of Wales, in the year of Culloden, showing the future king wearing a style of costume which, in that same year, was to be proscribed in the Highlands as a symbol of rebellion.

In the *Caledonian Mercury* of July 1732, a description of the Archers' dress avoids any suggestion that it was 'Highland' or even 'Scottish', but as follows: 'Antique Roman dress made of tartan, trimmed with green silk fringes; blue bonnet, trimmed with green and white ribbons, badge of St Andrew in front. Bows, swords etc. hung with white and green ribbons. Officers' dress same form and figure, but laid over with silver lace.'

There are few portraits of Archers painted during the second half of the eighteenth century but one in particular, although it does not show their dress, is of great interest to the student of sporting costume. It was painted in 1768 and shows William St Clair of Roslin who was a President of the Royal Company's Council, in the dress of the Honourable Company of Edinburgh Golfers. He wears a wide flat blue bonnet with a red binding, a red coat and waistcoat of the period, black breeches, white stockings and white gloves.

In 1789 the Council introduced a new uniform described as follows:

Common Uniform for all Ranks; A short frock, short lapelled, yellow gilt metal buttons, having struck or engraved thereon a royal crown, pair of cross-arrows and a thistle below. White cloth waistcoat and breeches, small buttons, same pattern as on the frock. White silk stockings.

Shooting Uniform for the Members. A worsted tartan short jacket, the tartan same pattern as the 42nd Regiment, green velvet capes, shoulder-straps and wings, trimmed with fringe corresponding to the frogs; the front of the jacket-pockets ornamented with frogs of blue, green and white silk. Sleeves and pockets slashed. Waistcoat, breeches and stockings, the same as the common uniform, with small black cloth half-gaiters. Blue worsted bonnet, bordered with green and white ribbon; a painted Saint Andrew, crown and thistle, in front, handsome black feathers on left side; insertion of the feathers covered with a cockade of green and white ribbon, tuft in the middle. Cross white leather belts for hanging a green tassel on the right, and green leather quiver on the left side. The belts fastened with a gilt plate, on which is engraved the arms of the Royal Company.

There is a proviso to the effect that the Captain-General was permitted to 'fix every part of his own dress', although the other general officers were regulated to 'Handsome epaulets, frogs, blue and green silk and silver. Bonnets blue velvet, with a St Andrew &c embroidered in front.' They were also to be distinguished by different colours of feathers in their bonnets.

It is this 1789 uniform which is shown in the full-length picture of Doctor Nathaniel Spens, painted by Sir Henry Raeburn in 1791.

In 1813, there were further changes. The bonnet was now to be chequered green, white and red with alterations in the badge and feathers. Minor changes were made to the coat, the white cross-belts were replaced by a plain patent waist belt, but the waistcoat, breeches and gaiters continued as formerly. The new uniform was worn by the Royal Company when they competed for the King's Prize in July 1813.

A 'dinner coat' was approved at this time and it was worn at balls and other social events. On such occasions the feathers were removed from the bonnets.

When King George IV made his state visit to Scotland in 1822, the Archers were very much in evidence. They became recognised as the only official King's Body Guard for Scotland and this provided the opportunity for another change of dress. Strangely enough there is little documentation regarding this change but it is said that Sir Walter Scott was responsible for the design, which was certainly 'Romantic', although perhaps slightly absurd. However, a Council Resolution of August 1822, refers the Archers to 'a proper uniform' to be seen at Hunter and Company, Princes Street.

There are many pictures of the 1822 uniform and several actual specimens have survived. The bonnet was made wider than ever before and surmounted with eagle feathers according to rank, one for a private, two for an officer and three for the Captain-General. An incongruous white ruff was worn up to the ears, and the tunic was once more slashed and also puffed out at the shoulders. Large leather gauntlets and a wide buff waist-belt were added. The rather clumsy short trousers showed red and white diced hose at the ankle. Both tunic and trousers were of 42nd tartan.

Many artists came to Edinburgh in 1822, and their records of the Archers range from the dignified gentlemen by Sir David Wilkie and Denis Dighton to the strange figures in tartan pantaloons drawn by Reinagle.

88 *The Royal Company of Archers' present day dress. Additional distinctions of rank are shown by the number of feathers worn in the bonnet*

In 1829, the Council appointed a committee to consider the introduction of certain changes in uniform, particularly the abolition of the tartan. The resulting report was rather extraordinary. The committee claimed that the original dress of the Royal Company was made of 'Border-green cloth' and that tartan had been 'merely introduced in the year 1745, to favour a political spirit and gratify the feelings of an unfortunate Prince.' Did they choose to ignore the evidence of their own records of 1713, the de Ryck and Waitt portraits, and the *Caledonian Mercury* of 1732?

Interestingly enough one of the earliest Scottish illustrations of tartan can be seen on a medal dated 1603. It is attached to the Musselburgh Arrow trophy and shows an archer wearing a tartan coat long before the Royal Company was formerly founded.

Nevertheless in 1829 the tartan was abandoned in favour of 'Border Green', and the correct use of the new uniform was taken very seriously. On one occasion an Archer who had won the coveted Saint Andrew Cross was disqualified as he had not been wearing the correct dress.

In 1834 Watson Gordon painted the 9th Earl of Dalhousie wearing the double-breasted coatee and holding in his left hand the Gold Stick of the Captain-General, which had been presented by King George IV. In the background of this picture we see two Archers wearing the ordinary Field Dress which was introduced in 1829, and which continued with slight modifications until the present day.

Although the Royal Company is not a military body, the distinctions between officers and the other members are quite pronounced in terms of their uniforms. The large eagle feathers worn in the bonnet are particularly noticeable as are the more splendid appointments of the senior officers. In 1863 the field or shooting uniform was slightly changed particularly in the style of head-dress and the abolition of shoulder straps which carried the officers badges. The latter were now transferred to the collar and a crimson cord was worn on the shoulder.

The dress of the Royal Company of Archers is unlike any other in the world, and it adds greatly to ceremonial spectacles in Scotland. Despite the expense which it imposes on the individual and its discomfort in certain weather conditions it continues to be worn with dignity and pride. The economic pressures of modern times are summarised by Ian Hay:

At the present time the dress of a member of the Royal Company consists, officially, of the familiar field uniform, Court uniform, and Mess uniform; to which in some cases must be added the undress shooting jacket, employed mainly in practice shooting. But Court uniform is seldom, if ever, seen today. The present tendency, however, towards greater simplicity in the Royal Company is no new thing; it began more than twenty years ago, and was greatly assisted by the avowed anxiety of King George V to cut down unnecessary expenditure and display in the increasingly difficult days of financial stringency following the industrial and economic slump of 1931.

14

♦

Highland Arms

THE HISTORY of Scotland unfolds against a background of external and internal warfare, and what is now accepted as the national dress perpetuates elements of this martial spirit. The arms and armament of the Highlander had many unique features which makes them of particular interest. However, of equal interest is their survival in association with the Highland dress into the present century. Indeed the majority of Highland portraits of Victorians show them carrying arms. In some cases the dirk only is worn but in others the weapons include a pair of pistols, a broad sword, the dirk and a powder horn. In addition the sword belt and waist belt are often heavily embellished with silver buckles and slides (*89*).

During the visit to Edinburgh of King George IV in 1822, there can have been only a very few amongst the hundreds wearing Highland dress who did not carry a weapon. Only the previous year Sir Walter Scott wrote: 'it is an ancient dress, a martial dress and a becoming dress.'

Whereas the ornamental use of Highland arms was widespread in the early nineteenth century, it was only a relatively short time since they had been used in warfare by large numbers of men who were not members of the official armed forces. The use of the sword, targe and dirk during the Rising of 1745 was a survival of a very ancient method of warfare. It is because of this late survival that we have so many fine examples of these characteristic arms (*90*).

Many of these weapons, targes and powder horns are works of art often decorated with delicacy and remarkable skill. But with the dawn of the nineteenth century and under the influence of the romantic revival there began a large production of ornamental and decorative 'weapons' to be worn with the latest styles of Highland dress. These costume weapons ranged from highly expensive dirks with ivory handles studded with semi-precious stones, golden or silver mounts and beautifully tooled scabbards, to vulgar monstrosities of crude workmanship with 'poached egg' cairngorms, which, had they all been genuine, would have razed that famous range of mountains to a plain.

We are only concerned here with those arms, and their associated items, which are characteristically Scottish, which means those used mainly by the Scottish Highlander.

Until now, the study of Scottish fighting weapons has been somewhat neglected with one outstanding exception. Charles Edward Whitelaw, a Glasgow architect, built up a splendid collection of Scottish arms which he studied throughout his life. Unfortunately, with the exception of a few monographs and *A Treatise on Scottish Hand Firearms*, he published very little and a vast amount of knowledge died with him.

193

89 *A modern Highland gentleman showing the survival of arms as part of the dress*

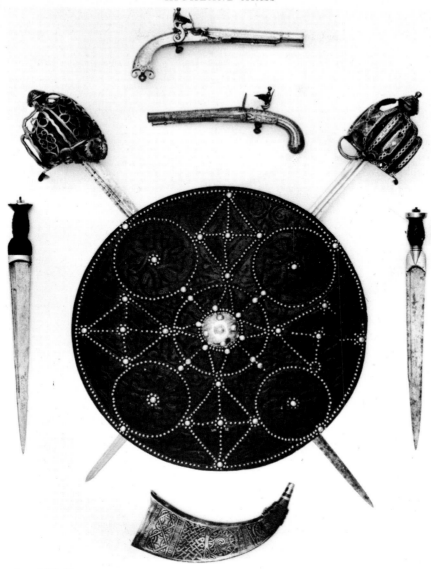

90 *A trophy of Highland arms*

However, a biographical dictionary of makers of firearms, edged weapons and armour working in Scotland from the fifteenth century to 1870, and based on Whitelaw's copious notes has recently been published under the title *Scottish Arms Makers*.

The weapons of the Highlanders varied greatly in quality. In September 1672, Denis de Repas, a monk turned arms-dealer, wrote that good arms in Scotland were 'very scarce and very much desired'. He therefore invested all the money he had in a cargo of arms from Holland which he imported into Scotland. He described their quality as 'indeed very fine' consisting of 'fusils of all sorts of size, pistols and mousquetons'. The deal took a month to negotiate and was finalised with a 'guft' to the Provost and Bailiffs of Edinburgh. Having achieved 'a very considerable advantage' on the sale of the arms, he invested the money in a load of 'Aberdeen stockings' which he shipped back to Holland, had them dyed and then sold them in Germany.

In 1724 General Wade was instructed by Royal Command to compile a report on the Highlanders. In it he has given an interesting account of their arms and also a brief but graphic description of their method of attack;

The Arms they make use of in War, are, a Musket, a Broad Sword and Target, a Pistol and a Dirk or Dagger, hanging by their side, with a Powder Horn and Pouch for their Ammunition. They form themselves into Bodies of unequal numbers according to the strength of their Clan or Tribe, which is Commanded by their Respective Superior or Chieftain. When in sight of the Enemy they endeavour to possess themselves of the highest Ground, believing they descend on them with greater force.

They generally give their fire at a distance, they lay down their Arms on the Ground and make a vigorous Attack with their Broad Swords, but if repulsed, seldom or never rally again. They dread engaging with the Cavalry and seldom venture to descend from the Mountains when apprehensive of being charged by them.

When that amiable traveller, Taylor the Water Poet, wrote his kindly account of a visit to Scotland in 1618, he described the weapons carried at a great hunt 'in the Brea of Marr' which he attended with a large assembly of nobility. 'Now their weapons are long bowes and forked arrowes, swords and targets, harquebusses, muskets, dirks, and Loquhabor-axes. With these armes I found many of them armed for the hunting.'

Thomas Morer, described as 'minister to St Ann's within Aldersgate', wrote his *Short Account of Scotland* 'when he was chaplin to a Scotch regiment. London, 1715.' His style of writing clearly indicates a man of character:

The quarrels and animosities between their great ones made it always necessary in elder times to be very well armed, and the custom continues to this day; so that you shall seldom see 'em, tho' only taking the air, without sword and dirk, which is a short dagger. In war, they had formerly bows and such kind of arrows as once entered the body could not be drawn out without tearing away the flesh with 'em; But now they carry muskets and other fire-arms; and when they are on the defensive part, they depend much on the targes or targets, which are shields of that form the Latines call by the name Clypeus, round and aquidistant from the center, and are made of the toughest wood they can get, lined within and covered without with skins, fenced with brass nails, and made so serviceable that no ordinary bullet, much less a sword, can penetrate to injure them or their masters, who have such an artificial way of twisting themselves within the compass of these shields, that 'tis almost a vain attempt for their enemy to seek to annoy 'em. And indeed they fight with too much odds, when they come so near us, because they not only have the protection of their bucklers, but are withal very expert at their swords, which consist of the best blades now in being, and were therefore much sought after by our officers and souldiers, who were very well furnished with 'em before wee (sic) left the High-lands.

This first-hand account is little known and seldom quoted but it contains a great deal of interesting information, such as the fact that the native sword blades were of a much better quality than the regular army issue. It was first published anonymously in 1702, and was described by Hume Brown as indubitably standing first in historic interest and value.

Morer's high regard for the targe seems to have been widely shared and Stuart Maxwell recounts a good story of a conflict between an English soldier and a Highlander engaged in combat at the battle of Killiecrankie; 'The Englishman understood the Back-sword very well, but the Scotchman received all the blows on his Target; and yet at the same time laid so hard at his Antagonist with his Broadsword that he cut him in two or three places; at which the Englishmen enraged, rather than discouraged, cried out to him; "You Dog, come out from behind the Door, and fight like a man".'

The everyday wearing of arms is remarked on by John Hume who wrote that the Highlanders 'always appeared like warriors . . . nay they went to church, with their broadswords and dirks; and in later times, with their muskets and pistols.'

Thomas Pennant visited Scotland in 1769, after the Disarming Act, and his account describes the effect of the Act and the change in Highland economy, on the use of arms;

Their antient arms were the *Lochaber* ax (sic), now used by none but the town-guard of *Edinburgh*; a tremendous weapon, better to be expressed by a figure than words.

The broadsword and target; with the last they covered themselves, with the first reached their enemy at a great distance. These were then antient weapons, as appears by *Tacitus*, but since the disarming act, are scarcely to be met with; partly owing to that, partly to the spirit of industry now rising among them, the Highlanders in a few years will scarce know the use of any weapon.

Bows and arrows were used in war as late as the middle of the last century, as I find in a manuscript life of *Sir Ewin Cameron*.

The *dirk* was a sort of Dagger stuck in the belt. I frequently saw this weapon in the shambles of *Inverness*, converted into a butcher's knife, being, like *Hudibras's* dagger

> *A serviceable dudgeon,*
> *Either for fighting or for drudging.*

The dirk was a weapon used by the antient *Caledonians*, for *Dio Cassius*, in his account of the expedition of *Severus*, mentions it under the name of *Pugio*.

The *Mattucashlash*, or arm-pit dagger, was worn there ready to be used on coming to close quarters. These, with a pistol stuck in the girdle, completely armed the Highlander.

The manner in which the Highlanders used their weapons has been narrated by a number of writers of the period. But there is one account which not only describes their battle tactics but also suggests the method whereby they might be defeated. In the Duke of Cumberland's Orderly Book there is an entry dated '12th January, 1745–46', which runs as follows;

The manner of the Highlanders' way of fighting, which there is nothing so easy to resist, if officers and men are not prepossessed with the lyes and accounts which are told of them. They commonly form their front rank of what they call their best men, or true Highlanders, the number of which being always but few. When they form in battalions, they commonly form four deep, and these Highlanders form the front of the four, the rest being Lowlanders and arrant scum. When these battalions come within a large musket shott, or three-score yards, this front rank gives their fire, and immediately throw down their firelocks and come down in a cluster with their swords and targets, making a noise and endeavouring to pierce the body or battalion before them, – becoming twelve or fourteen deep by the time they come up to the people they attack. The sure way to demolish them is, at three deep, to fire by ranks diagonally to the centre, where they come, the rear rank first, and even that rank not to fire till they are within ten or twelve paces; but if the fire is given at a distance, you probably will be broke, for you never get time to load a second cartridge, and if you give way, you may give your foot for dead, for they being without a firelock, or any load, no man with his arms, accoutrements, etc., can escape them, and they give no quarter; but if you will but observe the above directions, they are the most despicable enemy that are.

The Targe

The circular shield used by Bronze Age man in Scotland differed little from the Highland 'targe', 'tairge' or 'target'. From prehistoric times man relied on his shield for the defence of his life and possibly for this reason he frequently decorated it with all the skills available to him. The rectangular shields of the eighth-century warriors depicted on the sculptured stone of Birsay, in Orkney, are decorated with curvilinear designs. On the stone belonging to the same period at Aberlemno, in Angus, portraying Pictish warriors carrying shields, we see what could be claimed as forerunners of the targe. They are circular and embellished and strengthened with bosses, but are, however, convex in shape.

In the ninth century some of the Vikings who arrived in Scotland carried light circular wooden shields with metal bosses and handles, not far removed in design from the later Highland targe.

The real application of the word 'Targe', to identify the characteristic shield of the Scottish Highlander, belongs to the seventeenth century. By that time there are accounts in various records of targes 'of timber nails and hides' also of 'steill targets'. One of the earliest targes to survive to the present day is a very fine specimen bearing a shield of arms, the initials of the first Lord Reay, and the date '1626', all engraved on the flattened boss. It can be seen in the Hunterian Museum in Glasgow.

It was not until the early eighteenth century and the time of the 1715 Jacobite Rising that a significant number of targes were made, ensuring that enough survived to the present-day to be studied with a view to classification on stylistic grounds.

The strength of the wooden Highland targe lay in the use of cross-ply timber. Two sheets of fir or oak were placed one on top of the other and pegged together with the grain of one wood running at right angles to the other. They were then cut to a circular shape about 20 inches in diameter. The front was covered with leather which was almost always cow-hide, although the inner surface was frequently covered with goat-skin or deer-skin. There was usually a loop on this inner side through which the arm was thrust, and another loop which served as a hand grip.

Sometimes the central metal boss was fitted with a screw-hole into which a spike could be fitted, and an account published in 1753 describes a targe with a brass drinking cup, lined with horn which could be interchanged with the spike. It is interesting that whereas the spiked targe is occasionally illustrated, for instance in Morier's picture of Culloden, Jeremiah Davidson's picture of James Moray of Abercairney (*circa* 1739) and the Harlequin portrait of Prince Charles Edward Stuart, only one actual specimen seems to have survived, that in the collection of Major John Stewart of Ardvorlich.

In his *History*, published in 1749, James Ray describes 'forty or fifty stately fellows, in their hose and belted plaids, armed each of them with a well-fixed gun on their shoulders, a strong handsome target, with a sharp-pointed steel of about half an ell in length screwed into the navel of it'.

Only a few targes have dates on them, but Whitelaw managed to pioneer a dating classification based on their decoration. Later, Stuart Maxwell, who wrote an informative account of the targe, suggested that there are two main types as follows:

The flat circle of the targe with its dominating central boss has dictated the first and larger type within which three distinct groups can be recognized. The artist in the Celtic tradition liked to work in self-contained panels, and here the panels lie between circular lines round the boss and radii from it. In the first group there are two, three or four lines and four or eight radii; the nails used are small and there are no brass plates . . . The feature of group two is that within the same pattern star shapes, single or double and usually four or eight-pointed, are prominent, invariably emphasised by nails; a few have pierced brass plates and subsidiary brass bosses. The third group sometimes has a star, but is distinguished by having a series of almost semi-circular panels round the targe's circumference.

The main features of decoration which classify the second type are the large roundels usually six in number set around the central boss. The roundels often contain subsidiary bosses and have brass plates, frequently pierced and sometimes backed with red cloth, placed between them.

Maxwell illustrates his paper with photographs of targes, most of which are on public display. Perhaps the finest surviving example is the targe of Macdonald of Keppoch in the Royal Scottish Museum. Keppoch fell at the battle of Culloden and his heraldic arms are worked into the design on his targe.

In the Scottish National Museum of Antiquities there is a highly ornate targe which is known as 'The Prince Charlie Targe'. It has a pig-skin covered front embellished with silver in the French style. It is described as a 'Dress' targe.

The use of sword and target went out of practice in England about 1600 but survived in Scotland for a further century-and-a-half. It is the only truly defensive item in Scottish armoury and even when it ceased to defend it still had its purpose as described by Boswell in 1773: 'There is hardly a target now to be found in the Highlands. After the disarming act they made them serve as covers to their buttermilk barrels.'

The Sword

In an illustrated reference guide to Scottish edged weapons, John Wallace makes the fifteenth century his starting point as it was only then that a peculiarly Scottish type of sword emerged.

The sculptured stones and grave slabs of the Western Highlands and Islands illustrate two types of these early swords, the first being single-handed with quillons or cross-guard angled down in the direction of the blade and having flat spatulate terminals. Only two of these medieval Scottish swords seem to have survived.

It is, however, the second type which has caught the popular imagination. This is the *claidheamh-mor*, or great two-handed sword often referred to as the 'true' claymore. Its distinctive feature is the quillons, which slope down towards the blade and terminate in quatrefoils which are sometimes made in one piece and sometimes by welding or brazing four iron rings together.

Perhaps the earliest evidence of the claymore is the stone carving at Kirkapoll on the island of Tiree, dated to 1495. In some cases great prominence is given to such swords on these early tomb slabs, for example the carving of a claymore as the central feature of a slab on Oronsay dated 1539. A group of animals is carved around the pommel and grip, whilst the blade is flanked by carvings of foliage, and under the tip is a galley in full sail. This magnificent stone is one of many in which a claymore is the principal motif. It may well be that the sword in question had heroic associations.

One splendid claymore which can be seen in the Scottish National Museum of Antiquities has an overall length of $53\frac{1}{2}$ inches, the blade being over 40 inches long. Another sword in the same museum, with an overall length of 69 inches, is of a type which is heavier and usually less elegant than the claymore and is known as a 'Lowland' sword. There are a number of this pattern, their chief characteristic being the long quillons the ends of which turn sharply down and terminate in small knobs. These quillons are at right angles to the blade and do not slope downwards as in the case of the claymore.

Both these types of great sword continued in use into the seventeenth century and it is more than likely that even after they ceased to be used as fighting weapons, they were carried on ceremonial occasions. There is certainly evidence that the claymore was, in some cases, highly venerated, but Sir Walter-Scott's hero, Cospatrick, perhaps took this too far when he placed his great sword in bed alongside his various brides in order to seek its advice on the lady's virtue.

The title 'claymore' is now widely applied to the basket-hilted broadsword, a misnomer for which military authorities are largely responsible. I would like to add to what I have written elsewhere the more recent opinion of John Wallace on the ancestry of this world-renowned weapon:

> The basket-hilt may have come to Scotland directly from Germany. More likely, it travelled by way of England, or even by Scandinavia. What appears certainly is that a simple form of basket-hilt was known in England as early as the second quarter of the sixteenth century, and was the logical answer to the need for more protection to the hand as the use of the gauntlet decreased.
>   . . . .
> By this time, it would also appear that basket-hilts had become associated with the Scots in general, and the Highlanders in particular.

Wallace goes on to point out that because of the tendency of the English to lump the inhabitants of Ireland and the Scottish Highlands together, the term 'Irish hilt' was used to describe the basket-hilt. In Scotland it was also known as the 'Highland Hilt' or 'Highland Guard'

The early seventeenth-century basket-hilts were usually built up of bands of metal riveted together or cut out to form a cage of 'ribbons' around the grip. The blades were double-edged and nearly always wide and heavy. A great many of them were imported from Solingen and Passau. There is a sword which came from the fine collection of the late Major J. Milne Davidson which bears the seventeenth-century hilt-maker's name, John Simpson, Senior, of Glasgow. The blade is signed Herman Keisserr, and it bears the famous wolf mark of the Solingen workshops. It is also engraved with the arms of the Earl of Montrose and the date 1570.

From the beginning of the eighteenth century until the time of the Forty-Five, Scottish hilt-makers were designing and making magnificent broadsword hilts. Two silver basket-hilts in the Royal Collection have bars, fleur-de-lys members, plates and panels surmounted by the Crown, one containing the Cypher C. R., the other a thistle between the digits of the Roman numeral II. According to the inscriptions on the hilts they were given as prizes at race meetings held at Huntly Castle in 1713 and 1727. One hilt was made by William Scott the Elder, of Elgin, and the other by Robert Cruickshank of Aberdeen.

In 1934 Charles E. Whitelaw described a most important discovery which he had made regarding Scottish basket-hilts. Under the backguards of a number of hilts he noticed initials which he was able to identify with swordsmiths working in Glasgow and Stirling. Among them John Simpson and his son, Thomas Gemmil, John Allan and his son Walter, are all recognized today as great artists and craftsmen.

The blades too have their romantic associations. If they are two-edged they are known as 'broadswords', and if they only have a single edge they are 'backswords'. They were used according to the mode of fencing at the time, and when the Scottish courtiers came to London with King James VI, an English wit wrote of the change they made of their swords:

> *The sword at thy back was a great black blade,*
> *With a great basket hilt of iron made,*
> *But now a long rapier doth hang at thy side,*
> *And huffingly doth this Bonny Scot ride.*

But who was this 'Andrea Ferrara' whose name appears on so many swords and with so many spellings? Sir Walter Scott used the name in his novels, and Lord Archibald Campbell believed that he was a celebrated Spanish sword-smith who caught his apprentice spying on his secret methods and, having killed the lad, fled to Scotland, joined the court of James V, and once more set up this workshop.

How this story originated I have been unable to ascertain, but there was a Ferrera working in Italy during the sixteenth century. Unfortunately, however, the Scottish blades bearing that name belong to the seventeenth or eighteenth century and come from German workshops. There, the name which the Scots regarded as a mark of quality, was engraved just as were the words 'Gott Bewahr Die Oprecte Schotten' – 'God Protect the Honest Scots'.

The Gaelic bards made frequent reference to Spanish blades. Writing in the middle of the eighteenth century, John MacCodrum, bard to Sir James MacDonald of Sleat, refers to shearing Spanish blades which were as hard as a razor. In one of his Gaelic songs he describes the nobility of Clan Maclean flushed with wrath in the hour of battle and hacking flesh with strong polished Spanish blades that would split a man from his head to his brogues.

Leather or deer-skin linings to the hilts date back to the seventeenth century, but at that time they only covered the lower quarter of the hilt. By the end of the eighteenth century leather liners covered with red cloth or velvet enclosed the whole of the basket-hilt.

There are a number of sword-blades dating from the early eighteenth century bearing inscriptions which echo the sentiments of their long-dead owners. The earliest group demand the repeal of the Act of Union of 1707 and a splendid example can be seen in the National Museum of Antiquities of Scotland. On one side of this blade is inscribed PROSPERITY TO SCHOTLAND AND NO UNION, and in a panel below, the figure of Saint Andrew holding his Saltire Cross. The other side bears the words FOR GOD, MY COUNTRY, AND KING JAMES THE 8.

Several sword-blades belonging to the period of the Jacobite Risings of 1715 and 1745 are inscribed with the sentiments of their owners. But few Scottish swords can have greater interest than the silver-hilted back-sword said to have belonged to Prince Charles Edward Stuart himself. It is described by A. V. B. Norman in the *Proceedings of the Society of Antiquaries of Scotland*, Vol. 108, 1976.

This sword has a magnificent and intricate basket-hilt of silver decorated with human figures and trophies of arms. 'On the front is a figure of a woman, symbolic of War, seated on a cloud, her head forming the projecting "beak" of the hilt. The wrist-guard or rear quillon is formed like a crouching lion. The pommel, through which the tang is riveted, is formed as a horned owl.'

The blade is inscribed with the words '*Ne me tire Pas sans Raison*' – 'Draw me not without reason', and '*Ne me Remette Point sans honneur*' – 'Sheath me not without honour.'

Mr Norman describes the history of this sword which at one time was in the collection of George IV and is now to be seen in the National Museum of Antiquities of Scotland.

The Dirk

In the National Museum of Antiquities of Scotland we can see the ancestor of the Highland dirk – a ballock knife or dudgeon dagger belonging to the beginning of the sixteenth century. It would appear that it was about this time that the dagger took on certain characteristics which allow us to recognise it as a definite type of Highland weapon. The earliest had cylindrical grips surmounted with wide flat circular pommels and small rounded haunches. It was, however, a change in shape of these haunches from round to straight-sided that gave the weapon its Highland identity. In the above-mentioned museum we can see a very early example of the true dirk. Its 12½ inch blade, wedge-shaped in section, is surmounted by a wooden grip with two bands of interlacing pattern. This grip is four inches in length and would originally have had a metal pommel plate.

Two of the most popular inscriptions on these early daggers were MY HOPE AND TRUST IS IN THE LORD – in a variety of spellings, and similarly O LORD GOD BE MY DEFENDER.

The Highland dirk dates from the late seventeenth century and John Wallace points out that it was the faulty dating of a picture which led Whitelaw to give it an earlier beginning. The picture in question is in the Scottish National Portrait Gallery and is entitled 'Highland Chieftain'. It was said to portray the Earl of Moray, who died in 1638, but it is now known to have been painted about 1660 (*colour plate 1*).

Between the middle and the end of the eighteenth century the design of the dirk degenerated, possibly because it ceased to be in widespread use as a fighting weapon. The hilts began to assume a clumsy baluster shape and the haunch guards grew in size. At the beginning of the nineteenth century the top of the grip began to assume a 'thistle' shape and the pommel had a semi-precious stone or 'Cairngorm' stuck on top of it.

The inserting of a small knife and fork into the scabbard was popular from an early period. A dirk which belonged to Campbell of Glenfalloch has the small knife and fork attached to the scabbard by light silver chains. One of the silver mounts on the scabbard has his arms and motto engraved upon it and also the Edinburgh hall-marks of 1796–1797. The hallmarks on dirk mounts provide a valuable method of dating them and of course the military dirks which were by now coming into use can be dated much more easily than civilian specimens without hall-marks.

As far as pictorial evidence of dirks is concerned, perhaps the earliest example is on the monumental effigy of a knight in Ardchattan Priory carved in 1520. He carries what could be defined as a large dirk, in the scabbard of which is a small knife.

In the Inverness Burgh Records dated 1557 we read that 'Mans McGillmichell is jugit in amerciament for the wranguse drawin of ane dowrk to Andro Dempster, and briking of the dowrk at the said Androis heid.' The spelling of the word 'dirk' varies widely and its origin is obscure, but this is one of the earliest references to it.

Forty years later there is a reference in the Sheriff Court Records of Aberdeen to 'A helane durk with scheath and byknife'. This confirms the fact that by the late sixteenth century the dirk was recognised and described as a weapon of a particular Highland nature.

When Richard James visited Scotland about 1617 he drew attention to 'a longe kinde of dagger broade in the backe and sharpe at ye pointe which they call a durcke.'

Pictures of Highlanders swearing an oath with the dirk held to their lips were popular in Victorian times and, indeed, some Celtic Societies observed this custom at particular functions in the twentieth century. The custom is certainly ancient and was observed in Scotland in the eighteenth century, and possibly long before that. Hearing that members of Clan Cameron had taken such an oath, General Wade wrote a description of it. 'This oath they take upon a drawn dagger, which they kiss in a solemn manner, and the penalty declared to be due to the breach of the said oath is to be stabbed with the same dagger; this manner of swearing is much in practice on all other occasions to bind themselves to one another.'

Evidence that the highland dirk was often made by skilled craftsmen working on traditional lines is given by Professor Saint-Fond, who visited Dalmally at the end of the eighteenth century. On casting his eye around the workshiop of MacNab, the blacksmith, he noticed a very elegant dagger:

Its handle was made of wood only, but of a very hard kind. It was sculptured in a style of the most exquisite taste, and of the most perfect and finished workmanship. The sculpture consisted of vermiculated knots, formed in clusters, and passing and repassing each other in the most graceful manner, and without the smallest confusion.

This beautiful weapon was an ancient dirk which had been brought in for repair, and MacNab, responding to the visitor's praise, showed him several others of his own making whilst explaining:

We never deviate from this form, which is a very good one, being agreeable to the eye, and affording, at the same time, a solid hold to the hand which uses it. All the weapons of this kind which are made here, or in the neighbouring mountains, are of the same form with these, and that from time immemorial.

MacNab claimed that all his ancestors, over a period of 400 years, had been blacksmiths.

There remains of course that small ornamental knife which the modern 'Highlander' carries in his stocking. It is known as the *Sgian dubh* or *skene dhu* and probably only dates back to the end of the eighteenth century. The name is Gaelic and means 'black knife', referring to the colour of the hilt which in evening wear is often enbellished with 'Cairngorms' or coloured glass and silver or chromium studs.

Raeburn's portrait of Alasdair Macdonell of Glengarry, painted at the time of Waterloo, is, so far, the earliest illustration of the stocking knife. Even this is not of a type seen today as it consists of two small knives, one above the other. There is an actual specimen of this rather odd item in the National Museum of Antiquities of Scotland and one can only guess at its purpose.

The chromium-plated blade of the stocking knife might be regarded as only of use for domestic purposes, but a member of the mother of all parliaments thought otherwise. The following report appeared in the *Aberdeen Press and Journal* dated July 1931.

The question to be decided is whether or not a skean dhu is a lethal weapon, and the cause of its being raised is Mr T. B. W. Ramsay, who came to the House of Commons one night this week in full Highland dress. Before being allowed to enter the Chamber, Mr Ramsay had to leave his skean dhu behind him, as it was pointed out to him that it came under the category of lethal weapons, the possession of which is expressly forbidden inside the House.

The stocking knife is sometimes associated, without evidence, with a small knife said to be carried by some Highlanders and concealed in their armpit. The best reference I can find to this armpit knife is contained in *Letters from a Gentleman in the North of Scotland* by Captain Burt, who visited the Highlands in the 1830s. Writing of the Highlanders he says that 'some of them carry a sort of knife which they call a *skeen-ochles*, from its being concealed in the sleeve near the arm-pit.'

The Lochaber Axe

What a fine romantic ring the title of this Highland weapon has. Certainly the axe has been a favourite weapon of man since prehistoric times and a Highland version of it was recognised before 1501 when James IV bought a 'battle axe of Lochaber fashion'. The Lochaber axe consists of a head mounted on one side of the shaft only, this shaft terminating in a hook which would be of considerable use for dragging a mounted adversary from his horse. This was possible because of the unusual length of the shaft, which was five to seven feet, and it has been suggested that the axe got its name because Lochaber was a particularly heavily wooded part of the Scottish Highlands. The head consisted of a rectangular blade curving upwards and inwards and being much longer than it was broad.

One of the interesting points concerning this weapon is its long period of use. From the fifteenth century it survived into the late eighteenth, when it could still be seen in the streets of Edinburgh carried by members of the Town Guard. In an Inventory dated 1677 and recording the arms in Edinburgh Castle, 69 Lochaber axes are shown. In a book entitled *Weapons of War*, published in 1870, Auguste Demmin goes as far as to describe it as 'the national weapon of Scotland'.

Firearms

Hand firearms were certainly in use in Scotland during the fifteenth century and we know that James V shot a cow belonging to a Stirling woman. This event might have escaped the attention of historians had not the Lord Treasurer recorded the compensation which he paid to the lady.

By the second half of the sixteenth century muskets and 'hagbuts' were being carried in the Highlands by those who could afford them. In the inventory for the House of Balloch, dated 1600, there is an entry of 'ane lang hagbute that was maid in Dundie, gilt with the Lardis armis.'

During the fifteenth and sixteenth centuries every merchant who imported goods into Scotland from abroad had to bring in arms and armour to the equivalent value of such goods. Armour and bow-shafts gave way to hand firearms and the metal to make them, and the merchants received payment for these from the Exchequer. However, by the mid-seventeenth century, Scotland could supply her own arms and armaments and the merchants were then forbidden to bring in 'any musketts and bandeleers of any sort under the payne of confiscation.'

Hand guns had now become very beautiful objects engraved and inlaid with silver, copper and sometimes mother-of-pearl. One particularly beautiful specimen which has survived and is now in the Tower of London, is dated 1614, and the stock is decorated with silver thistles. It is signed 'R.A.' and was possibly made by Robert Alison of Dundee. The lairds of Grant had a particularly fine collection of long sporting guns in their armoury, including one the lock of which is signed 'I.T.' and dated 1671. The barrel is signed 'I.S.' and also bears the initials of Ludovic Grant, the first laird of Grant. However, the barrel also bears the date 1667, showing that a new lock had to be fitted at a later date. This is not unusual and there are some early guns with barrels almost a century older than the locks.

Michael Wright's portrait of the 'Highland Chieftain' shows a typical example of these long guns – usually about five feet six inches in length. The action was of the snaphaunce type, which probably originated in Sweden in the mid-sixteenth century and may have come here via Germany. Anyway, it has been said that the word 'snaphaunch' is derived from the German *schnapphahn*, meaning a 'poultry stealer'.

Like these long Highland sporting guns, the best of Scottish pistols are highly treasured in the major arms and armour collections of the world. They have also attracted the attention of art historians. Dr Joseph R. Meyer had a paper published by Rochester Museum, New York in 1940. In it he traces the generic relationships between the decorative motifs on a Highland pistol in his collection and decorations on a bronze brooch of the seventh century, the eighth-century Lindisfarne Gospel illuminations, and Bewcastle stone cross.

The earliest pistols which we can classify as Scottish were made of brass and had fishtail-shaped butts, and a similar type made of brass and steel with lemon-shaped butts. They were graceful and perfectly balanced weapons. These early pistols have been well described and illustrated by David Caldwell.

By the middle of the seventeenth century heart-shaped butts had come into fashion. Made entirely of steel, they were not so highly decorated as their predecessors but were still efficient fighting weapons.

Doune pistols have, of course, a world-wide reputation. Perhaps the earliest example is in Neuchâtel Museum, Switzerland. It is dated 1678 and is signed by the great master Thomas Caddell.

As Caldwell points out, these pistols were made 'in a Lowland tradition of craftsmanship, and not even the decoration on the pistols shows any clear trace of Highland influence.' They are all made of metal and have 'scroll' or 'ramshorn' butts, but whereas the action looks like that of the ordinary flint-lock, internally they have their own unique mechanism. The production of Doune pistols finished at the end of the eighteenth century.

We can now see how the evolution of Scottish armoury falls into two distinct periods. First, there was the widespread use of arms by a people constantly engaged in warfare. This ceased, rather abruptly, after the defeat of the Jacobite forces at Culloden, when the Highlanders were disarmed. Then, fairly quickly, as witness the portraits painted during the second half of the eighteenth century, these weapons became symbolic of the historic past. The advent of the Romantic period increased the demand for costume arms and this was met by the mass production of inferior specimens – a process which is likely to continue.

There is no other national costume which has such a close relationship with the arms of the fighting men of its past. These arms, because of their unique character, have a great romantic appeal, and their association with the dress serves as a reminder of the military aspect of Scottish national costume (*34*).

BIBLIOGRAPHY

P.S.A.S.   Proceedings of Society of Antiquaries of Scotland.
B.C.S.S.   Bulletin of the Costume Society of Scotland.

ANSTRUTHER, I., *The Knight and the Umbrella*, Bles, 1963.

BAINES, P., *Spinning Wheels*, Batsford 1977.
BENNETT, H., 'Early 18th century Grave', Lewis, P.S.A.S., 1975.
BOSWELL, J., *Journal of a Tour to the Hebrides*, London 3rd Edit., 1786.
BRERETON, W., *Travels . . . 1634 & 1635*, London, 1844.
BROWN, I., *Balmoral*, Collins, 1955.
BROWN, P. H., *Early Travellers in Scotland*, Douglas, Edinburgh, 1891.
BULLOCH, J. M., *The Gay Gordons*, Chapman & Hall, 1908.
BURT, E., *Letters from a Gentleman in the North of Scotland*, London, 1754.

CALDWELL, D. H., *The Scottish Armoury*, Blackwood, 1979.
— 'A Wooden-stocked Fishtail Pistol', P.S.A.S., 1976.
CAMPBELL, LORD A., *Highland Dress, Arms and Ornament*, London, 1899.
— *Records of Argyll*, Blackwood, Edinburgh, 1885.
CHAMBERS, R., *Traditions of Edinburgh*, Chambers, Edinburgh, 1823.

DONALDSON, M. E. M., *Further Wanderings – Mainly in Argyll*, Gardner, Paisley, 1926.
DRUMMOND-NORIE, W., *Loyal Lochaber*, Morison, Glasgow, 1898.
DUNBAR, E. D., *Documents Relating to the Province of Moray*, Douglas, Edinburgh, 1895.
DUNBAR, J. T. 'The Bannockburn Tartans', *Scots Magazine*, Oct. 1963.
— *History of Highland Dress*, Oliver & Boyd, 1962, Batsford, 1979.
— 'Sir John Sinclair of Ulbster', *Scotland's Magazine*, March, 1956.
— *The Official Tartan Map*, Elm Tree Books, 1976.
— 'Pioneer Historians of our National Dress', B.C.S.S., Spring 1972.

FRASER-MACKINTOSH, C., *Letters of Two Centuries*, Mackenzie, Inverness, 1890.

GARNETT, T., *Observations on a Tour through the Highlands*, London, 1800.
GRANT, E., *Memoirs of a Highland Lady*, Murray, 1898.
GRANT, J., *The Tartans of the Clans of Scotland*, Johnston, Edinburgh, 1886.
GULVIN, C., *The Tweedmakers*, Library of Textile History, Newton Abbot, 1973.

HALDANE, M. M., 'The Great Clan Tartan Myth', *Scots Magazine,* 1931.
HARRISON, E. S., *Scottish District Checks*, Wool Association, Edinburgh, 1968.
HAY, I., *The Royal Company of Archers*, Blackwood, 1951.
HOME, J., *History of the Rebellion in the Year 1745*, London, 1802.

JOHNSON, Dr S., *A Journey to the Western Islands of Scotland*, London 1775.

KAY, J., *Edinburgh Portraits*, Paton, Edinburgh, 1837.

LOGAN, J., *The Scottish Gael*, Smith Elder, London, 1831.

MAAS, J. *The Prince of Wales Wedding*, David & Charles, 1977.
McCLINTOCK, H. F., *Old Highland Dress and Tartans*, Tempest, Dundalk, 1949.
— *Old Irish and Highland Dress*, Tempest, Dundalk, 1950.
MACKAY, J. G., *Romantic Story of the Highland Garb and Tartans*, Mackay, Stirling, 1924.
MARSHALL, R. K., 'Three Scottish Brides, 1670–87', *Costume*, 1974. .
MARTIN, M., *A Description of the Western Isles of Scotland*, London, 1703.
— *A Voyage to St. Kilda*, London, 1753.
MAXWELL, Sir H., *Lowland Scots Regiments*, Maclehose, Glasgow, 1918.
MAXWELL, S., *The Highland Targe*, Glasgow Art Gallery, 1963.
— 'Highland Dress and Tartan in Ross of Pitcalnie Papers', *Costume*, 1976.
MAXWELL, S., & HUTCHISON, R., *Scottish Costume, 1550–1850*, A. & C. Black, 1958.
MILLER, A. E. H., 'The Truth about the Tartan', *Scotland's Magazine*, November, 1947.
MITCHELL, Sir. A., 'List of Travels and Tours', P.S.A.S. Vols. 35, 39 & 44.
MURRAY, M., 'Fife Fishermen's Clothing', B.C.S.S., Autumn, 1977.

NORRIS, H., *Costume and Fashion*, Dent, 1938.
NORTH, C. N. McI., *Book of the Club of True Highlanders*, London. 1881.

PAUL, J. B., *History of the Royal Company of Archers*, Blackwood, 1875.
PENNANT, T., *A Tour in Scotland, 1769*, Chester, 1771.
PLANCHÉ, J. R., *British Costume*, Knight, London, 1834.
PLANT, M., 'Clothes and the Eighteenth Century Scot', *Scottish Historical Review*, April, 1948.

RAY, J., *Compleat History of the Rebellion*, York, 1749.
— *Memorials of John Ray*, London, 1846.

SAINT-FOND, F., *Travels in England, Scotland and the Hebrides*, London, 1799.
SCOBIE, I. H. M., *Pipers and Pipe Music in a Highland Regiment*, Dingwall, 1924.
— 'Tartan and Clan Tartans', *Chambers Journal*, June, 1942.
SKENE, W. F., *Highlanders of Scotland*, Murray, London, 1836.
STEER, K. A., & BANNERMAN, J. W. M., *Late Medieval Monumental Sculpture in the West Highlands*, H.M.S.O., 1978.
STUART, J. S., *Costume of the Clans*, Edinburgh, 1845.

TAYLOR, J., *The Pennyless Pilgrimage*, London 1618.
THORBURN, W. A., *Uniform of the Scottish Infantry, 1740–1900*, H.M.S.O. 1970.
— 'The White Cockade', B.C.S.S., Spring 1973.

WALLACE, J., *Scottish Swords and Dirks*, Arms & Armour Press, London, 1970.
WEBB, W. M., *Heritage of Dress*, Richards, London, 1907.
WEBSTER, D., *Topographical Dictionary of Scotland*, Edinburgh, 1817.
WHITELAW, C. E., *Scottish Arms Makers*, Arms & Armour Press, London, 1977.
WORDSWORTH, D., *Recollections of a Tour made in Scotland AD 1803*, Douglas, Edinburgh, 1894.

INDEX